MORMON SETTLER
COLONIALISM

New Directions in Native American Studies Series

Liza Black and Colin G. Calloway, General Editors

MORMON SETTLER COLONIALISM

INVENTING THE LAMANITE

ELISE BOXER

UNIVERSITY OF OKLAHOMA PRESS : NORMAN

This book published with generous assistance from the Department of History, USD Foundation (James and Ruth Ann Weaver History Department Enrichment Endowment), and College of Arts and Sciences at the University of South Dakota.

Mormon Settler Colonialism: Inventing the Lamanite is Volume 25 in the New Directions in Native American Studies series

Library of Congress Cataloging-in-Publication Data

Names: Boxer, Elise author
Title: Mormon settler colonialism : inventing the Lamanite / Elise Boxer.
Other titles: New directions in Native American studies v. 25.
Description: Norman : University of Oklahoma Press, [2025] | Series: New directions in Native American studies ; volume 25 | Includes bibliographical references and index. | Summary: "This provocative book deepens the intersection of Mormonism, race (Indigeneity), and colonialism in a critical and necessary direction."—Provided by publisher.
Identifiers: LCCN 2025018576 | ISBN 9780806196046 (hardcover)
Subjects: LCSH: Church of Jesus Christ of Latter-day Saints—United States—History | Lamanites (Book of Mormon figures) | Settler colonialism—United States | Indians of North America—Social conditions | Racism—Religious aspects—Church of Jesus Christ of Latter-day Saints | BISAC: RELIGION / Christianity / Church of Jesus Christ of Latter-day Saints (Mormon)
Classification: LCC BX8627 .B6556 2025
LC record available at https://lccn.loc.gov/2025018576

The manufacturer's authorized representative in the EU for product safety is Mare Nostrum Group B.V., Mauritskade 21D, 1091 GC Amsterdam, The Netherlands, email: gpsr@mare-nostrum.co.uk.

For Hehaka Kuciya, Tatanka Wakiyan,
and Canku Maza Akicita

CONTENTS

PREFACE

My dad left Poplar, Montana, in the fall of 1990 to move to Toppenish, Washington. My father had a new job working for the Yakama Nation, a Tribal Nation in central Washington. One year later, we relocated to join him. I was apprehensive and angry about our move. I did not want to leave our home. I especially did not want to start a new school and make new friends. In the end, that transition to a new school was not as difficult as I had anticipated, but there was one transition that was not easy: church.

Every Sunday, my family would attend the Church of Jesus Christ of Latter-day Saints (LDS Church). I remember the first Sunday we went to church in Toppenish. As usual, our family was running a little behind schedule. When we arrived, the entire sacrament room was packed, with no place for us to sit together as a family. We waited in the foyer, and the usher quickly went about his job and took us one by one into the sacrament room, where he found each of us a seat. I was too scared to say no. He sat me by a random family, and I was in shock, exacerbating my feeling of being out of place. I felt as though this space was foreign and not just because it was new. When I looked all around me, the membership was predominantly white.

Once the sacrament meeting concluded, I located my family. Members recognized us as "new" and quickly helped us find our respective Sunday school classes. The members were friendly, and someone led me downstairs to join the other children my age. At this point, I had not been in a class with other children my age; it was usually just my siblings and me in our Poplar Branch primary, Sunday school classes for children age four to twelve. Our LDS congregation in Poplar, Montana, on the Fort Peck Assiniboine and Sioux reservation varied in weekly member attendance. At times there were other children, and we had a teacher, but I mostly remember it just being us, attempting to learn basic doctrine. We typically filled our primary time with church film strips and tapes. I remember "Benny the Builder" and other characters who taught us basic gospel principles. We also listened to LDS children's music from tapes or just colored to fill in the time. I remember enjoying this time with my siblings and the other children who would come and go.

As a child, I was timid in public spaces. I would rarely voluntarily speak in class, and I was more reserved because, in hindsight, I found my church experiences to be jarring or lonely without my sister. My oldest sister and I were only twenty-two months apart in age, so I had a built-in best friend and support system. I naturally gravitated toward her when we had shared classes. Our first year in Toppenish was excruciating because my sister stayed upstairs with her class while I went downstairs with other young girls under the age of twelve.

In primary, we had "sharing time." All the children would meet in the larger room for opening exercises, which included prayers, scripture, talk, songs, and brief lessons. During this time, we would often learn new songs. Many children would request "Book of Mormon Stories," a song with animated, choreographed movements and a rhythmic beat at the end of each line meant to mimic American Indian drums. The piano music also used a key to replicate stereotypical American Indian music. The lyrics read,

> Book of Mormon stories that my teacher tells to me
> Are about the Lamanites in ancient history.
> Long ago their fathers came from far across the sea,
> Giv'n the land if they lived righteously.
>
> Lamanites met others who were seeking liberty,
> And the land soon welcomed all who wanted to be free.
> Book of Mormon stories say that we must brothers be,
> Giv'n the land if they lived righteously.

I never learned this song and its associated movements until I attended church in Toppenish, but I still remember "Book of Mormon Stories" and the way other children would use their fists to pound on their scriptural books after every line. They made "feathers" using their hands held in a peace sign behind their heads at one point in the song. In general, everyone became animated and joyous, singing along, but I remember one specific incident that felt as though the other children were getting out of control with their "drumming." It was as if they were taking on these external markers of "Lamanite," or indigeneity, and getting into character by playing Lamanites. "Book of Mormon Stories" allows Mormon white children to "play Indian."

As you can imagine, this can be overwhelming to Indigenous children. It was for me. Almost thirty years later, I can remember what it felt like to be in that space. Those feelings of disgust and anxiety remain. I never participated in or sang this song, silently protesting by not singing or participating in what I found to be a problematic characterization of Indigenous people. I may not have had the language to articulate why this one song was so dangerous, but I knew how it felt to occupy a space in which I did not feel safe. And while I have experienced numerous microaggressions and blatant racism as a member of the LDS Church, witnessing other children sing and act out this song is seared into my memory.

In the song, Indigenous peoples are depicted as Lamanites, ancient people from the Book of Mormon who rebelled against God and his teachings. As part of their rebellious nature, they became spiritually and physically cursed by God with a "skin of blackness." Due to this fallen state, the erasure and marginalization of Lamanites is naturalized due to their wicked, rebellious nature. The song also indoctrinates young children with the notion that Indigenous people came from "across the sea" and could only remain and claim land if they "lived righteously." The portrayal of Indigenous peoples as Lamanites means that they exist within this narrow framework of indigeneity and normalizes the erasure of Indigenous peoples through the creation and application of this racialized subject position. Finally, this song also normalizes Mormon settler power to define the racialized Other, or Lamanite.

As a child, I grappled with the label "Lamanite" and asked myself what it meant. Who does it include? Why is it still used? As an adult, my questions became more complicated: How do white Mormon members view Indigenous peoples? Why are Lamanites integral to the construction of Mormon whiteness? Is this history? Or is it just a religious narrative? How do the LDS Church and its members reinforce racialized hierarchies based on doctrine?

I acknowledge that this may not be the experience of other Mormon American Indians. However, this is my experience, and it is valid. But because my experience is also not unique, it can be used to examine how Indigenous peoples have been uniquely othered within the LDS Church. My experience can be used to reclaim space and demonstrate the diversity of Indigenous experiences within the LDS Church. Those voices that are often promoted or recognized are those that accept the Lamanite label or are not critical of the LDS Church as an institution that perpetuates racist views or depictions of Indigenous peoples.

I also lay claim to this scholarly space of Mormon settler colonial studies in which the Mormon historical narrative naturalizes the colonization of Indigenous lands and peoples as it is whitewashed through the rhetorical construction and application of a Lamanite subject position. In doing so, I challenge the silencing or overlooking of Indigenous voices that do not support the mainstream Mormon narrative. By using a framework of Mormon settler colonialism, I expose and humanize the deceptive ways that Mormon settler colonialism shaped and operationalized indigeneity. I hope to give back this scholarly and religious space to empower Indigenous members who have resisted this Lamanite label because it is racist and paternalistic. I also hope to carve out a space for others whose experiences further complicate and elucidate the intersections of race, religion, and identity using a framework of Mormon settler colonialism. I want to acknowledge how different Mormon Indigenous spaces can be. Growing up in Poplar, Montana, and returning home each summer with my children, I return to this safe space found in our small Poplar Branch. Writing this book has given me the language and power to engage in these challenging, uncomfortable parts of our collective, shared past. In this space, we are relatives.

ACKNOWLEDGMENTS

From the start of this project, I have been blessed with and supported by those who believed in my voice and intellect even when I doubted myself. As a Dakota woman in academia, I undertook this project, which began as a dissertation, as a testament to the persistence and resilience of our people. I have written about the origins of this project in *Decolonizing Mormonism: Approaching a Postcolonial Zion*. I could not have imagined that one experience would shape the work I continue today. First and foremost, I do not intend to speak for Dakota people, my family, my community, Indigenous peoples, or members of the Church of Jesus Christ of Latter-day Saints. I offer up my voice and lens to complicate what it means to be Indigenous and Mormon. My book is meant to be a starting point for those writing about and wanting to better understand indigeneity and Mormonism from a theoretical framework that seeks to make visible Mormon settler colonialism. I hope that my book gives space to those living in the messiness and fluidity of faith and identity.

At various times throughout my academic career, grants and institutional support funded my research trips to the Church History Library owned by the Church of Jesus Christ of Latter-Day Saints in Salt Lake City, Utah; the Utah Division of Archives and Records Service; and the L. Tom Perry Special Collections at Brigham Young University. Thank you to all the archivists who assisted me throughout this process. I received generous funding as a doctoral student and an assistant professor from the Charles Redd Center for Western Studies. As a visiting assistant professor at the University of Utah and an assistant professor at the University of South

Dakota, I received funding and support to write and present the project at various stages. I thank the American Indian Studies Association, the Western History Association, and the Mormon History Association conferences for giving me the intellectual space to present my research.

Ella Deloria in *Speaking of Indians* writes that the "ultimate aim of Dakota life, stripped of accessories, was quite simple: One must obey kinship rules; one must be a good relative. . . . To be a good Dakota, then, was to be humanized[,] . . . to keep the rules imposed by kinship for achieving civility, good manners, and a sense of responsibility toward every individual dealt with" (25). Kinship made this process and project possible. While at the University of Utah I made many friends, including Alberto Müller, a kindred spirit. He was generous even when our paths took us away from Salt Lake City, letting me use his hotel discount to make conferencing and researching affordable. My dear friend, Martha Page, always opened her home to me and, later, my family when I traveled to and through Utah. Our conversations over good food sustained me when I felt I could not persevere. I did not imagine that when we met in 2005 our friendship would blossom and grow. I am so grateful to you and for your unapologetic will to live life on your terms. When Utah and the archives became too much during my doctoral work, Jen Davis and her mother, Debbie, invited me north to spend time with them in west Yellowstone. I did not realize how much I needed you two. I treasure those memories and your unwavering support and belief in me.

This project has been a labor of love sustained by those around me. I want to thank my mother, Julia Boxer. She demonstrates her love in her actions, showing up to do the hard work, which can often go unseen. I see her labor and love for me. More than anyone, she understands how difficult it was to leave my children. I often felt selfish, but she knew that I had to do what I had to do. In the summer when I would attend the Mormon History Association Conference, she traveled to South Dakota to be with my boys. She encouraged me to go to the office and get my writing done. In the summer when I traveled home, I could count on her to care for my boys while I went to write. My mother did the things I wanted to do with my children, including summer "homework." My boys now have these dear memories because they spent time with *abuelita*. This book is a testament to the unconditional love my mother has for me even if she may not always understand my work. Thank you, Mom. You made this possible.

Academia can be a difficult place to exist; forming good kin is key. As a doctoral student at Arizona State University, I had the privilege of knowing scholars whose work paved the way for many, including me. I count myself as an "Iverson student." The late Dr. Peter Iverson served as chair of my dissertation and doctoral work. Recently, I was reminded on my social media account that Dr. Iverson once advised me, "Your subject and verb should be within shouting distance of each other." I remember this now with joy, a reminder that writing is a process. I hope Dr. Iverson would be proud of my book and contributions to the field. I also had the privilege of working with Dr. Myla Vicenti Carpio, also an Iverson student. My dissertation committee represented three generations of scholars, and I hope to continue that legacy. Dr. Karen Leong's intellectual rigor, while intimidating, inspired me as I theorized about this project. Myla and Karen were vital to my well-being at Arizona State University and shaped how I mentor students. I also had the privilege of learning and being in kinship with Waziyatawin. Her fierce and unapologetic approach to history continues to shape how I teach and write. Her love for our Dakota people continues to influence how I think about a decolonial future for my family and our people.

There are many scholars who were influential to me, including David Lewis, Amanda Hendrix-Komoto, Gina Colvin, Ignacio Garcia, Molly Rozum, Jared Tamez, P. Jane Hafen, Joanna Brooks, Margaret Jacobs, Hokulani K. Aikau, and Sujey Vega. They embody the best of academia: they are generous with their intellect, time, and feedback. Special thanks to Molly Rozum for reading several chapters, providing valuable feedback, and being such a great colleague. Molly has been an invaluable friend and mentor. Thank you to my students, including Myah Red Horse and Gavyn Spotted Tail, who became part of our family.

Jerome Clark and I started the Kinship and Reciprocity Collective after a discussion at an American Indian Studies Association conference. We wanted to develop and support what we termed "Indigenous excellence." That summer, Jerome and I worked separately but checked in daily to hold each other accountable. He finished and defended his dissertation while I worked on my book proposal and tenure and promotion portfolio. Jerome's advice was invaluable even when it was tough. He changed how I saw myself as a writer, a space that I had been hesitant to claim. We wrote a book proposal and secured a contract with the University of Arizona Press just in time for the tenure process. Our edited volume *From the Skin: Defending Indigenous Nations Using Theory and Praxis* embodies Indigenous excellence. Our collective expanded to include Travis Franks, a settler scholar. This book is a testament to the unwavering support of Jerome and Travis even when I wanted to give up and move on to a new project. You two saw the value in my work and my voice and encouraged me in the final push to get it done. Your critical and helpful advice helped me push through when I simply did not want to write.

My sister, Majel Boxer, is my fellow academic and best friend. I am so grateful to have such a wonderful older sister who inspired how I teach. When I started teaching, she selflessly shared her teaching materials, answered questions, and was my go-to as we navigated Indigenous studies and academia together. I am blessed that we get to attend conferences with one another, and I continue to learn from Majel.

Those who know me know that I take my role as mother and wife seriously. I met my husband, Samuel Valdez, while I lived in Utah, and when my job took us to Vermillion, South Dakota, he left the life he had built in Provo, Utah. I recognize the bravery in deciding to start our life in an unfamiliar place and region. One year later, we started our family. Our sons are our greatest joy, but I also recognize that they are a lot of work too. Sam is the reason our children's lives went uninterrupted when I left for work. We made the decision for Sam to be the stay-at-home parent, and I will be forever grateful that he always prioritized our children. He sacrificed these last ten years to be the steady presence at home. Our children embody the best of us and our people. Thank you for supporting my dreams and being such a wonderful father and partner. The final push to finish revisions was challenging. Those long hours and days would not have been possible without you and your sacrifices. I love you, Sam.

My boys, Hehaka, Tatanka, and Canku, you are the reason I finished this book. I want each of you to know that you can do anything you set your mind to. The time I spent away from you was difficult, but I did so because I imagined a better world where you could exist on your terms. You are why I get up, go to work, and dare to dream of a world that recognizes our humanity. I am hopeful that I have created a good life for you and that you can hold onto this little piece of something I created with you in mind.

NOTE ON TERMINOLOGY

Throughout the book, I employ the term "Indigenous" in my analysis to challenge the usage of "American Indian," "Native American," "Natives," and, within the Mormon context, "Lamanite." The deliberate use of "Indigenous" acknowledges those who originated from this land. Daniel Health Justice in *Why Indigenous Literatures Matter* also utilizes Indigenous: the "capital 'I' is important here as it affirms a distinctive political status of peoplehood."[1] Indigenous Nations have their creation stories that connect them to specific places and, in doing so, recognize this connection and relationship to the land and the world around them. I also use this term to recognize the diversity of Tribal Nations, peoples, and their connection to the land. Indigenous peoples are not settlers or immigrants, even when they have been pushed from their traditional homelands. Seminole historian Susan Miller asserts that "Indigenousness does not connote merely the earliest occupation of a region; rather[,] it is a pattern of characteristics shared by polities that have not adopted the nation-state type of organization."[2] Thus, kinship becomes a governing principle in the lives of Indigenous peoples. Kinship dictates behavior, family life, and relationships, including those to nonhuman beings and the natural world. Indigenous peoples have a reciprocal relationship to all kin; this is particularly important when examining their relationship, or kinship, to the land. This connection to the land is vital to the well-being and survival of Indigenous peoples. Removal and dispossession had and continue to have an impact on Indigenous peoples; settler colonialism severed this intimate relationship with the land and the health of the nation and people. Finally, I use "Indigenous" to recognize the distinct political status as sovereign nations and citizens. When possible, I employ tribally specific names.

The terms "American Indian," "Native American," "Native," and "Lamanite" continue to categorize a diverse group of Indigenous people using homogenous terms that fail to recognize their place in and of the land. These terms appear when employed by settler nations and institutions, including the Church of Jesus Christ of Latter-day Saints (LDS Church). These labels have also been pivotal in shaping and racializing Indigenous peoples as the Other on their homelands. These terms categorize and define Indigenous peoples in context to the creation of the United States as a nation even though Indigenous peoples have existed since time immemorial, much longer than the founding and existence of the United States. The usage of these terms naturalizes the racialization of Indigenous peoples and is also dangerous because they acknowledge only federally recognized Tribes. There are many Indigenous peoples and nations whose treaties have not been ratified by Congress or who chose not to have their existence recognized by the United States. Indigenous peoples and communities understand the complications of indigeneity, which is why I use "Indigenous" or tribally specific names when possible to challenge the "arbitrary colonial standards of 'authenticity' that have *always* functioned to diminish Indigenous rights and access to land."[3] When using the term "Lamanite," I deliberately want to distinguish it as a category constructed and applied by the LDS Church, religious texts, and its members to Indigenous peoples. In essence, Lamanite becomes the first settler subject position as Mormon settlers attempted to claim a settler status to justify their claims to land. I use "Lamanite" throughout the text, but this subject position was constructed by Mormon settlers. The Lamanite subject position is the Mormon settler colonial Other. Lamanite is central to the Mormon settler colonial project and Mormon settler infrastructures.

Although many Indigenous peoples have used the terms "Native," "Native American," "American Indian," and "Lamanite" as markers of their indigeneity, it is crucial to understand and recognize how settlers created and used these subject positions to mark and racialize Indigenous peoples. The categorization of indigeneity was part of the settler colonial processes. Disrupting the use of "Lamanite" is not meant to completely disregard how individuals choose to identify themselves but instead is meant to recognize that settlers created these subject positions to erase individual and collective markers of indigeneity while constructing specific definitions of indigeneity to suit the Mormon settler colonial project. The term "Lamanite" as a discourse and subject position also erases the process of Mormon settler colonialism.

According to the "Style Guide—The Name of the Church," the official name is "The Church of Jesus Christ of Latter-day Saints. The full name was given by revelation from God to Joseph Smith in 1838."[4] Today, the official name is the preferred name: The Church of Jesus Christ of Latter-day Saints. Although the preferred shortened version is either "the church" or "Church of Jesus Christ" or "restored Church of Jesus Christ," I do not use "the church" because it privileges the LDS Church over other Christian denominations. I use the shortened version, LDS Church, to include the early formative period before 1838 to avoid confusion over early variations of what would eventually become the LDS Church. When writing about the LDS Church, the style guide explicitly states that "Mormon" is not an "authorized title, and the Church discourages its use." I employ the term "Mormon" throughout the book to reflect its common and popular usage in the nineteenth and twentieth centuries by the LDS Church, leaders, and members.

I also use the terms "settler" and "settlers" when discussing the early LDS Church and its membership. Even though Blacks and Lamanites would join the early LDS Church, they did not make up a numerically significant portion of the early LDS Church membership or leadership. White Mormons, especially religious leaders such as Joseph Smith, shaped early Lamanite discourse and subject position.

I recognize that "settler" is also a complicated term, and Daniel Heath Justice's *Why Indigenous Literatures Matter* discusses these debates and ongoing "conversation. Either way, we must name our violent history to understand its continuing effects."[5] I use "settlers" to describe the predominantly white membership in the LDS Church and recognize that many members had immigrated into the United States and, whether knowingly or not, contributed to the loss of Indigenous people's land, ways of living and being, and lives to settler presence.

Brigham Young statue in front of the Abraham O. Smoot Administration Building. Photo courtesy of Brigham Young University Police.

INTRODUCTION

THE MORMON SETTLER COLONIAL PRESENT

On the morning of June 15, 2020, two unknown individuals vandalized a statue of Brigham Young on the Brigham Young University (BYU) campus in Provo, Utah. The Young statue stands in front of the Abraham O. Smoot Administration Building, at the heart of BYU campus. Red paint ran down Young's chest, pooling at his feet and dripping down the base of the statue. "Racist" was emblazoned in bold red letters across the statue's base signage.[1] The Smoot Building, named after Abraham O. Smoot, a prominent member of the Church of Jesus Christ of Latter-day Saints (LDS Church), former Provo mayor, and slave owner, was also spray-painted with a red "X" over building signage.[2]

Defacing the Young statue and the Smoot Building signage caused immediate public outrage, but not for the same reasons. On one end of the spectrum, individuals responded with anger toward the individuals who would brazenly write "racist," damage private property, and smear the legacies of Young and Smoot. Others championed and supported the act because it challenged the memorialization of racist Mormon settlers' and their attitudes and actions toward Indigenous and enslaved peoples. Although these differing responses were at odds with one another, an uncomfortable dialogue ensued. The defacement forced the public, including many LDS members, BYU students, and administrators, to contend with Young's and Smoot's racist pasts memorialized in monuments and structures marking Mormon settler space. BYU, owned by the LDS Church, faced criticisms in its response to the vandalism, which led to discussions of campus diversity and belonging. Due to increasing scrutiny by BYU students, alumni, and the general public, BYU announced the creation of the BYU Committee on Race, Equity, and Belonging and tasked the committee with examining race and inequality at BYU on June 17, 2020. The committee was charged with "review[ing] processes, laws, and organizational attitudes regarding racism and root[ing] them out once and for all."[3] Many praised the formation of this eight-member committee; however, not one Indigenous person was appointed to the committee. It took external pressure for BYU administrators to appoint BYU Seneca professor of law Michalyn Steele a month later.[4] In February 2021 the BYU Committee on Race, Equity, and Belonging released its report, including a note on how BYU can address "historical issues associated with racism" and specifically addressing the call to rename buildings on the BYU campus. Despite acknowledging the painful experiences of students who are Black, Indigenous, and people of color (BIPOC), the committee "fully understand[s] that the naming and renaming of buildings is not among the responsibilities of or within the prerogative of the university president or the President's Council."[5] Ultimately, the committee made recommendations to "effectuate historic and transformative change," including renaming all buildings to functional names and creating a memorial honoring early BIPOC LDS members. At this moment in 2025, no monuments have been removed or constructed, no buildings have been renamed, and no changes have been made to campus signage.

The defacing of Young's statue and the Smoot Building's signage was an anti-colonial act that confronts the structures of Mormon whiteness. These acts challenge how Mormon institutions such as BYU memorialize their settler-colonial past as they push these institutions to (re)right and (re)write Mormon settler history. (Re)naming Mormon settler colonial structures confronts the invisibility of Mormon whiteness.

I begin with the defacement of Young's statue in front of the Smoot Building on BYU campus, a recognizable Mormon figure and space, to illustrate how Mormon settler colonialism functions and continues to maintain Mormon white supremacy in the present. Prior to the defacement of Young's statue, there was not an active public discussion regarding contestations over memory and Mormon monuments. Even though the committee's report acknowledges how these Mormon structures carry meanings that are often polarizing, what is missing is the framework to make sense of how Mormon settler structures work to sustain Mormon whiteness. I put forth the phrase "Mormon settler colonialism," defined and discussed in more detail below, to understand how Mormon settlers wielded their authority, or whiteness, to construct indigeneity and justify Indigenous dispossession as they secured their belonging to the land. Mormon structures, such as the Young statue and BYU campus, are a tangible manifestation of Mormon whiteness embedded in and onto the land. Mormon discourse, including structures, are signs of Mormon white possession and highlight "territory that has been marked by and through violence and race."[6]

SETTLER COLONIALISM, WHITENESS, AND POSSESSION

I utilize settler colonialism as a theoretical framework to elucidate the ideology of Mormon whiteness and possession and the processes employed by Mormon settlers to fulfill their ideological goals of creating a Mormon empire beginning in the nineteenth century. The Mormon subject position, in which identity is not an individual choice but operates at the macro, ideological, and structural levels, is a fluid social construction in which Mormon settlers' behaviors and choices are influenced by Mormon settler colonial ideologies. The Mormon subject position is the result of processes meant to carry out Mormon settler colonial ideologies. This book also makes Mormon white supremacy, an expression of Mormon settler colonialism, visible through an examination of how the construction and application of indigeneity resulted in both a racialized and racializing experience for the Lamanite subject position. The LDS Church believes the Book of Mormon to be a religious, historical text of the American continent beginning in 600 BCE. Lehi, his family, and followers faced religious persecution and fled Jerusalem for the American continent. Eventually, dissent divided Lehi's family and followers into two categories: righteous and wicked. Those who rebelled became Lamanites, led by Lehi's eldest son, Laman, and were cursed by God with a "skin of blackness" that would follow them for many generations and would continue into modern times.[7] In the nineteenth century Joseph Smith, the first prophet of the LDS Church, and his followers believed American Indians to be descendants of Lamanites living in a degraded state of savagery because they no longer followed God's commandments. Their degraded status is a physical representation of their spiritual demise. I explore in chapter 2 how the production of a Lamanite subject position and discourse as a discursive field of knowledge was a manifestation and technology of Mormon settler colonialism.

According to Māori scholar Linda Tuhiwai Smith, colonialism and, I would add, settler colonialism are expressions of imperialism. Smith defines imperialism as "economic expansion[,] . . . subjugation of the 'others,' [the] idea or spirit with many forms of realization, [and a] discursive field of knowledge."[8] All four definitions can work alongside or against one another and are useful for understanding the "different layers of imperialism." Imperialism, like settler colonialism, is tied to the land, including the transfer of Indigenous lands and resources to the settler society. Patrick Wolfe's influential essay "Settler Colonialism and the Elimination of the Native" has articulated that "settler colonizers come to stay: invasion is a structure not an event," an ongoing process that continues today.[9] Wolfe further articulates that settler colonialism "destroys to replace." In my work on Mormon settler colonialism, I further articulate that Mormon settlers asserted their right to possess Indigenous lands and in the process destroyed Indigenous identity, history, and land. In this process, Mormon settlers possessed Indigenous peoples by imposing Lamanite, a subject position and discourse. In this book, I argue that Lamanite discourse operates as a discursive field of knowledge that Indigenous peoples "were brought" into and still exist within this imposed subject position.[10]

Mormon settler colonialism is about the "structures of dominance" over the Lamanite subject position, and Mormon dominance is not relegated to one time, period, policy, or individual.[11] Maile Arvin's *Possessing Polynesians: The Science of Settler Colonial Whiteness in Hawai'i and Oceania* is useful for contextualizing whiteness as possession and as "one strategy deployed within the ideological power of settler colonialism." Arvin places emphasis on the logic of possession as a contrast to Wolfe's definition of settler colonialism as eliminatory. Possession allows for "the ways in which settler colonial practices of elimination and replacement are continuously deferred . . . [and] expressing more precisely the permanent partial state of the Indigenous subject being inhabited (being known and produced) by a settler society."[12] Mormon settlers possessed Indigenous peoples by defining and operationalizing the Lamanite subject position and discourse as a means to possess Indigenous land. The very nature of the Lamanite subject position was meant to be controlled, produced, and operationalized by Mormon settlers through the LDS Church and related religious ideologies. The widespread depiction of American Indians as "savage" reinforced their cursed status as Lamanites whose history can be found in the Book of Mormon. Mormon settlers used their subject position to create a uniquely racialized identity and category of race: Lamanite. The Mormon settler subject position relies on the othering of Indigenous peoples as the Lamanite subject position to secure their move to whiteness. Initially, Smith understood American Indians to be descendants of Lamanites who, when (re)introduced to Mormonism, would recognize their former, elevated status and (re)claim their subject position and place within the LDS spiritual belief system and Mormon settler infrastructures. Doing so also meant dropping their cursed status—their blackened skin. However, Indigenous peoples would never become the Mormon subject position or be assimilated into mainstream Mormon settler society despite their conversion because their skin would continue to mark Indigenous peoples as *the* spiritual outcast; thus, God sanctioned the dispossession of Indigenous lands to make way for the Mormon settler empire, or Zion. This religious insight serves two purposes, marking Indigenous peoples as the Lamanite subject position and impeding their complete move into Mormon whiteness. Because Indigenous peoples are a quasi-saved people, the liminal Lamanite subject position fits the needs of Mormon settlers in their quest to create a Mormon settler society that conceals their status as settlers. Indigenous peoples had to remain Lamanite to justify Mormon possession.

Arvin uses Hawai'i and Polynesia broadly to contend that settler colonialism "is fueled by a logic of possession through whiteness[,] . . . possessions that never have the power to claim the property of whiteness for themselves."[13] While Arvin focuses on Polynesians as *almost* white, they can never claim whiteness because being white meant that one could possess land. Arvin's work is useful for thinking about the use of the Lamanite subject position to mean that while LDS discourse articulates a move to literal whiteness, Indigenous peoples could never *be* white because their claims to land contradicted Mormon settlers' claim to land. Instead, white settlers claimed "indigeneity in Polynesia," and "according to this logic, whiteness itself is indigenous to Polynesia." Mormon whiteness functions similarly: Mormons as white settlers normalizes their presence on this continent as they move the Lamanite to the category of Other. The Lamanite subject position prevents Indigenous peoples from fully accessing their whiteness because their cursed status will never fully be removed. Thus, Mormon white settler presence is naturalized, and their claim to land is "rightful and natural."

Ultimately, this concept of whiteness empowers Mormon settlers to secure their belonging using religious ideologies as a means to possess land and replace Indigenous identity with the Lamanite subject position, including Indigenous people's relationship to land and the nonhuman world.[14] In this book, I focus on how Mormon settlers operationalized and affirmed their whiteness as Indigenous peoples became Lamanite, an expendable category within Mormon settler structures. Indigenous peoples are only ever useful when in service to Mormon settler ideologies that sustain Mormon whiteness. K. Mohrman's *Exceptionally Queer: Mormon Peculiarity and U.S. Nationalism* also explores how the LDS faith reinforces US settler colonial ideologies of whiteness and belonging, Mormon settlers reaffirm their whiteness and belonging as settlers using a very specific brand of US exceptionalism.[15] Mohrman's work reaffirms Mormon whiteness as central to the national project of white supremacy. The fluidity of Mormon whiteness reflects the power of Mormon settlers to function within the US colonial empire because their goals merge and support US settler colonial ideologies. My critique of Mormon settlers' production and operationalization of Lamanite as a subject position is based on my contention that this category of race, beyond a social construct and a subject position, is vital to Mormon settler possession of land. The Mormon settler subject position requires the religious and racial othering of Lamanites to secure their whiteness as a means to claim and possess Indigenous lands.

In *The White Possessive: Property, Power, and Indigenous Sovereignty*, Goenpul scholar Aileen Moreton-Robinson asserts that Indigenous peoples—and, as I argue throughout the book, Lamanites as a subject position—did not produce the Book of Mormon. The Book of Mormon is not Indigenous history, yet the Mormon subject position deliberately produced and used the Book of Mormon to give meaning to indigeneity. The Mormon settler construct of the Lamanite subject position shaped the lives of Indigenous peoples. While Moreton-Robinson focuses on the Australian Aboriginal context, I find her work useful for understanding how "race and state operate in tandem to condition each other."[16] In the Mormon-Lamanite context, the Lamanite subject position also functions as a category of race, while the LDS Church functions as a state or settler colonial center. The LDS Church produced a Lamanite subject position as a means to control Indigenous peoples, especially as this construct was designed to serve the logics of Mormon settler possession. Mormon possessive logics operationalized Lamanite discourse to circulate meanings about Indigenous peoples, which was necessary for Mormon settlers to construct their subject position at the apex of a racial, patriarchal hierarchy in the LDS Church. Throughout the book, I use the Mormon and Lamanite subject positions to better understand and illuminate the ideologies of Mormon settler colonialism as they are "operationalized, deployed, and affirmed" in LDS Church infrastructures, including policies to possess the Lamanite subject position.[17] In this introduction, I extend Moreton-Robinson's argument by showing how the Lamanite subject position has been deployed, operationalized, and affirmed to justify Mormon possession of Indigenous lands. Moreton-Robinson's concept of "possessive logics" signifies "a mode of rationalization . . . that is underpinned by an excessive desire to invest in reproducing and reaffirming the nation-state's ownership, control, and domination" of Lamanites.[18] Mormon possessive logics have "circulate[d] sets of meanings about ownership of the nation, as part of the commonsense of knowledge, decision making, and socially produced conventions," including the Lamanite subject position. In chapter 1, I explore the creation of Lamanite discourse and how religious texts are utilized to formulate this commonsense knowledge about Indigenous peoples and how this knowledge about the Lamanite subject position informed LDS Church policies and infrastructures. In chapter 2, I use the Council of Fifty, a political and hierarchical organization within the LDS Church, to operationalize Mormon empire onto Indigenous lands. In chapter 3, I utilize the move west by Mormon settlers as an example of how discourse and decision-making worked in tandem to create Mormon infrastructures to possess Indigenous lands.

These chapters work together to highlight the fluidity of the Lamanite subject position and discourse to suit the ever-changing desire of Mormon settlers. It is in these processes and infrastructures that Mormon settlers secure their whiteness. Their ability to define and dominate Indigenous peoples as the Lamanite subject position elucidate how Mormon settler colonial ideologies functioned to assert the Mormon settler subject position as the "pinnacle of its own racial hierarchy."[19] Mormon settler whiteness is the pinnacle of the racial hierarchy within the LDS Church, and, as a result, Black and Indigenous peoples became the Other in these defined racial categories.

Much like Erika Marie Bsumek's *The Foundations of Glen Canyon Dam: Infrastructures of Dispossession on the Colorado Plateau*, each chapter in my book takes an episodic approach to Mormon colonization in which Mormon settlers claimed and altered land using physical and social infrastructures. Mormon settlers actively shaped their built environment, but these Mormon settlers and Mormon monuments are part of the built environment, used as a means to mark, shape, and possess land as Mormon settler land. However, there are other invisible structures that carry out, or operationalize, Mormon settler ideologies, embedding Mormon whiteness onto Indigenous land, peoples, and narratives. Bsumek's definitions of infrastructures is useful to understand the various structures at play. Bsumek defines social infrastructure as "the key social systems that dominant society impressed upon the land and people," and I include religion and physical infrastructure as "the buildings, roads, ditches, and dams needed to support the operation of the dominant society."[20] Bsumek's use of physical and social infrastructures demonstrate that possession is not relegated to the built environment but is also the systems in which we exist. I also argue that religion is an important part of the social and physical systems that order and carry out Mormon settler colonial ideologies. Both social and physical infrastructures work together to dispossess Indigenous peoples and benefit settler society. These settler colonial processes work in tandem to possess and dispossess Indigenous peoples. Mormon whiteness gets embedded in these social, religious, and physical infrastructures as physical manifestations of Mormon settler colonialism.

I am interested in how these physical, social, and religious infrastructures assert and reify Mormon whiteness as a function of Mormon possession. Cynthia Prescott's *Pioneer Mother Monuments: Constructing Cultural Memory* explores the use of monuments in the American West to reinforce myths and imagery of pioneers moving west by tracing how these portrayals from the late nineteenth century throughout the twentieth century changed over time. Prescott specifically examines the symbol of white motherhood, or pioneer mother, and its importance in constructing US national identity embodying white civilization. These pioneer mother monuments become essential in how memory and commemoration intersect in public spaces. Subsequently, monuments are used to erase Indigenous claims to land and instead mark land and space as belonging to settlers so as to reinforce other narratives, such as Mormon and US settler colonial narratives of exceptionalism. *Pioneer Mother Monuments* is also helpful in understanding how settler colonialism continues to persist, because these monuments serve to normalize "white conquest of Native lands and peoples."[21] Young's statue on the BYU campus serves a similar purpose: a commemoration of Mormon civilization while staking claim to Indigenous lands as Mormon possessions. US *and* Mormon empires are both built on the possession of Indigenous homelands. The dispossession of Indigenous peoples is manifested in Mormon settler monuments as a means to possess and mark land as belonging to Mormons. These monuments become part of the physical and social infrastructures and the means to map settler authority and possession of Indigenous land.

Mormon settlers and their descendants marked land as Mormon or white using physical infrastructures and historical narratives to shape Mormon possession of land. These structures and narratives of possession shape Mormon settler infrastructures and are not just about Indigenous dispossession and possession of lands; they are also used "in tandem with historical narratives" that "naturalize and legitimize settler sovereignty."[22] Tracey Banivanua Mar examines how history has been "constructed, produced and made" in Australia and how efforts to decolonize the past and colonial settler narratives make visible Indigenous peoples. Her work is useful for exploring how Mormon settler colonialism produced Mormon settler narratives and landscapes, or physical infrastructures, thus possessing Indigenous peoples and narratives around Mormon settler presence. These physical structures of Indigenous dispossession are then inscribed with distinctly Mormon settler names and histories. The Mormon settler colonial project required the dispossession and possession of Indigenous peoples in all forms in order to access land, the primary goal of Mormon and US settler colonialisms.

The production of Mormon settler spaces was limited not just to the claiming and marking of land but also in the production of Mormon settler history designed to mark Indigenous peoples as the first settlers. For example, the Book of Mormon names and identifies American Indian peoples as descendants of Lamanites, the first immigrants to this continent. Consequently, the participation of Mormon settlers in the violent dispossession of Indigenous peoples is not only naturalized but also justified. Lorenzo Veracini refers to this settler tradition as a settler fantasy, in which "settler projects," including Mormon settler projects, "are inevitably premised on the . . . *violent* replacement and/or displacement of Indigenous Others," including Lamanites and, I argue, possession of Indigenous peoples and lands.[23]

The Book of Mormon is a production of Mormon settler history that constructs and gives meaning to indigeneity beginning in 1830 with the first printing of the text and continues with every print that goes into circulation today. Smith marked American Indian peoples as Lamanite based on Mormon settler history found in the Book of Mormon. The Book of Mormon is the ideological foundation of Mormon settler colonialism because the text purports to document Mormon settler origins and history, including Lamanites. The text as Lamanite discourse becomes part of the Mormon settler discursive field of knowledge about Indigenous peoples. Mormon settler colonialism, like US settler colonialism, sought to possess the Lamanites by defining and giving meaning to indigeneity as a means to claim Indigenous land and resources. In doing so, the Book of Mormon serves as a tool to operationalize Mormon settler colonial ideologies about Indigenous identity, claims to land, and history. The possessive nature of Mormon settler colonialism was to remake Indigenous identity. Mormon settlers such as Smith played a key role in the introduction of this Lamanite history and subject position to American Indian peoples. Once American Indians recognized their history and authentic identity as Lamanites, they would convert and embrace this subject position. In a sense, American Indians' acceptance of this Lamanite subject position signaled their willingness to not just assimilate but also assume an important place in Mormon settler society. In the Mormon settler context, American Indians floundered in a state of savagery because they lost their original teachings recorded in the Book of Mormon. LDS leaders sent missionaries to American Indian nations to (re)introduce the Book of Mormon as their *true* history and identity because Mormon settlers' eternal salvation was dependent on the religious uplift of Lamanites. Indigenous peoples could only ever assume a Lamanite subject position and could not bring their indigeneity into Mormon settler structures. This Mormon-Lamanite subject position reproduced the US-Indian relationship in which the Great White Father, Joseph Smith, or other prophets tried to save Indigenous peoples from their savage state. Ultimately, both US and Mormon settler colonial projects relied on the othering and assimilation of Indigenous peoples so that settler possession of land could be justified. US and Mormon settler colonial projects operationalized systems of whiteness to exert and maintain power over Indigenous peoples.

Mormon settler colonialism relies on the production of distinctly Mormon settler spaces that obscures and normalizes settler invasion by marking Indigenous peoples as foreign, or Lamanite, as well as violent and marking land as terra nullius. In any of these variations, Mormon settler violence and marking of space that erased and dispossessed Indigenous peoples of their lands is necessary to create what Mar terms "a cultural *terra nullius*[,] . . . [which] ensures that the history of frontier violence and massacres are 'unremembered' and repressed."[24] The defacement of Young's statue confronts how Mormon history is constructed and remembered and challenges how settlers have claimed and owned Indigenous spaces. Instead, Young's statue becomes a symbolic and physical representation of how Mormon settler sites of dispossession continue to be naturalized. The defacement was a direct challenge to how Mormon settler history, infrastructures, and landscapes are produced to secure and maintain Mormon whiteness. The entire BYU campus is just one of many spaces and places demarcated as Mormon settler, while Indigenous people become the forgotten Other, written out of the settler colonial narrative of the BYU campus, the region, and the memory of the land. This is how the ideologies of whiteness and possession of Mormon settler colonialism function and structure the lives of Indigenous peoples.

MORMON SETTLERS AND THE RACIALIZED OTHERS: INDIGENEITY AND BLACKNESS IN THE LDS CHURCH

The defacing of Mormon structures sparked and interrogated how race and meaning are embedded in Mormon infrastructures. The defacement of the Brigham Young statue moved the conversation regarding race beyond the Black/white binary, particularly how these social and physical infrastructures impact the experience of BYU BIPOC students. However, this discussion must move beyond the individual to expand to the include infrastructures of race, especially Mormon whiteness, as an expression of Mormon settler colonialism. Building on the work of previous scholars, I argue that Mormon white supremacy and settler possession are embedded in and on the land and within Mormon settler structures. Joanna Brooks, the author of *Mormonism and White Supremacy: American Religion and the Problem of Racial Innocence*, examines anti-Black racism within the LDS Church and how Mormons became invested in their whiteness. Although her book primarily focuses on the Black/white binary, her framework of Mormon white supremacy is useful for understanding anti-Indigenous sentiments in the LDS Church, including policies and doctrine. The racialized hierarchy in the LDS Church continues to maintain Mormon white supremacy and possession, as exhibited by the public backlash against the vandalism of Young's statue and the Smoot Building signage.

In an episode of the podcast *Mormon Land*, hosted by Peggy Fletcher Stack and David Noyce, Brooks discusses the vandalism of Young's statue as an act of resistance in challenging the production of Mormon white supremacy through monuments. Brooks argues that during Young's tenure as both LDS Church president and Utah territorial governor, he set forth racist policies in his desire to create a Mormon theocratic empire in which "white men" ruled.[25] Young was not the only one who held this view. Although it was "easy to say that Young was racist," he systematically institutionalized these racist views when he became the second LDS prophet on December 27, 1847. The issue is not whether Young, as an individual, was or was not racist. Brooks argues that Young implemented policies driven by racist or racialized views of Blacks and Indigenous peoples, thus embedding his views in the infrastructures and policies of the LDS Church.

At the same time, Young served as territorial governor of Utah from 1850 to 1858, later establishing a "territory, a system. And . . . the territory did not remake that system[,] and . . . Mormonism still has not remade that system . . . that privileged white voices, white lives, and white participation over Blacks."[26] I also argue that the dispossession of Indigenous peoples was necessary to realize this Mormon subject position. Brooks argues that American society, including Mormons, exists within a system of white supremacy; however, only those at the apex of this system, Mormon white men, directly benefit from these structures of power. Brooks's argument connects the institutionalization of race within the LDS Church to the larger US settler colonial project in which the enslavement of Blacks and Indigenous dispossession are coconstitutive subject positions. Mormon settler structures also signal to the larger US settler colonial society that Mormons are in fact settlers. The innocuous nature of Mormon white supremacy and possession normalizes the oppression, racialization, and dispossession of Indigenous peoples and Blacks as the Other.

The Mormon settler colonial present continues because these narratives, discourse, monuments, and thefts of Indigenous land remain invisible within Mormon history and the larger history of the American West. According to Brooks, Mormon white supremacy—and, I add, the ideologies of Mormon settler colonialism—renders "invisible the racist histories of the architectures [infrastructures] we live in every day. . . . We don't see the structures of power that make life dangerous for Black people in the U.S. Black people know these histories."[27] Mormon white supremacy and the logics of possession influenced LDS Church policies regarding Indigenous peoples and lands. Indigenous peoples exist as the Lamanite subject position, a fluid construct that changed over time and place to serve the needs of Mormon settler colonial power. The Mormon settler subject position can only exist concomitantly with the Lamanite subject position in which Indigenous peoples are uncivilized, a problem to Mormon empire. As *the* problem, Lamanite subject status means that Indigenous peoples have no right to possess land, and the Mormon settler subject position provides the means to control constructs of indigeneity and possession of land. Mormon settler narratives are a form of possession; Indigenous peoples exist only when they are in service to the goals of Mormon settler colonialism.

The inclusion of Indigenous peoples complicates the insidious ways the Mormon settler colonial project constructed and gave meaning to race and how Mormon settler colonialism, specifically systems of Mormon whiteness, were predicated on their ability to construct Indigenous peoples as the Lamanite subject position. Mormon whiteness was constructed and reaffirmed in Mormon religious texts, structures, and the Lamanite subject position. The move to whiteness meant that Mormon settlers would secure their place to the land, while the Lamanites would never become white enough to possess and remain on their homelands. Black and Indigenous people's experiences within Mormonism are also fundamentally different due to Indigenous people's unique political status as sovereign nations. The racialization of Black and Indigenous peoples functioned together, despite their differences and status as "cursed" people, and can expand our understanding of race within and outside the LDS Church. The status of Blacks as a "cursed" people was similar to the status of Lamanites, except Indigenous peoples could potentially leave behind their status as fallen people with skins of "blackness" by accepting and converting to Mormonism. Indigenous peoples could be saved because of their potential to be Mormon, or white. Lamanites must simply adopt Mormonism and return to their *real* traditions, or the acceptance of the Book of Mormon as a history of their ancestors, to access their whiteness. Yet Indigenous peoples, much like Blacks, could never fully shake off their racialized status. I explore this more in detail in chapter 1, particularly regarding the fluidity of the Lamanite subject position to serve the changing desires of Mormon settler colonialism.

Blacks as the racialized Other could not attain full membership in the LDS Church until 1978. Black men could not have the priesthood, the "power and authority that God gives to man to act in all things necessary for the salvation of God's children."[28] Without the priesthood, Black men and women could never be full members, since membership for adults meant that individuals must participate and complete various ordinances such as baptism and temple marriage (endowment). These ordinances must be performed by men who held the Melchizedek priesthood, the highest-ranking form of priesthood held by only men in the LDS Church. Only men with the Melchizedek priesthood can lead and conduct religious services, including temple ordinances. Mormon men must have the Melchizedek priesthood to participate in these ordinances, the apex of religious authority, which Black men could not attain until after 1978. The temple endowment is the most important Mormon ordinance required of individual members to achieve eternal exaltation. Black members could not fulfill this ordinance required by the faith, since they could not participate in temple ordinances and could never be full members of the faith and were thus relegated to a lower, cursed status.

On June 8, 1978, then-president Spencer W. Kimball declared in the "Official Declaration 2" the "desire to extend to every worthy member of the Church all of the privileges and blessings which the gospel affords."[29] Race, or racialized status, could no longer be used to justify the exclusion of Black members from full membership in the LDS Church. Black men could receive the Melchizedek priesthood, and both Black men and women could now enter the temple and participate in temple ordinances fundamental to being Mormon. This moment marks a shift in policy, but racist interpretations of Black status in Mormon discourse persisted. The Black priesthood ban did little to end racism in the cultural fabric of the LDS Church and within its membership ranks because religious rhetoric and teachings continued to exist in Mormon discourse, such as the curse of Cain. Rather than acknowledge and recognize Mormon white supremacy and racism embedded in Mormon religious discourse, Mormon settler fantasies continue to articulate that "all are alike unto God" while ignoring culpability in the oppression of racialized members of the Mormon faith.[30] Instead, the Mormon subject position laid blame on wicked ancestors of descendants who carry the mark of the Other. Black and Lamanite skin became physical manifestations of unrighteous heritage, and Mormon settler fantasy reigns because Mormon religious rhetoric justified any critique and responsibility for Mormon settler policies driven by race.

TRIANGULATING US-MORMON SETTLER COLONIALISMS

The majority of Mormon race scholarship has largely been dominated by scholars writing about the Mormon Black experience, many focusing on the history of the priesthood ban.[31] There are books that discuss the Mormon–American Indian experience, including two edited volumes.[32] One such book is Farina King's *Diné dóó Gámalii: Navajo Latter-day Saint Experiences in the Twentieth Century*, in which King utilizes her family's conversion to the LDS Church and experiences to examine the complexities of being Diné and Mormon. While these individual, family, and community experiences enrich the spectrum of Mormon Indigenous experiences, my book provides the necessary framework to understand the decisions these individuals made to exist within Mormon and US settler colonial infrastructures. Individuals lived within these Mormon settler structures, and while King's father and many others could balance or remain Mormon Diné members, they did so within these settler colonial structures, including religious institutions. For example, many felt ostracized or not completely embedded in either their Diné or Mormon community. Many also felt pressures from their Indigenous communities, not feeling Indigenous enough, much like contestations over indigeneity that include blood quantum, enrollment status, and living in one's community.

All of these constructs of indigeneity are settler interventions; removing the infrastructures to better understand indigeneity or, more specifically, the Lamanite subject position is another form of settler colonialism. Mormon settler colonial ideologies must be made visible in addition to a theoretical framework to provide the necessary context for the difficult decisions made daily to exist as Indigenous. In doing so, we can better understand the spectrum of Mormon-Indigenous experiences and how many choose to reject these settler colonial structures as an anticolonial act. LDS discourse defined, shaped, and operationalized Indigenous identity in the nineteenth, twentieth, and twenty-first centuries and at moments replicated US settler definitions of indigeneity. The Mormon subject position relied on constructions of indigeneity to give meaning to white identity and place and in the ability to define and subjugate the Other, or Lamanite.

Mormon settlers highlight the nuanced ways in which they are both the settler and the exogenous Other as they seek to assert their sovereignty against the US nation-state and other settlers. They claim their exogenous status in opposition to Indigenous peoples when it serves their political purposes in disentangling from other settlers but move toward settler status to secure and legitimize their claims to land. This triangulation between the three subject positions (settler, exogenous

Other, and Indigenous) becomes important in marking Mormon settlers as a politically sovereign people and the fluidity to move between three subject positions. [33] The US settler colonial enterprise marked Mormon settlers as exogenous, which aligns with Mormon narratives of marginalization or religious persecution. Mormon settlers never remained exogenous; instead, as they moved west they secured their settler status because of their ability to claim others' territories. However, at the same time, their relationship to and with the United States and Indigenous peoples shows that they are still settlers, or settlers of a different religion. The categories are fluid and support Veracini's claims that these subject positions are "ongoing and protracted contestation, are never neatly separate, mutually shape each other, and are continually tested and reproduced."[34] Settlers want to possess Indigenous peoples to undermine Indigenous claims to land and move them even farther west, or to Indian territory. "Indian territory" became code for land that settlers have yet to claim. US and Mormon settler colonialisms are about the control and management of Indigenous peoples, which is why these categories are not finite; they are in constant movement to accommodate settler desires. However, it is important to note that Indigenous peoples will never become settlers even when they act like settlers, because Indigenous peoples do not have the power to define the settler as the Other or even remain in possession of their land. In the Mormon context, American Indians will never fully become Mormon. Indigenous peoples will always be relegated to the Lamanite subject position. Indigenous peoples as the Lamanite subject position is necessary for the Mormon settler colonial project to be complete. Yet the Mormon settler colonial project will never be complete, because the Lamanite subject position is necessary for the "vanishing endpoint," or the "moment of colonial completion . . . when the settler society will have fully replaced Indigenous societies on their land, and naturalized this replacement."[35] The Mormon settler colonial project has not completely replaced Indigenous peoples as the Lamanite subject position; thus, the Mormon vanishing endpoint has yet to occur, which is the purpose of Mormon settler colonialism. Mormon settler colonialism is malleable so as to serve Mormon settlers' needs across place and time. These hierarchical subject positions reinforce their claims to land as legitimate because it was sanctioned by God and coded in religious texts. Mormon settlers' claims to land will always be more righteous than the claims of Indigenous peoples because of the settlers' desire to "uplift," "elevate," and "raise indigenous communities."[36]

This triangulation between settler, Mormon settler, and Indigenous illuminates the process in which Mormon settler colonialism functions as a direct challenge to US sovereignty while also replicating violent policies of assimilation against Indigenous peoples. Mormon settlers experienced violence, but this vio-lence was not used as a tool to assimilate or subjugate them. Violence was used as a tool to mark Mormon settlers as distinctly different from other Christian settlers in order to force their removal from Missouri and Illinois, just to name two places. Mormon settlers refused to assimilate and take on traits of the larger settler society; instead, they wanted to create their Zion, a Mormon nation-state. The othering of Mormon settlers was distinctly different from the othering of Indigenous peoples by the United States. Mormon settlers relied on their whiteness to migrate, claim land, and exercise economic and political power at each new Mormon settler site. The Mormon center moved to accommodate the needs of those with power in the LDS Church. This Mormon settler narrative of violence and expulsion ultimately justified their presence and participation in the making of a Mormon settler empire predicated on the removal, erasure, and possession of Indigenous peoples.

Mormon studies and history have been utilized to embed and normalize Mormon whiteness, reinforcing the settler colonial process. The dominant Mormon narra-tive continues to claim an exogenous or othered settler status for Mormons due to religious persecution by the larger US nation. This is simply not the case: Mormon settlers have always relied on their proximity and access to whiteness. When placed in the context of settler colonialism, Mormon whites acted as settlers. It was their whiteness that sanctioned their movement across space and time. Mormon settlers moved with their sovereignty, a function of their whiteness. Mormon scholars have conflated the rejection of Mormon settlers as a racialized Other due to their chal-lenge to US sovereignty and refusal to accept established Christian and social settler colonial norms. However, Mormon settlers as the Other, or the Indigenous, must be confronted to demonstrate the nuanced ways settler colonialism functions to main-tain these power structures. The Mormon settler colonial present exists because the scholarship, monuments, and discourse continue to fulfill this function.

The naturalization of Mormon whiteness has been effective in maintaining these infrastructures of power within the LDS Church and normalizing the Mormon settler subject position and presence and Mormon settlers' power to define the Other to claim land and assert sovereignty. For example, W. Paul Reeve's *Religion of a Different Color: Race and the Mormon Struggle for Whiteness* argues that Mormon settlers assumed this othered status because they have been racialized, extermi-nated, and pushed to the periphery of American society. Mormon settlers have been marginalized and harassed because of their religious beliefs and close association with freed Blacks and Indigenous peoples. However, the violence enacted against Mormon settlers based on their religious belief systems does not change the fact that they are still settlers and can access and use their whiteness to erase their violence toward Indigenous peoples.

Other scholars of Mormon history focus on Mormon settlers as a racialized people and offer up a different perspective of whiteness in which Mormons became nonwhite, their bodies marked as the Other, but I argue and demonstrate throughout this book that Mormon settlers do not always exist in this marginalized status. In fact, Mormon settlers became white enough as they differentiated themselves from Black and Indigenous bodies and sought to maintain their supremacy in their bid to build a Mormon empire. This body of scholarship is also useful to understand how Indigenous peoples have been written out of the Mormon historical narrative or simply exist at the margins, where their experiences matter only in the context of Mormon settler history. Mormon settler history and fantasy work together to naturalize the ways in which Mormon settlers have utilized their whiteness to enact violence on the land and Indigenous peoples.

Mormon historians draw upon various examples of religious persecution to demonstrate how Mormon settlers have been racialized by conflating and comparing violent methods used to subjugate or eliminate Indigenous peoples, including policies of extermination. For example, Reeve's *Religion of a Different Color* uses the 1838 massacre of three boys at Hawn's Mill, located in Caldwell County, Missouri, to illustrate the dehumanization of Mormon settlers by comparing it to the 1864 Sand Creek massacre of Arapaho and Cheyenne peoples. Colonel John M. Chivington ordered and led the military campaign that killed over 150 Cheyenne and Arapaho people on November 29, 1864. Most victims were children, women, and the elderly. The Cheyenne and Arapaho Tribes had already surrendered when Chivington and his men charged through camp. Chivington encouraged those under his command to kill indiscriminately and yelled "kill and scalp all, big and little; nits make lice."[37] This phrase is critical because Chivington sanctioned the killing of Cheyenne and Arapaho women and children, women who sustained and gave life to the next generation. Chivington destroyed generations of Cheyenne and Arapaho people by killing children at Sand Creek. The violence used by Chivington was not just about the dehumanization of Cheyenne and Arapaho people but was also the deliberate genocide of a people by using violence, including violent acts committed against Cheyenne and Arapaho women and their bodies. Settlers used violence as a means to carry out settler colonial ideologies, policies of elimination, and possession.

The Sand Creek massacre occurred more than twenty years after the Hawn's Mill massacre, making it difficult to influence Mormon extermination or racial othering by non-Mormons or to be utilized as a comparative example of US genocidal policies.

This comparative example attempts to make the connection between Indigenous peoples and Mormon settlers as nonwhite, marginalized due to their racial status, yet what is missing from this analysis is the framework of Mormon settler colonialism to understand the malleability of whiteness and how Mormon settlers could be white *and* marginalized due to their religious beliefs, which is really the core of non-Mormon ire. Mormon settlers became a threat to the existing US settler colonial project by resisting efforts to join a homogenized settler society. Instead, their religious beliefs and practices, such as polygamy, marked Mormon settlers as the Other. Despite violent harassment by other settlers, Mormons remained white. Mormon settlers have always been white and accessed their whiteness when they moved west and beyond the peripheries of US colonial society. I utilize this specific narrative to illustrate how Mormon scholars aid in the move of Mormon settlers to innocence by equating violence with US eliminatory policies toward Indigenous peoples. The move to innocence begins when Mormon settlers' experiences are equated to the massacre of Cheyenne and Arapaho peoples at Sand Creek. Indigenous peoples are moved to the margins of Mormon settler history as Mormon settlers occupy the center; their histories and experiences become the normative experience and subject position. The Sand Creek massacre, as the largest massacre in US history, matters only when it can be used in service to Mormon settler experiences and narratives about non-Mormon violence.

The first publication of the LDS Church's *Evening and Morning Star* was produced in Independence, Missouri, beginning in 1832 and ending in 1834, when the printing press was destroyed by non-Mormon settlers. In the July 1833 issue, William W. Phelps, editor and printer, wrote an article, "Free People of Color," to dissuade free Blacks from migrating to Missouri "as members of the church" by citing state law that required proof of citizenship by court seal.[38] Despite Phelps's editorial to clarify the Mormon stance on migrating free Blacks to Missouri in which slaves were considered "real estate," his efforts did little to assuage non-Mormon concerns. In fact, tensions escalated between these competing settler groups. Mormon settlers wanted to create Zion in Jackson County, Missouri, while other non-Mormon settlers saw the steady surge of Mormon settlers into the region as a direct threat to their existing settler infrastructures, including those that relied on slave labor. Missouri became a place in which US and Mormon settler colonial powers clashed as each competed for the right to occupy the apex of the racialized and political hierarchies. Ultimately, Mormon settlers lost and were expelled from the state due to their perceived willingness to convert free Blacks. Mormon settler attitudes toward American Indians mimicked US settler colonial attitudes driven by desires to civilize and assimilate Indigenous peoples. Mormon settlers remained white, even during their Missouri occupation, because they adopted larger US colonial attitudes toward Blacks and Indigenous peoples so they could reaffirm their whiteness and take on the mantle of US exceptionalism, which coincided with Mormon settler ideologies. Mormon settlers secured their whiteness as they enacted violence against Black and Indigenous bodies and the land. The institutionalization of race was pivotal in creating racial hierarchies and policies to maintain these white infrastructures of power in the LDS Church and among their membership for generations. Black and Indigenous peoples may have rejected, navigated, or existed within these infrastructures of Mormon power, but this does not negate how these ideologies of Mormon settler colonialism impacted their lives and how they continue to live in US and Mormon colonial systems.

In the Mormon historical narrative, Mormon settlers claimed and perpetuated their status as the Other to justify their possession of Indigenous lands. Critical examination of the Mormon historical narrative, especially the production of Lamanite subject position discourse, is necessary because it is part of how the Mormon settler colonial project functions. The Mormon historical and religious narrative rewrites settler discourse, especially Lamanite discourse and subject position. Scholars of Mormon history have attributed this to the marginalization of Mormon settlers who do not "enjoy inherent rights and are characterized by a defining lack of sovereignty entitlement."[39] This is simply not the case. Mormon settlers moved and carried their sovereignty with them as they moved from one place to another. Mormon settlers' whiteness meant they could move west and assert their claims to land for a Mormon empire. Like other settlers, Mormons asserted their sovereign authority over Indigenous peoples, Blacks (including the enslaved), and other settlers, since Mormon settler desires were even more exceptional, supported by religious discourse as with the Book of Mormon.

Indigenous possession continues when scholarship about Mormon Indigenous history centers Mormon settlers' history in the production of historical narratives that legitimize settler policies and sovereignty premised on the possession, including religious and cultural, of Indigenous peoples. For example, Matthew Garrett's *Making Lamanites: Mormons, Native Americans, and the Indian Student Placement Program, 1947–2000,* purports to be a history of the Indian Student Placement Program (ISPP) and only focuses on Indigenous voices of those students who "enrolled year after year, engaged with, and even embraced part or all of the foreign identity ISPP provided."[40] Thus, Indigenous voices and histories continue to be erased to center a Mormon settler institutional history of the ISPP. The "foreign identity" is in fact a subject position produced and operationalized by the LDS church as a means to assimilate Indigenous children. *Making Lamanites* demonstrates how Indigenous peoples exist in Mormon history when Indigenous history begins to intersect with Mormon settler history, specifically when LDS Church policies shaped how Mormon settlers interacted and viewed Indigenous peoples as the Lamanite subject position.

Mormon settler colonial ideologies embedded in policies and structures impacted the ways in which Indigenous peoples made sense of their identity, because Mormon settler colonial policies or beliefs about Indigenous peoples affected their lived experiences within these infrastructures. Indigenous voices are the possession of the ISPP settler colonial narrative, their existence literally written out of the narrative if they do not conform to the Lamanite subject position. *Making Lamanites* excludes Indigenous experiences and the voices of those who did not continue their participation in the ISPP and the LDS Church or embrace this Lamanite subject position.[41] Thus, the complexity of Indigenous identity within Mormon settler structures is silenced and erased from the historical narrative on the ISPP and larger Mormon-Indigenous history. Ultimately, Garrett's book is more about the LDS Church and the Mormon settler colonial views of Indigenous peoples and corresponding policies that operationalized programs, such as the ISPP, to assimilate and erase Indigenous children's identity, spirituality, history, and connection to community. Mormon-Indian histories remain squarely rooted in Mormon history and primarily do not use Indigenous theories or methodologies to understand the structures and functions of settler colonialism in the LDS Church. Many Mormon scholars who are not familiar with Indigenous studies or are dismissive of the use of anticolonial or decolonial theories and instead center Mormon settler voices and histories on the agency of individual Indigenous peoples render Mormon settler colonialism invisible. The focus on individual agency fails to consider the Mormon settler colonial infrastructures in which the individual lives. The dismissal of settler colonialism or other Indigenous theories fails to consider settler colonial infrastructures and systemic issues such as racism embedded in these structures.

Mormon settlers enticed Indigenous peoples with the promise of whiteness as a means to become civilized, meaning access to land. However, Lamanite redemption could not interfere with Mormon settler policies. Both Black and Lamanite as categories of race exist relationally to Mormon whiteness, and Mormon whiteness must be made visible by illuminating the mechanisms of settler colonialism with the LDS Church. Reading Mormon settler colonialism back onto the land and into the historical narrative makes visible the subtle ways in which Mormon settlers preserve their whiteness and the functionality of Mormon settler colonial logics. Finally, the existence of a distinct Mormon settler society in the intermountain West, the center of Mormon settler authority in what is now Utah, demonstrates the success of Mormon settler colonialism in the late nineteenth century and into the modern era.

The expansion of US empire necessitated the removal of Indigenous peoples to the West, or unceded Indigenous lands, to open land for settler society. Indigenous peoples could assimilate or be pushed to the periphery of settler society and into Indian lands because Indigenous presence impeded settler progress, civilization, and possession of the land. The boundaries of Indigenous lands were constantly in flux to make way for settler society as settler demand for land intensified. Ultimately, most of Indian territory would be reduced to reservations to increase settler access, both public and private, to land. Settlers needed land to realize their goals of settler empire, including Mormon settlers. Access to land meant that Indigenous peoples often had to be forcibly removed from their homelands to justify settler claims. US and Mormon colonialism created these relationships of power between the colonizer/colonized and settler/Indigenous or settler/Lamanite to justify their violent policies of removal and assimilation. Empire building on this continent by settlers necessitated the possession of Indigenous land and the Lamanite subject position, marking Indigenous peoples as foreign.

Mormon settlers directly benefited from the US dispossession of Indigenous peoples while also contributing to Indigenous displacement, because Mormon settlers claimed Indigenous land as Mormon and wanted to exist outside the geopolitical boundaries of the United States as a Mormon empire. Mormon settlers also established themselves as the normative subject position, recognizably different from other US settlers especially in their relationship with Indigenous peoples as Lamanites, who would be saved from their fallen status. Mormon settlers, like other US settlers, "control indigenous policy" and did so within their civilizing policies and religious and secular education to uplift Indigenous peoples and possess Indigenous lands. Mormon settlers, like other settlers, sought to civilize Indigenous peoples as a means of possession and to assimilate into settler society. Settlers, including Mormons, feared that Indigenous rejection of their civilizing efforts via religious conversion would threaten settler society or settlers' belonging. Settler anxieties drove assimilation policies, including Mormon-Lamanite policies that relegated Indigenous peoples to a subject position that benefited their settler desires.[42] Settler sovereignty seeks to manage "their respective domestic domains" and relieve their anxiety of losing control or access to lands by Indigenous people's rejection of the policies designed to bring about their elimination and possession. Rejection of

Lamanite subject position and discourse thus confronts Mormon settler impulses of possession and claims to Indigenous lands and bodies.

Mormon settlers did not intend to become an extension of US settler empire. Instead, they intended to create their distinct settler society, Zion, based on Mormon settler religious ideologies. For example, Mormon settlers who moved to Independence, Missouri, and to Nauvoo, Illinois, and eventually to the Salt Lake Valley in Utah did so because they wanted to possess land and resources to create a distinctly Mormon space and place as prophesied and recorded in Mormon religious discourse. At each site, Mormon settlers tried to create their sovereign space, a Mormon settler empire, and moved outside the geopolitical boundaries of the United States to realize their goal of a Mormon nation-state. Mormon settlers fused a religious and political mandate to create their Mormon empire. Although Mormon scholars have argued that Mormons had been marginalized and dispossessed from their homes, Mormon settlers could choose to move to other locales in their bid to create Zion, or a Mormon settler society. Mormon settlers wanted to make their distinct "country" and "establish a better polity" to form an "exemplary model of social organisation" to the United States and other settlers.[43] As outlined in chapter 2, Mormon settlers sought to create a Mormon nation-state, but the Nauvoo experience, as just one example, fell short due to a variety of reasons, including their proximity to the US geopolitical boundaries and non-Mormon settler conflict. There are various moments in which the US settler empire converged with US settler desires of expansion, such as their move west to colonize Mexican territory. This was yet another attempt to create the Mormon empire by possessing the Indigenous land but also shows how Mormon settler colonialism functions at the margins and as an extension of the United States.

Mormon settler colonialism advanced a Mormon project of empire that reaffirmed Mormon settlers' sense of belonging by excluding Indigenous peoples from the Mormon center and apex of racial hierarchy. Mormon settler belonging was manifested in their move to belong, and Indigenous peoples became the settler by assuming their Lamanite subject position. The logics of Mormon settler colonialism required the move to whiteness by Mormon settlers and the use of infrastructures to embed and naturalize their belonging and possession of Indigenous land. The Mormon settler subject position has largely been excluded from the discourse on US settler colonialism because Mormon scholarship is a subfield in US history, much like Indigenous history. Mormon history, like Indigenous history, is central to understanding how Mormon settler colonial processes operated to create the American West as a place and structure. Mormon and Indigenous histories are central to the history of the United States.

Public structures have been deliberately built and curated to celebrate and reinforce Mormon settler narratives in which settler presence, settler subject position, and possession are naturalized. The LDS Church utilized statues, monuments, and buildings (physical infrastructures) to mark Mormon space and highlight the ideologies of Mormon settler colonialism: whiteness, possession, and Lamanite subject position discourse function together. Mormon settler monuments, such as Young's statue, are "an act of possession" that upholds and sustains Mormon settler colonialism.[44] The statues of Young on the BYU campus and at This Is the Place Heritage Park celebrate his role as prophet and governor while also naturalizing and reifying Mormon whiteness as Indigenous peoples are dispossessed from the land and the narrative. The statue, building signage, and park are part of the uninterrupted Mormon settler colonial project to unsettle Indigenous claims to land. Mormon settler belonging is also cemented in the built environment via infrastructures to reflect Mormon possession.

OVERVIEW OF BOOK

This book is not a decolonization project, nor is it about Indigenous refusal. That is, I am not calling for individual Mormon Indigenous members to denounce their membership or dismantle the LDS Church as a structure of Mormon settler colonialism. Instead, I seek to uncover Mormon settler colonial structures of power and push back on the centering of the Mormon settler subject position by making visible Mormon settler colonialism and identifying how Mormon settler colonialism functions to possess Indigenous peoples and lands. This book is meant to make visible the Mormon settler subject position as innocent, the center in which Mormon settler power emanates, and *the* normative Mormon subject position. The function and operationalization of Mormon whiteness is pivotal to understanding race in and outside the Mormon context, first by acknowledging and recognizing the formation of the Mormon settler subject position and dissemination of the subject position in LDS Church discourse, including in and through the Lamanite subject position, and narratives produced by Mormon settlers about themselves and Indigenous peoples.

I use settler colonialism to understand how Mormon settlers created narratives of belonging to justify their possession of land. My intention is to make visible how Mormon settler colonial processes function at various moments to serve the Mormon settler colonial center and explore the ways in which these Mormon settler colonial ideologies drove these processes that shaped indigeneity historically and into the present. While individual agency/experience is important, Indigenous experiences happen in a larger context of US and Mormon settler colonialism. Mormon settlers became the normative subject position and center in Mormon settler discourse, thus making invisible the processes in which Mormon settlers have literally and figuratively dispossessed and disappeared Indigenous peoples. Mormon settler narratives focus on their experiences of religious persecution and, in doing so, normalizes the production of Mormon settler narratives to secure their belonging.[45] My book is about illuminating the logics of Mormon settler colonialism, specifically how structures and policies function in tandem using Mormon settler texts, policies, and discourse to construct indigeneity and dispossess Indigenous peoples of their identity and lands. Mormon history is the beginning of settler history, and scholarship must mark Mormon settlers as the Other. The purpose of my book is to locate the formation of Mormon settler colonialism to deepen our understanding of race in the LDS Church and in the US Mormon settler constructions of the Lamanite subject position, or indigeneity, which can be useful to make sense of how Mormon settlers utilized religious ideologies to uphold Mormon white supremacy and possession of Indigenous peoples and lands.

When I initially began this project, I was not immersed in theory to better understand the Mormon-Indian experience. Over time, my approach and use of theory have changed and will continue to change as I seek to make sense of Indigenous people's lives when they intersect with settler structures, such as the LDS Church. The initial interaction I had with an educated, Mormon white settler female piqued my interest and confused me because her Mormon experience became *the* Mormon experience.[46] I walked away from that discussion realizing that while I grew up in the LDS Church and considered myself to be a faithful member, others did not see me as fully Mormon because I am seen first as Indigenous, or Dakota. Damakota, which means "I am Dakota." I will always be Dakota, but I was also raised as Mormon, yet that is not a visible subject position I carry that can be recognized by others.

My worldview and academic training are centered within the discipline of Indigenous studies. This project is meant to be a starting point for scholars and lay Mormon members to think more critically about Mormon and Indigenous histories and how settler colonialism functions and operates in our daily lives. How do our histories as Indigenous peoples change our understanding of Mormonism? How do we as Indigenous peoples confront the ways in which our histories are told and written about by those who do not recognize settler colonialism as an ideology and how these ideologies influence infrastructures and processes? How do Mormon-Indigenous histories change when we name Mormons as settlers or identify the structures and function of Mormon settler colonialism or white supremacy? Mormon and Indigenous history does not begin in 1830, yet that is the first time the Book of Mormon references Lamanites, or the Indigenous peoples of this continent.

Our histories begin in our creation stories, which connect us to very specific places. Our stories are erased when histories do not begin with the land. If Indigenous peoples existed prior to the founding of the LDS Church, how does settler understanding around the origins of the LDS Church change? My book hopes to answer the following questions: Does the LDS Church's relationship to Indigenous peoples change when framed within settler colonial studies? How does Mormon settler colonialism function if we do not critically examine within the context of the US settler colonial project? How have Mormon settlers remade space to be distinctly Mormon as they erase Indigenous presence? How does Mormon settler understanding of Indigenous peoples as Lamanites inform the construction of indigeneity? Mormon settlers and Mormon settler colonialism are largely absent in Indigenous studies, and too often the focus on indigeneity is relegated to the US-Tribal context. Each chapter in this book is meant to highlight how Mormon settler colonialism functions through the production of Lamanite and Mormon settler subject positions and discourse. Mormon possession of Indigenous lands was integral to the making of the Mormon empire in which Mormon settlers relied on religious ideologies and narratives to justify their possession of Indigenous lands, resources, and bodies to the Mormon settler center as they created the Mormon empire.

The Mormon settler colonial present has roots in the founding of the LDS Church and intersects and advances US colonialism and settler colonialism into the modern era. This book renders Mormon settler colonialism visible because the Mormon settler is decentered, made visible, so as to understand how race and whiteness have been constructed in and by the LDS Church. The structures and processes of Mormon settler colonialism must be named and explored in all their forms, and I do so in each chapter, where I illuminate one aspect of Mormon settler colonialism. Each chapter examines an aspect of Mormon settler colonialism, starting from the establishment of the LDS Church, the publication of religious texts such as the Book of Mormon, and the ISPP as ideology and structure premised on the Lamanite subject position. I choose various moments beginning in the early and late nineteenth century and in the twentieth century to show the range and depth of the Mormon settler colonial project.

Mormon Settler Colonialism is divided into four chapters. This introduction, where I take a chronological, episodic approach to illuminating Mormon settler colonialism, provides the theoretical framework for each chapter of the book. I began with the origins of Mormon settler colonialism, which coincides with the founding of the LDS Church, and moved to how the Lamanite subject position was constructed using religious texts. The examples I used in this introduction demonstrate the fluidity of the Mormon settler and Lamanite subject positions and policies to suit Mormon settler desires.

Chapter 1, "Mormon Settler Colonialism and the Production of Lamanite Discourse and Subject Position," introduces Mormons as settlers and their racialization of Indigenous peoples. As interactions with Indigenous peoples increased, boundaries between Mormon settlers and Indigenous peoples became fluid, changing to reflect Mormon settler tendencies at various moments and places. Mormon settlers' othering of Indigenous peoples is not at all unique, because all settlers have othered Indigenous peoples. However, I argue that what is unique about Mormon settlers' othering of Indigenous peoples is that they do so with the creation of the Lamanite subject position. While this subject position comes with all kinds of unique characteristics and narratives, at its core it is doing the necessary work of dispossession and elimination. My book, then, is about making the Lamanite subject position visible as a process of settler colonialism; contextualizing Mormon settler ideologies and how the LDS Church and its members implemented, produced, and applied these narratives; and deconstructing Mormon settler colonial processes. Chapter 1 also explores how Joseph Smith played a pivotal role in creating and disseminating the Lamanite subject position. Using the Book of Mormon and Doctrine and Covenants, a modern religious text, this chapter focuses on the early origins and understanding of the Lamanite subject position and how Mormon leaders interacted with American Indian peoples based on Mormon religious beliefs about Lamanites. Chapter 1 contextualizes the Lamanite subject position within a broader framework of Mormon and US settler colonialism and shows us how Mormon settler colonialism functioned by defining and giving meaning to Indigenous identity via the creation and application of the Lamanite subject position. Mormon settler colonialism constructs of indigeneity do not limit identity to citizenship or enrollment. In the Mormon context, Indigenous identity is based on lineage, specifically as Book of Mormon descendants, and Mormon settlers used the Lamanite subject position to define indigeneity as it pertained to their settler identity.

Chapter 2, "Council of Fifty: Operationalizing Mormon Settler and Lamanite Ideologies onto the Land," examines the ways in which Mormon settlers began to advance the Mormon settler colonial project based on their religious ideologies, including the building of Nauvoo, Illinois, and the establishment of the Council of Fifty to oversee Mormon settler desires to expand. This chapter charts how Mormon settler ideologies about Lamanites, including missions, and land influenced early LDS Church structures and efforts to locate and build a Mormon empire. The chapter begins with the establishment of Nauvoo, a Mormon settler colonial outpost along the Mississippi River and part of the "frontier" of US settler society. Nauvoo becomes the haven for Mormon settlers seeking refuge from religious and political violence in other Mormon settler sites, such as Missouri. Mormon settlers escaping Missouri violence and expulsion chose Nauvoo for its strategic location along the river. Nauvoo would be made into a Mormon settler space and would serve as the religious and political center for Mormon settlers under the leadership of Joseph Smith. Under Smith's leadership, Mormon settlers built Nauvoo infrastructures and created the Council of Fifty due to their interest in Indigenous peoples, or Lamanites, and oversaw the exploration of lands in the West. Using the minutes of the Council of Fifty, chapter 2 illuminates the important role of the council, a group of white Mormon men charged with creating a Mormon theocratic nation. The council also played an important role in early LDS Church diplomatic relations with American Indians and the exploration of potential sites for Mormon empire in the American West. Mormon missionary efforts and the expansion into Indigenous land reflect the ways in which Mormon settlers also sought to civilize Indigenous peoples via religious conversion and claim Indigenous land as their own. Mormon manifest destiny moves beyond American manifest destiny because God privileged Morman claims above all others. Mormon civilizing efforts were rooted in the notion of American Indians as Lamanites, which meant that Indigenous claims to land could be terminated since Indigenous peoples did not fulfill the prescribed Mormon subject position. Mormon settlers continued to explore the West and identified future potential sites for Mormon settlement. The Council of Fifty became pivotal in the operationalization of Mormon settler structures that advanced US and Mormon settler colonialism rooted in the possession of Indigenous peoples to access land and resources. Chapter 2 uncovers the nuanced ways in which Mormon and US settler colonialism intersected and simultaneously existed in opposition to one another.

Due to ongoing and escalating religious persecution, Mormon settlers began to look at the West as a place of refuge. Chapter 3, "The Mormon Pioneer Settler Landscape: Embedding Mormon Identity onto the Land," examines how this shared experience of religious persecution became the catalyst behind a Mormon pioneer subject position to secure Mormons' whiteness. While many Mormon historians frame this persecution as an example of the marginalization and racialization of Mormon settlers, I argue that Mormon settlers maintained their ability to move west and claim land because of their status as settlers and secured their belonging to land through narratives and structures that embed the Mormon settler subject position. Mormon settlers accessed and utilized their whiteness at times when it advanced their claims to Indigenous land. These experiences became vital in understanding how Mormon settlers secured their belonging because they moved with their settler sovereignty. Historian Lisa Ford defines settler sovereignty as the interconnectedness of jurisdiction, empire, and sovereignty predicated on "indigenous subordination."[47] Settlers, including Mormon settlers, sought to legitimize their presence and did so by limiting or destroying Indigenous jurisdiction and claims to land. Empire and sovereignty "grew at the same time and in dialogue" by "set[ting] the conditions for conquest, defined what land was empty, what land was as good as empty, and which sorts of political communities could exercise rights over land and people and under what conditions."[48] Mormon settlers tested and exercised their settler sovereignty in the US geopolitical margins as they asserted their right to claim land to build a Mormon empire. In doing so, Indigenous peoples became displaced from the land and religious discourse as the Other. The Mormon settler subject position gave meaning to the Lamanite subject position as the LDS Church built a Mormon settler society. "Pioneer" is a Mormon settler subject position; specifically, Mormon settlers' use of "pioneer" conceals and naturalizes Mormon settler processes. Chapter 3 also explores how Mormon settler subject position functioned by marking place and history as Mormon. Brigham Young, the second president and the prophet of the LDS Church, declared of the Salt Lake Valley "This is the place!" on July 24, 1847. The date of Young's declaration has been marked as important to not just Mormon history but also Utah state history, which declared this day a state holiday only two years after Mormon settler arrival. Young's statement led to the colonization of the region by Mormon settlers and erased Indigenous peoples from the historical narrative but also from the memory of the land when a historic site was constructed in 1947 to commemorate Mormon pioneers/settlers at This Is the Place Heritage Park in Salt Lake City, Utah. Indigenous peoples became the Other on their land as Mormon settlers continued to create and propagate this pioneer subject position. The possession of Indigenous peoples is central to Mormon settler colonialism, in which Indigenous peoples become either the Other on their land or are completely physically or metaphorically pushed to the periphery of the historical narrative. The infrastructures of Mormon settler colonialism and how Mormon settlers possess and mark land as Mormon become visible in this chapter.

Chapter 4, "'The Lamanites Shall Blossom as a Rose' The Indian Student Placement Program and Redemption of Lamanite Children," examines how Mormon settlers built infrastructures, such as the ISPP, to aid in the operationalization of a

Lamanite subject position. Mormon settlers used the intimate spaces of their homes to extend Mormon infrastructure to possess Indigenous children and sever their connection to their families and communities. The ISPP was designed to further embed and render Mormon settler colonialism invisible by the LDS Church. Touted as a foster care program, the ISPP was the manifestation of Lamanite policies designed to move Indigenous peoples to a status as the Other because they served Mormon settler colonial ideologies about the racialized Other. Indigenous peoples as Lamanites meant that they could never become fully Mormon because their subject position was predicated on their racialization. This racialized hierarchical status within the LDS Church cemented Mormon whiteness and further marked Indigenous peoples as the religious and racialized Other. Mormon settler education shaped and redefined indigeneity and would have a negative impact on Indigenous children, who would remain on the margins of Mormon settler colonial society. Indigenous children made sense of their indigeneity within US and Mormon settler colonial structures that oftentimes were detrimental to their sense of self and belonging, whether in a tribal, religious, or national context.

In the conclusion, "Mormon Settler Colonialism's Endpoint: Enduring Mormon Settler and Lamanite Discourse in Mormon Infrastructures," I utilize two more contemporary examples to demonstrate how Mormon settler colonialism continues to be produced and persists in the modern era. Indigenous peoples remain and are assigned a Lamanite subject position in published religious discourse and moved to the margins when their histories conflict and challenge Mormon settler presence. The 2020 *Come Follow Me* handbook published globally by the LDS Church and disseminated to members used racialized language to describe Indigenous peoples as uncivilized Lamanites. This manual is evidence of how Mormon discourse maintains these hierarchical categories of indigeneity and whiteness. The following year, the Manti Utah Temple, located in Manti, Utah, began renovations, and initial plans marked murals painted by Minerva Teichert, a Mormon artist, for removal. The mural removal became contentious within public discourse, much like the contestations over defacement of Young, and calls for the preservation of Teichert's mural arose. Ultimately the LDS Church decided to preserve the mural, an ode to Mormon settler life and a vision of empire on this continent despite protests to disrupt Mormon settler infrastructures and narratives. The Mormon "pioneer" and settler subject position and narrative persists in the twenty-first century.

Mormon settler colonialism, including Mormon settler fantasies, constructs and institutionalizes the Lamanite subject position. The Mormon settler fantasy provides a way to escape culpability for enacting violence against Indigenous peoples as Mormon settlers have simultaneously experienced violence. According to Veracini, civilized modern settler societies must reject the very violent settler processes and institutions that created settler societies. The Mormon settler fantasy of Indigenous peoples as the Lamanite subject position fulfills this objective; this subject position and narrative make it possible for Mormon settlers to distance themselves from the removal, dispossession, and genocide of Indigenous peoples despite being active in Indigenous possession. The Mormon settler narrative reaffirms this settler fantasy; Mormon settlers can ignore their violent acts of Indigenous removal as they signal their innocence to the larger settler society in the production of Lamanite discourse. Indigenous peoples as Lamanites places blame squarely back onto Indigenous peoples, thus removing Mormon settler culpability.

The use of theory such as settler colonialism and whiteness not only decenters settler history but also names and explores how settler colonialism has impacted Indigenous peoples and communities historically and into the present. While individual agency and experience is important, Indigenous experiences happen in a larger context of US and Mormon settler colonialism. My book is about illuminating the logics of Mormon settler colonialism, specifically how infrastructures and policies function in tandem using Mormon settler texts, policies, and discourse to construct indigeneity and dispossess Indigenous peoples of their identity and lands. Mormon-Indigenous history begins with the founding of the LDS Church and religious rhetoric on how Mormon settlers encountered Indigenous peoples and how Indigenous peoples functioned within Mormon settler structures.

My intention with this book is to show how Mormon settler colonialism is embedded in the structures and discourse of the LDS Church. Mormon Indigenous peoples must navigate within these structures, but their experiences must move beyond individual agency and instead be placed within the framework of Mormon settler colonialism. I pick key episodes to highlight how Mormon settlers operationalized Lamanite and settler colonial policies. Mormon settler colonialism has been ignored within Indigenous and settler colonial studies. Mormon settler colonialism contracts and moves with the US settler colonial project. Vital to the Mormon and US settler colonial projects is the racialization of Indigenous peoples as the Other to secure access to and possession of land. In chapter 1 I begin with the origins of Lamanite discourse and subject position, which have provided the necessary justification for racializing Indigenous peoples as the Other.

1 MORMON SETTLER COLONIALISM AND THE PRODUCTION OF LAMANITE DISCOURSE AND SUBJECT POSITION

And this testimony shall come to the knowledge of the Lamanites and the Lemuelites, and the Ishmaelites, who dwindled in unbelief because of the iniquity of their fathers, whom the Lord has suffered to destroy their brethren the Nephites, because of their iniquities and their abominations. And for this very purpose are these plates preserved, which contain these records—that the promises of the Lord might be fulfilled, which he made to his people. And that the Lamanites might come to the knowledge of their fathers, and that they might know the promises of the Lord, and that they may believe the gospel and rely upon the merits of Jesus Christ, and be glorified through faith in his name, and that through their repentance they might be saved. Amen.

DOCTRINE AND COVENANTS, 3:18–20

In this chapter, I examine the origins of Lamanite discourse beginning with Joseph Smith, the first prophet of the Church of Jesus Christ of Latter-day Saints (LDS Church), alongside religious texts such as the Book of Mormon and Doctrine and Covenants, to make visible Mormon settler belonging and displacement of Indigenous peoples and illuminate the processes of Mormon settler colonialism. The story of Joseph Smith, his desire to find the *truth*, becomes the catalyst for Mormon narratives around faith, place, and belonging. Smith was a young man during the Second Great Awakening and joined thousands of others searching for belonging within religious infrastructures. I am not interested in debates on whether Smith was a *real* prophet or if the LDS Church's religious ideologies are true; rather, my fascination lies in how his experiences have been parlayed into narratives about religious doctrine and belonging, particularly how Mormon belonging and religious beliefs are tied to land. Joseph Smith's religious experiences, including the unearthing of the Book of Mormon, becomes symbolically and ritually important to Mormon belonging in the United States while also legitimizing his authority in creating and becoming the center of Mormon settler colonial power. Smith was a quintessential American settler. He lived on Indigenous lands while dispossessing Indigenous peoples from their lands. Mormon religious ideologies drove Mormon settler desires tied to the land. America was the land of promise, a future Mormon empire, or Zion.

In order to realize their Mormon settler desires, Indigenous peoples had to be displaced, yet Smith and Mormon settlers were invested in the redemption of Indigenous peoples as a means to realize their goals of empire. However, Mormon settler desires and Indigenous redemption could not exist alongside one another, which is why Indigenous people's presence within Mormon settler colonial ideologies matters. Mormon settlers needed Indigenous peoples to authenticate and substantiate their presence and claims to land. The Mormon move to innocence that secures Mormon settler belonging occurs when Indigenous peoples do not become Lamanite. When Indigenous peoples do not subscribe to Mormon settler religious ideologies, their removal and disappearance from the land and narratives about place and belonging are justified. The construction and discourse of a Lamanite subject position becomes necessary for Mormon settlers' claims to Indigenous lands and resources while securing Mormon settler presence and belonging to land.

In this chapter I do not include how Indigenous peoples navigated within this space or Lamanite subject position, because I want to make visible Mormon settler colonial processes, including racial formations. I am interested in the Mormon settler colonial imaginary to understand how the LDS Church "envisions its relationship to the world in a particular way and generates a hegemonic discourse and symbolic system to enforce that perspective" using primarily Smith's religious experiences, the Book of Mormon, and the Doctrine and Covenants.[1]

I specifically focus on the production of the Lamanite subject position to highlight how Mormon settler colonialism functions and do not focus on how Indigenous peoples engage in and with the LDS Church as Lamanites. Instead, I focus on how Mormon settlers relied on Mormon texts and speeches to produce the Lamanite subject position to serve the Mormon settler goals of empire. As I demonstrate, the Lamanite subject position shifts to assert and maintain Mormon white supremacy in the nineteenth century.

The founding of the LDS Church and the publication of its religious texts illustrate how the formation of Mormon settler colonialism has been utilized to possess Indigenous people's identity, history, and land. I begin this chapter with a brief history of Joseph Smith and his role in translating and publishing the Book of Mormon to highlight the production of Mormon settler narratives that create Mormon community and belonging. This early history of Smith and the LDS Church is also necessary to understand the Lamanite subject position and discourse and the Mormon settler desire to belong on Indigenous lands. The origin story of the LDS Church and the patriarchal power of Smith tied Mormon settlers to the land and, in doing so, moved Mormon settlers to the center of power, including the power to produce and define the Lamanite subject position based on their religious texts. The Book of Mormon defined and embedded a Lamanite subject position and history into the foundation of the LDS Church. The Mormon settler colonial project racialized the Lamanite subject position as a means to access land and naturalize Mormon settler presence and possession of Indigenous lands. US and Mormon settlers marked Indigenous peoples as the Other because settler presence required Indigenous dispossession to legitimize their God-given settler right to possess and mark Indigenous land as Mormon settler land. These Mormon settler texts, as a function of Mormon settler colonialism, aid in the Mormon settler move to innocence. The Book of Mormon as a religious text is a manifestation of how the Mormon settler fantasy functioned on this continent. Smith wielded his authority as prophet of the LDS Church to construct the Lamanite subject position as a means to possess Indigenous peoples. The Book of Mormon serves the Mormon settler colonial center, and Smith gained religious power from the text and used his position as prophet to give meaning to the Mormon settler experience. While Smith was just an individual, he illuminated how he parlayed his desires to belong that were part of his very American experience. Smith's desire to belong provided a pathway to secure his patriarchal power and status as a white settler man. Mormon settlers' move toward innocence occurred as they distanced themselves from the violent removal and dispossession of Indigenous peoples as they remade Indigenous peoples into Lamanites. The Book of Mormon normalizes the origins of the Mormon settler subject position and history by focusing on the genesis of Lamanite peoples and discourse later in this chapter. According to Lamanite discourse, Lamanites descended from the first immigrants to this continent, thus justifying Mormon settler claims to land. I seek to disrupt the invisibility of Mormon settler colonialism, especially the processes around the production of indigeneity as Mormon settlers relied on a fluid Lamanite subject position to serve Mormon settler logics of possession. Mormon settlers justified their righteous claims to Indigenous lands and resources because Mormons were a "promised people," unlike the fallen Lamanites, or Indigenous peoples.

JOSEPH SMITH AND BOOK OF MORMON ORIGINS

Joseph Smith formally founded and organized the Church of Christ, later changed to the Church of Jesus Christ of Latter-day Saints officially on April 6, 1830.[2] He played an important role as founder and as first prophet, influencing early beliefs about American Indians as Lamanites based on the Book of Mormon. The LDS Church's early formations are pivotal to understanding Mormon settler colonialism and how Mormon settler and Lamanite subject positions are coconstituted. Mormon settlers sought to possess Indigenous land and used Lamanite discourse to aid in the dispossession of Indigenous peoples from their lands. Smith's spiritual experiences and personal revelations from God and Jesus Christ were used to assert and claim that American Indians were descendants of Lamanites, as found in the Book of Mormon. Smith used the Book of Mormon as evidence of the first settlers to this continent: Lamanites. The Book of Mormon was also pivotal in disseminating Mormon religious worldviews that connected Mormonism to the Christian tradition, dating back to Jerusalem, despite its very American roots. Thus, when taken together, Smith's spiritual revelations, the origins of the Book of Mormon, and textual examples found in the Book of Mormon became the foundations of the Mormon settler subject position, narrative, and history. Smith's use of the Book of Mormon also demonstrates how Mormon settler ideologies function within Mormon settler infrastructures.

The Book of Mormon is a Mormon settler text about the history of "God's dealings with ancient inhabitants of the Americas and contains the fulness [sic] of the everlasting gospel [Mormonism]."[3] The Book of Mormon is a chronological history organized into books written by fourteen different prophets that document their people's spiritual and secular history on the American continent. Ancient prophets wrote on gold plates, and a prophet, Mormon, would later compile these records into an abridged narrative that would be buried. Joseph Smith would unearth this record and lead the effort to translate the gold plates into English for public distribution. Book of Mormon history begins with the arrival of migrant settlers from Jerusalem beginning in 600 BCE and is "an abridgment of the record of the people of Nephi, and also of the Lamanites." For the purpose of this book, I am going to focus on the Book of Mormon as a history of settler migrations into the American continent, where eventually "all were destroyed except the Lamanites." The Book of Mormon is a foundational religious text to the LDS Church because it documents the "personal ministry of the Lord Jesus Christ among the Nephites soon after His resurrection. It puts forth the doctrines of the gospel, outlines the plan of salvation, and tells men what they must do to gain peace in this life and eternal salvation in the life to come." Jesus Christ's visit to the Americas connects the Book of Mormon to Jerusalem and the larger Christian tradition that places Christ at the center of LDS religious teachings. Like the Bible, the Book of Mormon contains teachings given by Jesus Christ to Book of Mormon peoples that are foundational to modern LDS Church teachings and beliefs. Ultimately, Smith claims that the Book of Mormon is "the most correct of any book on earth, and the keystone of our religion, and a man would get nearer to God by abiding by its precepts, than by any other book." The Book of Mormon ends around 421 CE when Moroni, the last prophet of the Book of Mormon era, "sealed the sacred record."[4] Thus, the Book of Mormon contains *the* true history of Lamanites, written by Lamanites, on this continent and the restoration of Jesus Christ's gospel to the world according to the text.

Mormon discourse about the Lamanite subject position is formed around these Mormon settler colonial ideologies. The Book of Mormon is pivotal to this shift from Indigenous peoples being *of* the land to being recent migrants to this continent. The text and narratives around Joseph Smith and the Book of Mormon become central to the formation of race within the LDS Church. These narratives also serve another purpose in that Smith and the Book of Mormon are established as the center of power in developing Mormon settler infrastructures that also produced narratives about indigeneity on this continent. The Book of Mormon, a settler text or foundation for Mormon settler colonialism, was unearthed by Smith in 1823. His spiritual experiences are pivotal to understanding the origins and processes of Mormon settler colonialism through the recovery and production of the Book of Mormon as a Lamanite text. Smith uses the Book of Mormon to establish Mormon settler colonial power, a manifestation of settler presence on Indigenous lands, and the subsequent disappearance of Indigenous peoples from the narratives and land by imposing Mormon settler constructions of indigeneity.

A short biographical sketch of Joseph Smith is useful for understanding his desires to belong. His interest in religion was driven by his desire to belong to a place where his experiences and understanding of the world mattered. Ultimately, the life of Smith inspires others seeking out a community to belong to, and the narrative itself became part of Mormon settler structures and narratives about place that secure Mormon settler presence. On December 23, 1805, Smith was born to Lucy Mack and Joseph Smith Sr. in Sharon, Vermont. The Smiths came from parents whose families influenced their relationships to and with religion. For example, Joseph Sr.'s maternal great-grandfather had been a Congregational deacon, while Lucy's father had "lived without religion most of his life" until his conversion in later years.[5] While his father "hovered on the margins of the churches," Joseph Sr. had a "brief flirtation with Universalism" in 1797. Lucy fell ill in 1803, which renewed her interest in religion.[6] She eventually joined the Presbyterians after the Smith family moved to Palmyra, New York.[7] Joseph Smith Jr. did not join or attend church with his mother. The family subscribed to and drew from various denominations that were not "ranked by recognized authority[,] . . . all available for adoption as personal whim or circumstances dictated. The result was a religious melee."[8] Joseph Smith's family fostered an environment of religious inquiry that reflected the world around them. During his formative years, the Smiths lived in a region and a county consumed by religious fervor, or the Second Great Awakening. The religious landscape in Palmyra, New York, was dotted with various church denominations. Like his mother, Smith sought a religion that "was not then upon the earth."[9] His story is important because it positions Smith as a young innocent boy seeking religious enlightenment but also begins the process of positioning him as *the* authority that led to the origins of the LDS Church and as an extension of God's authority. Mormon settler presence and authority is a fulfillment of religious ideologies from the Book of Mormon.

According to the Book of Mormon, as a young boy Smith decided to pray and find out which church he should attend. He recounts his prayer and subsequent religious experience that becomes part of the Book of Mormon narrative:

> When the light rested upon me I saw two Personages, whose brightness and glory defy all description, standing above me in the air. One of them spake unto me, calling me by name and said, pointing to the other—*This is My Beloved Son. Hear Him!!* My object in going to inquire of the Lord was to know which of all the sects was right, that I might know which to join. . . . I was answered that I must join none of them, for they were all wrong; and the Personage who addressed me said that all their creeds were an abomination in his sight. . . . He again forbade me to join with any of them.[10]

Smith received his answer. He was to join no church because "they were all wrong." This "First Vision" would lead to the origins of what would become the LDS Church and the spiritual power bestowed by God to Smith. Smith's vision also claims that the Mormon faith is the only "true" Christian sect globally. Ultimately, this imbues Smith with a power that cannot be denied or dismissed. His religious and political power was derived directly from God, recognizing Smith as a modern Mormon prophet with divine power. Thus, Smith becomes the vessel in which revelation and religious doctrine and policies regarding Lamanites shape

Mormon settler power and relationships to and with Indigenous peoples. Smith becomes a powerful force in defining and shaping Mormon theology, including Lamanite discourse that becomes the only *truth* about Indigenous peoples on this continent and erases Indigenous sovereignty as Mormon settlers stake an authoritative claim over the Lamanite subject position. Smith's claims of American Indians as Lamanites drove Mormon settler policies that continue to extend beyond Smith's tenure and into the twenty-first century.

Smith's formative spiritual experiences also became part of the Mormon settler narrative that shaped early LDS Church history and beliefs, including the origins of the Book of Mormon. According to Smith, the Book of Mormon documents the origins of Lamanite people and their history. He had a second vision where the Book of Mormon was disclosed to him by the spiritual apparition Moroni, a prophet who kept a history of his people on gold plates, or the Book of Mormon. Smith recalled seeing an individual in

> a loose robe of most exquisite whiteness. It was a whiteness beyond any earthly thing could be made to appear so exceedingly white and brilliant. . . . [H]e was a messenger sent from the presence of God to me, and that his name was Moroni; that God had a work for me to do; and that my name should be had for good and evil among all nations, kindreds, and tongues. . . . He said there was a book deposited, written upon gold plates, giving an account of the former inhabitants of this continent, and the source from whence they sprang.[11]

Moroni, prophet-historian from the Book of Mormon, reappears as a spirit to Smith to inform him of the gold plates and the rich history and teachings found within the text. Lehi, whom I discuss in more detail later in this chapter and his family and followers were also "former inhabitants." Moroni completed the Book of Mormon before burying the record. Smith's second spiritual experience would direct him to the exact location of the gold plates on the Hill Cumorah, located in present-day Manchester, New York.[12] Smith's second vision further solidifies Smith's role as a spiritual leader in the modern LDS Church but also just as importantly secures the validity of the Book of Mormon to faithful followers. Smith, the Book of Mormon, and his spiritual experiences secure his belonging to a very American religion. A distinct Mormon settler subject position emerged based on Smith's spiritual experiences and religious texts. This power translated into religious and political power as an American leading the Mormon settler colonial project of empire.

Smith became the mouthpiece for the LDS Church and spoke with authority as he established the center of Mormon settler power. The language used in Smith's second spiritual experience encodes and embeds racialized language into the text by equating whiteness with righteousness. For example, Smith described the angel Moroni's clothing as the "most exquisite whiteness. It was a whiteness beyond any earthly thing could be made to appear so exceedingly white and brilliant." These terms embed Mormon whiteness by connecting to spirituality beyond human context and comprehension. The language utilized reaffirms Mormon settler whiteness as civilized because the trope of righteousness and one's spiritual status have been used to mark the racialized Other as the spiritual Other. Smith's account also legitimizes claims made about the gold plates, a history of this continent's "former inhabitants," or Indigenous peoples. Later, Indigenous peoples disappear from the land and narratives because this record is about Lamanites, and as such stories from Indigenous peoples get ignored in lieu of privileging the Book of Mormon as the only source of truth about Indigenous people's history on this continent. This text then becomes the only record of Lamanite history and written document of Indigenous people's existence and ties to this land. This is how Mormon settlers wielded their power, marking Indigenous peoples as the Other based on the narratives found in religious texts written by Lamanites. This is an act of Mormon settler possession, the ability to produce and give meaning to Indigenous history and peoples by asserting Lamanite discourse onto the bodies and lands of Indigenous peoples.

The ability to produce a Lamanite subject position and discourse relied on the premise of Indigenous peoples as immigrants to the American continent. The Book of Mormon, much like the Bible, begins in Jerusalem, thus connecting the LDS Church to Christianity and holy lands. This connection to Jerusalem is vital to the claims made in the Book of Mormon: Lehi, his family, and his followers fled Jerusalem to the American continent for religious refuge. In the nineteenth century, narratives about the United States as a site of religious freedom were common, and Mormon claims about this continent resonated and reinforced those beliefs about land. The settler subject position came from narratives about the land as terra nullius, ready for colonization by those seeking a better life including those seeking religious freedom. The Book of Mormon produces narratives about the land, including Mormon settlers' exceptional claims to land. The Book of Mormon foretold the arrival of settlers seeking religious refuge, and this narrative resonates with Smith and Mormon settlers who are also seeking freedom to practice religious ideologies that secure their claims to land. Their settler claims to Indigenous land, or Lamanite land, would be cemented by claims made in the Book of Mormon, beginning with an account written by Nephi, a son of Lehi, a leader who fled from Jerusalem with his father, his family, and other followers.

Nephi recounts his favored status as he documents the "true" history in the "language of the Egyptians."[13] Lehi, like Smith, has a dream where he sees God and twelve others, who give him a book to read.[14] The book prophesied the fall of Jerusalem because of its inhabitants' wickedness, which meant that Jerusalem "should be destroyed, and the inhabitants thereof; many should perish by the sword, and many should be carried away captive into Babylon."[15] Lehi publicly shared his spiritual experience with others in hopes of converting followers but instead became the target of religious persecution. The parallels between Smith and Lehi are significant: God visited them in a life-changing spiritual experience and gave them crucial religious teachings, and they proselytized among unbelievers as prophets. I utilize these two examples to demonstrate how white patriarchal power is produced within and by Mormon settler texts and how these prophets become the center of Mormon power and empire. These individual settlers use their power to produce the religious Other, or Lamanite subject position, in religious discourse about rightful claims to land. Thus, Mormon settler presence is justified and in fact is a fulfillment of prophecy. The Book of Mormon also simultaneously constructs a narrative about the land and settler presence by naturalizing Mormon settler claims to land and resources. The narratives about Smith and Lehi also become central to the construction of Mormon settler structures and narratives about belonging.

The production behind the Book of Mormon, including narratives around Smith's discovery and founding of an American religion, become important in constructing Mormon whiteness, belonging, and Mormon settlers' move to innocence. After a copyright was secured, the first Book of Mormon was printed and published in 1830. The book was disseminated to a larger Mormon settler readership who would take seriously the claims made by this settler text as a literal history of Indigenous peoples on this continent. Lamanite discourse worked because it reinforced widely held beliefs about Indigenous peoples: Indigenous peoples needed to be civilized, as they stood in the way of settler progress. The civilization process could begin when Indigenous peoples were introduced to the Book of Mormon via missionary efforts to Tribal Nations. Smith used modern revelation to reinforce Mormon settler claims to land, and this text advances settler sovereignty, although not always visible, as Mormon settlers moved from place to place. Mormon whiteness, including Smith's, meant that the settlers could access their whiteness at moments that advanced their desires to create Mormon Zion. The purpose of this religious text is twofold: outline religious ideologies, which in turn would sanction Mormon settler claims to land. These claims to land were fluid and ever changing to serve Mormon settler colonial desires. Smith, the center of Mormon settler authority and power, moved the center of Mormon empire several times, including to Nauvoo, Illinois, which I discuss in chapter 2. This move to Ohio, Missouri, Illinois, and eventually the Salt Lake Valley became part of the Mormon settler narrative about sacrifice and faith, the foundation of Mormon settler belonging. Mormon settlers moved from place to place to practice their religion freely, yet at the same time their movement aligned with the US settler colonial project of expansion. Mormon settlers relied on religious texts and prophetic revelations to locate their next Mormon settler site. The language around the establishment of Mormon empire is tied to religious texts and leaders who claimed land exclusively for Mormon settler use. Mormon settlers created and embedded empire onto the land, whether through infrastructures that marked land as distinctly Mormon and in narratives that carved out and justified these claims to land. The power of the text itself extends the processes of Mormon settler colonialism. According to God's commandments, Mormon settlers would claim "this land, which is the land of Missouri, which is the land which I have appointed and consecrated for the gathering of the saints. Wherefore, this is the land of promise, and the place for the city of Zion."[16] While the language refers to Missouri, definitions of "this land" changes, especially when Mormon settlers migrate west to the Salt Lake Valley, proof of the fluidity of Mormon settler colonial desires for land to build empire. The language used in these Mormon settler texts produces the rhetoric around Mormon settler colonialism, ever changing to suit the needs of Mormon settlers and the center of Mormon power. As the LDS Church expanded globally, settler texts validated the Mormon settler colonial project and coincided with the fluidity of Lamanite discourse, and expansion of the Lamanite subject position was purposeful and coincided with the expansion of LDS missionary efforts. LDS missionaries sought to convert Indigenous peoples globally by making an ancestral connection to the Book of Mormon, a means to connect them to the modern LDS Church.

THE BOOK OF MORMON AND THE PRODUCTION OF LAMANITE DISCOURSE AND A SUBJECT POSITION

The production of Indigenous peoples as Lamanites was necessary to the Mormon settler colonial project. Central to Mormon settler colonialism was the production and categorization of indigeneity using "Lamanite," a label to reference the diverse Indigenous nations and peoples on the American continent. This unifying subject position was meant to control indigeneity and legitimized Lamanite discourse, particularly the category of Lamanite as the racialized, religious Other. Lamanite discourse as a discursive field of knowledge silenced Indigenous voices, experiences, and worldviews, which were replaced with Mormon settler narratives about a people and land that centered the settler. Even if Lamanites wrote the Book of Mormon, their narratives about the land sever their relationship to it when they become unrighteous. As unrighteous peoples, their claims to land were tenuous at best, and therefore Indigenous peoples disappear from the narratives and from the land, further entrenching this racialized status and normalizing Mormon settler presence and subject position.

Mormon settler colonial ideologies relied on religious, racialized ideologies to erase Indigenous claims to lands, an extension of the larger American colonial project of removal and assimilation of Indigenous peoples. Mormon settlers severed Indigenous claims to land by marking Indigenous people as the descendants of Lamanites, settlers of this continent. The production of Mormon settler colonialism was based on Mormon settler texts, which elucidate how settlers name Indigenous peoples as Lamanites to disrupt connection and sever their access and connection to land. Mormon settlers, just like other settlers, made claims to land that directly challenged Indigenous peoples' rights to land because Mormons' righteous claims, or manifest destiny, were supported by religious texts. Joseph Smith could articulate Mormon settlers' primacy to land using religious rhetoric, specifically their Lamanite discourse that made it possible to live their settler fantasies driven by their desires to belong as they secured their whiteness. Settlers displaced Indigenous peoples and remade society, so the settlers, including Mormons, became the center. Settlers' experiences and presence became normalized as they racialized the Other, or Lamanites, in a hierarchal settler society. Their settler status, or whiteness, marked their possession of Indigenous land as inevitable, even justifiable since Lamanites were unbelievers, savages living in a degraded state. In the Mormon context, Indigenous peoples were simply other settlers who could be displaced by righteous, white settlers. Indigenous people's uncivilized ways paved the way for settler claims and the (re)making of land tied to Mormon whiteness.

The (re)making of narratives around land can also be found throughout the Book of Mormon. Nephi writes an account of his family and his father Lehi's foreshadowing of the destruction of Jerusalem. Lehi is commanded to take his family and "depart into the wilderness."[17] Lehi and his family left to live in the "wilderness" until God instructed him to leave Jerusalem with his wife, sons, daughters, the sons' wives, and other followers. The language used to describe the wilderness echoed other descriptions of the American continent as this group departs for a "land of promise."[18] Like other migrants, Lehi, his family, and followers seek religious freedom and frame their arrival as one of religious necessity. Read another way, Lehi and his people claimed migrant status because of their desire to practice their religion freely; they did not intend to create a settler society. However, Lehi's group came to stay. They had no intention of leaving this land of promise. In fact, the language used to describe their migration and arrival meant that they would establish infrastructures to sustain their people. These settlers from Jerusalem displaced Indigenous peoples already living here, even if Nephi does not explicitly discuss other civilizations prior to their arrival. This further justifies their arrival and claims to land, and when discussing the formations of Lamanites, they can be settlers because Lehi's family and followers secure their settler status in their attempt to stay and establish Zion.

Upon the group's arrival to the American continent, a "land of promise," Nephi recorded their arrival, internal family conflicts, and an extensive history of their people. Nephi kept two records; one recorded the "reign of the kings, and the wars and the contentions of my [Nephite] people," and another was about the "the ministry," or religious contestations, from their arrival to their fall.[19] Nephi begins his record of their family's migration across the ocean, arriving on the American continent around 600 BCE. Eventually, the history of the rise and fall of two great nations that originated from Lehi and his family, the first settlers on this continent, became the foundation for Lamanite discourse and gives meaning to the Lamanite subject position. This origin story of Lehi and his family and followers shapes a narrative in which their settler ideologies, presence, and right to land becomes naturalized, coded as sacred, protected from criticism. Their narrative casts Indigenous peoples as settlers, thus securing Mormon settlers' belonging to the land and move to innocence. For the purpose of this book, I am focusing on this origin story of Lamanites to demonstrate how the production of Lamanite discourse relies on the othering of Lamanites to displace and undermine their claims to land, or being *of* the land. For example, after their arrival, there was immediate discord in Lehi's family. Laman and Lemuel, the two eldest sons, did not want to follow their father or youngest righteous brother, Nephi. Instead, they rebelled while Nephi heeded his father's warning to follow God. Nephi became the patriarchal leader of the group and decided to separate from his brothers and take his "family, and . . . all those who would go with [him] were those who believed in the warnings and the revelations of God" to create a separate, righteous civilization.[20] Righteousness marks the difference between these two groups and becomes the genesis of a racialized Lamanite subject position and discourse. According to the Book of Mormon, Lamanites would be "cut off from his [God's] presence. And He caused the cursing to come upon them[;] . . . as they were *white*, and exceedingly *fair* and *delightsome*, that they might not be enticing unto my people [Nephites] the Lord God did cause a *skin of blackness* to come upon them. And thus saith the Lord God: I will cause that they shall be loathsome unto thy people, save they shall repent of their iniquities. And cursed shall be the seed of him that mixeth with their seed; for they shall be cursed even with the same cursing."[21]

Lamanites became cursed and marked with a "skin of blackness" due to their lack of faith, yet this categorization becomes necessary for Lamanites to be racialized and for their subject position to exist. Lamanites as a category of racialized difference justify their savage status and the difference between settlers and Indigenous peoples. This curse becomes the racialized delineation between the two civilizations based on notions of righteousness, or civilized status. This language is similar to the racialized and religious language used in papal bulls issued by the Catholic Church and the pope to colonize the religious Others, including Indigenous peoples living throughout the American continent. Lamanites became a cursed people, marked with a "skin of blackness," while Nephites remained "white, and exceedingly fair and delightsome." Nephites' literal whiteness is a reward for their righteousness, their marked status as a chosen people, or a civilized people. This marking of the body, becoming white, was not just symbolic but also advanced the logics of Mormon settler colonialism. Indigenous peoples disappear as a people *of* the land. Instead, the Book of Mormon advances the claim that Lamanites were part of the first wave of settlers on this continent, marked with a "skin of blackness" due to their savage state. Lamanite origins begin once God curses them because of their unrighteous, or savage nonbeliever status. Lamanites become outsiders, the Other, in their lands because of their inferior status. Nephites, and eventually righteous Mormon settlers, use and center their whiteness to claim the normative settler subject position and center of settler society. Despite being recent settlers from Jerusalem, Lehi, Nephi, and others become the progenitors of white civilization on the American continent. It should be nearly impossible for Nephi and his followers to claim whiteness because they migrated from Jerusalem, but there is power in this status and in their ability to access and wield their whiteness as a tool to possess Indigenous peoples. Nephites became physically white as a manifestation of their settler status, coded as "righteousness." In this settler text, the racialization of Indigenous peoples is vital to the Mormon settler colonial project: the production of indigeneity vis-à-vis Lamanite meant that settlers could assume a righteous settler status to possess land as Indigenous claims were severed. Nephi and the Book of Mormon also rely on the tired trope of the American continent as "empty," due to the fall of great civilizations, to legitimize their presence and possession of Indigenous lands and resources. Consequently, Indigenous peoples as Lamanite descendants meant they could never have primacy over land, especially given their uncivilized, fallen state as Lamanites.

This Mormon settler narrative is essential to understanding how Mormon settlers claimed a hierarchical, racialized status over Lamanites. Nephites became responsible for saving their Lamanite relatives who could not save themselves because they continued to live in a degraded status well into the twentieth century. Lamanites remained in this savage state until they recognized their "true" identity and heritage as Lamanite by converting to the LDS Church. For example, there is a brief account of how Nephites must "restore the Lamanites unto the true faith in God" but refused to do so because their "hatred was fixed, and they were led by their evil nature that they became wild and ferocious, and a blood-thirsty people, full of idolatry and filthiness."[22] The language utilized to describe Lamanites becomes part of the discourse produced by the Book of Mormon to maintain the marginalized status of Lamanites. This Lamanite discourse embeds a hierarchical status in which power is wielded by those defining and maintaining the narrative in which they, Nephites/settlers, exist at the apex. It does not matter whether Lamanites convert or follow God's teachings; their initial refusal provides the necessary justification to Nephites to become a chosen people as they assert religious and political power over Lamanites. The status between Nephites and Lamanites changes over time, but Lamanites as unrighteous and marked with a skin of blackness persists into the modern era.

Lamanites' rejection of God means that Indigenous claims to Lamanite land can be superseded by other settlers, especially Mormon settlers. Smith, based on the Book of Mormon and other religious texts and experiences, believed initially that American Indians were Lamanites who had forgotten their Lamanite heritage and became even more "wild, and ferocious." Later in the text, Lamanites became nomadic, wandering, which means that they were not tied to specific homelands, making settler claims to land even stronger. The Book of Mormon perpetuates US settler colonial views of Indigenous peoples as nomadic to erase the literal presence and connections of Indigenous peoples to their homelands. Nephite and later Mormon settlers marked and made claims to the land and, in this process, became native to the land. The use of Lamanite discourse becomes important in the process to possess Indigenous lands. The Book of Mormon perpetuates settler ideologies about the land, as settlers' move to innocence is secured by their righteous settler status. Nephites' move to the center happens simultaneously as Lamanites become the Other, nomadic migrants on their land. Finally, Mormon settlers employ and rely on settler fantasy narratives in which the American continent was a virgin wilderness, set aside for their explicit use. The land is a religious refuge for Lehi and his family and followers, which is replicated by Smith and his followers centuries later. According to the Book of Mormon, the arrival of Lehi and his family, and his followers and their claims to land supersede Indigenous claims because Lamanites were unworthy to be of the land. Smith and his adherents follow a similar pattern. Their righteous settler desires make them worthy of land, especially when Indigenous peoples were not willing to claim their Lamanite status, thus securing for Smith and his followers their whiteness and their claims to land legitimized by their civilized status.

EMBEDDING LAMANITE DISCOURSE INTO THE BOOK OF MORMON AND PRINT CULTURE

Lamanite discourse extends beyond the text and is embedded within Mormon infrastructures, including art that depicts settler migration to the American continent. This art inserts Lamanites in the Mormon settler colonial imaginary where Lamanites become descendants of white-complected, righteous settlers. These images further inscribe a settler subject position as natural, depicting Lamanites as the first settlers on this continent. For example, the well-known painting depicting a scene in the Book of Mormon, *Lehi and His People Arrive in the Promised Land* by Arnold Friberg, illustrates the crossing of Lehi, his family, and his followers to the American continent, or the "Promised Land." This painting is one of twelve Book of Mormon paintings commissioned in 1950 by Adele Cannon Howells, president of the Primary Association, an organization in the LDS Church established to educate children and during the fiftieth anniversary of *The Children's Friend* magazine commissioned a series of paintings by Friberg based on the Book of Mormon.[23] Eventually, every Book of Mormon published for the next fifty years included Friberg's paintings as illustrations alongside the text. In this depiction of the first settlers from Jerusalem, the artist's rendition takes liberty in his portrayal of Lehi and his family and followers. In the painting, Lehi is looking upward to the sky, presumably looking to God, and Lehi's wife Sariah is holding and leaning onto his shoulder. In the distance there is a mountainous landscape, partially covered by clouds. There are several individuals leaning over the right side of the boat, and one man stands on the bow, pointing to the distant land as others also cast their eyes in the same direction. Just behind Lehi and Sariah stands an imposing man, presumably Nephi. What is striking in this specific depiction is that the individuals depicted appear white, with very light complexions, despite being from Jerusalem. The use of art in the Book of Mormon and other Mormon spaces reinforces this racialized narrative of those who were righteous, or civilized, as white. This painting naturalizes the power of whiteness. The art embeds the belief that Lehi and his people as the first settlers to this continent seeking religious refuge and appears in every Book of Mormon printed and distributed globally. The arrival of Nephi and his family and followers signaled the fulfillment of religious ideologies as they made claims to land. While seeking religious refuge, these settlers would displace, marginalize, and remove unbelievers, including Lamanites. Racialized language and imagery further reinforce the difference between Nephites and Lamanites, in which the Lamanite curse becomes the identifier of the Other. Consequently, the curse makes easier identifying Indigenous peoples as outcasts suitable for removal and assimilation into Mormon settler society.

As a function of Mormon settler colonialism, Mormon settlers controlled the production and dissemination of the Lamanite subject position by publishing religious texts and speeches that established a clear relationship of power between Mormon settlers and Indigenous peoples, in which settlers occupy the apex of this racial hierarchy. The existence of Indigenous peoples confirmed Mormon settler claims that Lamanite descendants carried the curse of their ancestors. Lamanites could become white, indicating their righteousness, when they returned to God's presence. For example, the Book of Mormon states that "their scales of darkness shall begin to fall from their eyes; and many generations shall not pass away among them, save they shall be a white and a delightsome people."[24] This racialized language constructs Lamanite savagery and correlation to their ancestors' wickedness. Lineage becomes vital in determining one's place in Mormon theology. However, Lamanites could become righteous if they reclaimed their chosen status as God's children, or one of Israel's lost tribes, alongside Mormon settlers. There was value in being righteous, and one's status conveyed the power to literally become white. As chosen people, Mormon settlers could claim a space to fulfill religious mandates while reaffirming Book of Mormon prophecies. At its core, Mormon settler colonialism sought to disrupt Indigenous land claims by maintaining that Lamanites came from original settler stock and descended from the first immigrants to the Americas. Lamanites could secure their chosen status and restore connection to land by accepting the Book of Mormon as their history, further legitimizing claims made in these religious texts. The first edition of the Book of Mormon and the testimony of three witnesses—Oliver Cowdery, David Whitmer, and Martin Harris—confirms the belief of Indigenous peoples as Lamanites. They wrote, "Be it known unto all nations, kindreds, tongues and people, unto whom this work shall come, that we, through the grace of God the Father, and our Lord Jesus Christ, have seen the plates which contain this record, which is a record of the people of Nephi, and also of the Lamanites, his brethren[;] . . . we also know that they have been translated by the gift and power of God."[25]

The testimony of the three witnesses was meant to confirm the validity of the Book of Mormon, especially as a historical record of Lamanites. Smith shared these Mormon beliefs with others in hopes that they would convert or accept the teachings about this land. For example, Smith wrote a letter to Noah C. Saxton, editor of the *American Revivalist, and Rochester Observer*, a weekly evangelical newspaper dedicated to the "free discussion and critical investigation of the doctrines and duties of Christianity."[26] In this letter to the editor on January 4, 1833, Smith wrote, "The Book of Mormon is a record of the forefathers of our western Tribes of Indians. . . . By it we learn that our western tribes of Indians are descendants from that Joseph that was sold into Egypt, and that the Land of America is a promised land unto them, and unto it all the tribes of Israel will come."[27] In this letter, Smith clearly articulates that western American Indian tribes are Lamanites, a lost tribe of Israel, and that the Book of Mormon was a record of their ancestors. According to Smith, this land of promise was pledged to Lamanites and all other tribes of Israel, but this promise was never realized. Smith's letter effectively dismisses Indigenous histories that connect them to land and instead connects these western tribes to another continent and as settlers. Smith's initial definition of Lamanite was limited to western tribes because this definition coincided with Mormon settler interests in the region.

Mormon settler colonialism and the Lamanite subject position were rooted in the land and predicated on the removal and possession of Indigenous people's bodies, histories, and lands. Indigenous people's bodies became marked for removal due to their spiritual status as Lamanites. Lamanites became inherently wicked due to their ancestor's cursed status, while Nephites, or settlers, remained white and righteous. While these categories change over time, what emerged in the nineteenth century was Lamanite discourse of Indigenous peoples as religious, racialized Lamanites. Thus, the removal and disappearance of Indigenous peoples could be justified when indigeneity was also a spiritual, religious category. The Mormon settler colonial project necessitated Indigenous dispossession via absorption or expulsion from the Mormon settler body. When Mormon settlers encountered Indigenous peoples, many rejected their fallen status as Lamanites, which further reified Mormon settlers' views of Indigenous peoples as savage, while also playing into widely held tropes of American Indians as uncivilized.

THE FIRST LAMANITE MISSION

Joseph Smith's belief of Indigenous peoples as Lamanites shaped how the LDS Church functioned and developed policies to convert Indigenous peoples. Smith's religious experiences would continue to influence how Mormon settlers dealt with Lamanite peoples. Similar to US settler colonial policies of assimilation, Smith and his followers also sought to assimilate Indigenous peoples using religion. While other settlers used Christianity to signal civilization, Mormon settlers did not believe that they were civilizing agents because they were simply reuniting Indigenous peoples with their correct teachings. Lamanites must be civilized through LDS missionary efforts to introduce the LDS Church and Book of Mormon. During a church conference in Fayette, New York, in September 1830, Smith shared a recent revelation with the audience that the church would send missionaries to the Lamanites. Smith stated to Oliver Cowdery, "I say unto you that you shall go unto the Lamanites and preach my gospel unto them; and inasmuch as they receive thy teachings thou shalt cause my church to be established among them."[28] In order to expand church membership, Smith needed missionaries to attract new American Indian converts to fulfill religious ideologies about the Book of Mormon and Lamanites. The first Lamanite mission would introduce Indigenous peoples to the Book of Mormon, a history of their ancestors on this continent as a means to entice conversion. The Lamanite mission embodied paternalistic attitudes and fundamental Mormon beliefs about Lamanites, including the Book of Mormon as their history. Mormon missionaries were critical to Lamanite civilizing efforts, especially as the first Mormon missions had been sent among western tribes, a fulfillment of religious ideologies about Lamanites as a fallen people in need of redemption via baptism. The mission gave meaning to Mormon settler ideologies and their subject position as they sought to restore Indigenous peoples to a settler status. Many early converts and leaders secured their place within LDS Church leadership as they carried out Mormon settler desires to possess Indigenous peoples. For example, Oliver Cowdery, a recent convert, wanted to carry out Smith's settler desires guised as spiritual revelation and published his own commitment in the *Ohio Star* on October 17, 1830. Cowdery wanted to "go forth unto the Lamanites to proclaim glad tidings of great joy unto them, by presenting unto them the fulness of the Gospel, of the only begotten son of God."[29] David Whitmer, Parley P. Pratt, Ziba Peterson, and Peter Whitmer would join Cowdery in the first Lamanite mission to western tribes. Their public support for Smith's religious claims about Indigenous peoples justified their settler colonial desires to convert and civilize them as Lamanites. They were carrying out God's will.

Smith and Cowdery's spiritual experiences reaffirm their commitment to the Lamanite mission and erasing Indigenous spirituality, a manifestation of Mormon settler colonialism. Mormon spiritual leaders, including missionaries, claimed spiritual lordship over Indigenous peoples. Mormon missionaries believed the Book of Mormon to be a Lamanite text that could save themselves from their degraded, uncivilized status. Read another way, if Indigenous peoples just recognized their Lamanite history and heritage, they would no longer be constrained by their degraded status and could reclaim *real* indigeneity as a Lamanite. The Lamanite mission is an example of how Smith operationalized Lamanite policies that aligned with the desire to also build a Mormon empire. Missionaries could explore other possible sites for Mormon empire while trying to convert unbelievers, which I explore in chapter 2. Mormon missions constructed indigeneity by replacing indigeneity with a Lamanite subject position, history, and narrative.

Mormon empire and missionary efforts coincide in the first Lamanite mission. Cowdery and the other Mormon settler missionaries traveled west "to the borders of the Lamanites."[30] Indigenous peoples had been pushed to the periphery of constantly changing political boundaries in the United States, and Mormon settler missionaries took advantage of and benefited from chaos and contestations over land. These constantly changing borders would become contested territory between Indigenous peoples and settlers. Placed into the context of US-Indian relationships, the Lamanite mission to western Tribal Nations took place the same year as the passage of the Indian Removal Act, passed by Congress on May 28, 1830. Smith later writes about the US government's policy in regard to Indigenous Americans and President Andrew Jackson's removal policy, and at this moment Mormon and US settler interests converge:

> The plan of removing the aboriginal people who yet remain within the settled portions of the United States, to the country west of the Mississippi River, approaches its consummation. It was adopted on the most mature consideration of the condition of this race, and ought to be persisted in till the object is accomplished and prosecuted with as much vigor as a just regard for their circumstances will permit, and as far as their consent can be obtained. All preceding experiments for the improvement of the Indians have failed.[31]

Smith's attitudes toward "aboriginal people" echoed those of President Jackson, who campaigned on an anti-Indian platform. Smith attributed Indigenous removal west of the Mississippi to Indigenous people's failures to improve their condition or become civilized, not to the fact that their removal was principally due to settler desire and the demand for land and resources. Smith played upon these notions of civilization and used this rhetoric to justify Indigenous dispossession for their inability to become civilized. According to Smith and Mormon religious ideologies about Lamanites, Indigenous people could become civilized by recognizing their status and heritage as Lamanites, an important branch in the House of Israel, by becoming Mormon. Mormon settlers benefited from the removal of Indigenous peoples in 1830, and the Lamanite mission echoed US policies of assimilation and civilization. On January 13, 1831, Mormon settler missionaries arrived at Independence, Missouri, the closest town to dispossessed Tribal Nations along the western border of the United States. Independence, Missouri, would serve as a base of operations for Mormon settler missionaries and later would be identified as the future site of Mormon Zion. Cowdery and others crossed the "frontier line and commenced a mission among the Lamanites."[32] Mormon settler missionaries asserted their settler sovereignty and visited the Shawnees and Delawares in western Missouri and Indian territory.

Mormon settler missionaries relied heavily on the notion that Indigenous peoples would recognize the Book of Mormon as a literal history of their ancestors. In a speech to the Delawares, Cowdery stated that "[we] are glad of this opportunity to address you as our red brethren and friends[;] . . . thousands of moons ago, when the red men's forefathers dwelt in peace and possessed this whole land, the Great Spirit talked with them, and revealed His law and will, and much knowledge to their wise men and prophets."[33] In this speech, Cowdery introduces the Book of Mormon to Lamanites under the guise of sharing religious beliefs. Cowdery recalled how the "red man's" language was used and that Smith, a "pale-face," had to translate this Indigenous language. The rhetoric used by Mormon settler missionaries echoed US settler colonial discourse around land and civilization. Cowdery connected Mormon settlers to Lamanites. They had a shared heritage on this land, and Mormon settlers possessed their true knowledge. Cowdery and the other missionaries then presented the Delaware chief with a copy of the Book of Mormon in hopes that it would be "read and known among his tribe; it will do them good."[34] The ritual of presenting the Book of Mormon to the chief was important and signified the recognition of Mormon settler and tribal sovereignty. In addition to the physical presentation of the Book of Mormon, Indigenous peoples were expected to accept this history as their people's history. The presentation of the book also represented a political and religious negotiation between Mormon settlers and Indigenous peoples. The Delaware chief responded, "'We feel truly thankful to our white friends who have come far and been at such pains to tell us good news . . . concerning the Book of our forefathers, it makes us glad in here,' placing his hand over his heart."

According to Cowdery's account, the Delawares accepted the Book of Mormon as their history, and for the next several days the missionaries continued to discuss the Book of Mormon with them. Historian Warren Jennings argued that this was because the Delawares had their own "sacred books of pictorial symbols engraved on wood . . . [that] told of the Delawares' past, of their wanderings, and like the *Book of Mormon*, chronicled periods of peace followed by periods of disaster."[35] This is interesting, because Jennings acknowledges the two texts but also the willingness of the Delawares to accept Mormon teachings simply because they had preserved similar teachings on wood. The Delawares' acceptance of the Book of Mormon as their history cannot be assumed to be accurate because Mormon settler missionaries kept the only written record of these encounters.

The LDS Church had sent its missionaries to western tribes to fulfill its settler desires to enlighten Indigenous peoples of their true identity. As a result, Mormon settler missionaries' presence caused tension between other settlers, missionaries, and federal Indian agents because they did not have permission to be in these Tribal communities. These Mormon missionaries met resistance from other Christian missionaries and Indian agents and were "soon ordered out of the Indian country as disturbers of the peace, and even threatened within the military in case of non-compliance."[36] Mormon and US settler interests diverge at this moment; Mormon settlers did not acquiesce to US settler authority over Indigenous nations and lands. Instead, their focus remained on Indigenous peoples because the Lamanite mission served their religious and political interests. The expulsion of Mormon missionaries became particularly interesting because during this first mission to the Lamanites, Mormon settlers set out to Indian country based on a religious mandate to share the Book of Mormon without consulting any federal Indian agents. Even though Mormon settlers had not developed specific policies to remove Lamanites, their missionary efforts fit into larger federal Indian policies of assimilation and removal. Settlers pushed Tribal Nations out of their homelands and into the margins, or the borders between civilization and "savagery." However, Tribal Nations and peoples were never completely out of danger of constant removal and the push for assimilation. Mormon settlers used the Book of Mormon and missions as a civilizing tool against Indigenous peoples since the first Lamanite mission in 1830. Indigenous peoples would convert and be expected to give up traditional spiritual beliefs and connections to the land. If Indigenous peoples claimed the Book of Mormon as their own, Mormon civilizing efforts would have been successful. Ultimately, this first Lamanite mission was a failure, as the missionaries did not convert large numbers of Indigenous peoples. Instead, the missionaries' presence was an affront to US settler colonial power, so they were pushed off Indigenous lands. Cowdery declared, "[It is the end] of our first Indian mission, in which we preached the Gospel in its fulness and distributed the record of their forefathers to three tribes." Yet despite distributing a record of their ancestors, American Indians did not convert in huge numbers, and as a result, Mormon settlers continued to migrate and make claims to land.

Mormon settler origins in the United States become essential in understanding Mormon settler colonial fantasy: Mormon settlers used their power to assert and articulate indigeneity via a Lamanite subject position to justify their participation in the removal of Indigenous peoples from their land. The Book of Mormon produced indigeneity to serve the Mormon settler colonial project of empire, including Indigenous people's physical and metaphorical dispossession. LDS Church leaders and members relied on Mormon settler texts to create and operationalize Lamanite discourse, which required the civilization of Indigenous peoples, communities, and nations.

Religion became a civilizing tool, but other settlers and US settler colonial policies and Mormon understanding of Lamanites as American Indians fulfilled a similar purpose: civilization via (re)conversion to Mormonism. Mormon settler texts and Smith articulated the belief that Indigenous peoples were descendants of Lamanites who once had the *truth*. Mormon settlers were simply (re)introducing Lamanites to their original beliefs given to them by God and recorded in the Book of Mormon. Mormon settlers' desire to assimilate and remove all Indigenous claims to land paved the way for Mormon empire and become the driving force behind constructing a Lamanite subject position and discourse. In the Mormon settler colonial context, Mormon settlers utilized religious theology to justify their assimilation policies, which required Indigenous peoples to recognize and claim their Lamanite subject position, a racialized status within Mormon settler society. Mormon settlers believed that Lamanites would play an essential role in the gathering and building of Zion, but this would never be realized. Eventually, Mormon settler views shifted when they met resistance from Indigenous peoples and other settlers. Mormon settlers ultimately would rely on mainstream US settler colonial categories of indigeneity as they also imposed their version of indigeneity. These settler categories of indigeneity led to and justified the removal and civilization of Indigenous peoples.

ANOTHER MORMON SETTLER TEXT: THE DOCTRINE AND COVENANTS AND LAMANITE DISCOURSE AND SUBJECT POSITION

In addition to the Book of Mormon, Smith utilized another text, the Doctrine and Covenants, published in 1835 that continued to define Lamanite subject position and discourse. In addition to the Book of Mormon, Smith also produced modern religious texts and ideologies that further shaped Mormon settler discourse about Lamanites. In another spiritual experience in the home of Peter Whitmer Sr., Smith recorded being informed by God that "there shall be a record [Doctrine and Covenants] kept among you; and in it thou [Smith] shalt be called a seer, a translator, a prophet, an apostle of Jesus Christ, an elder of the church through the will of God the Father, and the grace of your Lord Jesus Christ."[37] The text also established Smith's religious power. Like Book of Mormon prophet-historians, Smith documented early church history in what would become the Doctrine and Covenants, a modern settler text. This religious text was also used to racialize Indigenous peoples in Mormon settler structures and was central to the making of Mormon subject position, history, and belonging. The Mormon text shows how Smith organized and documented early church history. In the last gathering held on the Whitmer farm on January 2, 1831, he received a revelation that Mormon settlers had to gather in Ohio to "escape the power of the enemy, and be gathered unto me a righteous people, without spot and blameless.... I [God] gave unto you the commandment that ye should go to the Ohio; and there I will give unto you my law; and there you shall be endowed with power from on high."[38]

These religious texts worked in tandem regarding Mormon religious ideologies about Indigenous peoples as Lamanites and Mormon settler ideologies rooted in the land. Smith used these texts to define indigeneity while carving out a Mormon settler subject position and discourse around Mormon settlers' presence to secure their belonging to the land. I draw upon these settler texts to elucidate how Mormon settlers produce meaning about Indigenous peoples as Lamanites that naturalizes Mormon settler colonialism. The LDS Church considers the Doctrine and Covenants a modern text containing "revelations given to Joseph Smith ... for the establishment and regulation of the kingdom of God on the earth in the last days."[39] This text of modern prophetic revelations became important in making and maintaining the Mormon settler subject position while also legitimizing Mormon settlers' religious claims about Indigenous peoples and the desire to build Mormon empire.

The Doctrine and Covenants was written primarily for members of the LDS Church but could be useful for everyone, including non-Mormons, because the "messages, warnings, and exhortations are for the benefit of all mankind and contain an invitation to all people everywhere to hear the voice of the Lord Jesus Christ, speaking to them for their temporal well-being and their everlasting salvation."[40] This Mormon settler text is meant to establish Mormon religious authority, especially Smith as the prophet over LDS members and Indigenous peoples. Smith organized members in Kirtland, Ohio, to publish the text that would become known as the Doctrine and Covenants in 1835. The 1835 edition also contained the "Lectures on Faith," "seven theological lectures delivered in the School of the Elders in Kirtland, Ohio in the winter of 1834–35" meant to extrapolate on religious teachings by Smith and these texts.[41] The Doctrine and Covenants contained 103 revelations from God to Smith about how to organize the LDS Church, reference to the Book of Mormon and Moroni, and tenets of the faith.

The Doctrine and Covenants, along with the Book of Mormon, became foundational to the formation of Lamanites as a religiously, racialized people and the discourse about their degraded status. The Doctrine and Covenants supports and reinforces the Book of Mormon as a settler text, a record preserved for the explicit purpose of reminding Indigenous peoples of promises made to their ancestors and, by extension, them if they embrace their Lamanite heritage and repent of their rejection of Christ's teachings.[42] The Doctrine and Covenants reinforces claims made in the Book of Mormon, especially since Lamanites were central to the formations of the early church, the Book of Mormon is considered to be Lamanite history, and early LDS missionary efforts were intended to convert and save Indigenous peoples. These religious texts fortify narratives around Mormon settler ideologies about the history and subject position of Indigenous peoples as Lamanites.

These texts construct and give meaning to indigeneity, spirituality, and land. Like the Book of Mormon, the Doctrine and Covenants reinforces teachings about Lamanites as the racialized, spiritual Other. Lamanite history would not have been preserved had it not been for settler recordkeeping that was then translated into English by Smith. For example, the Doctrine and Covenants references Lamanites as unbelievers who must be saved and says that the Book of Mormon was key to saving them. According to the text, "the Lamanites . . . dwindled in unbelief because of the iniquity of their fathers. . . . And for this very purpose are these plates preserved, which contain these records . . . that the Lamanites might come to the knowledge of their fathers, and that they might know the promises of the Lord, and that they may believe the Gospel and rely upon the merits of Jesus Christ, and be glorified through faith in his name, and that through their repentance might be saved."[43]

The Doctrine and Covenants, along with the Book of Mormon, claims that Indigenous peoples were a fallen people, unbelievers because of the sins of their ancestors. They have carried this degraded status for generations, and the only way to be redeemed is to take the Book of Mormon as their history, where they can learn correct teachings and traditions. Only then can they be saved. Smith continued to receive revelation about Lamanites' need to "come to the knowledge of their fathers." This reference implies that the traditional teachings and stories that Indigenous peoples knew were in fact not accurate in terms of their *original* teachings as recorded in these Mormon settler texts. In this regard, Mormon settler texts produce meaning and knowledge about Indigenous peoples and are purveyors of truth and civilization. Thus, Mormon settlers know more about Indigenous peoples than Indigenous peoples themselves. Mormon settler colonial processes erase Indigenous ways of knowing and being and instead impose settler constructs, such as the category of Lamanite. Smith and other Mormon settlers viewed Indigenous peoples as Lamanites, which shaped their interactions with Indigenous peoples.

Mormon settler narratives further enact violence against Indigenous peoples in their assertion of Lamanite as rebellious, wild, savage, or less than human. These sentiments appear throughout the Book of Mormon. For example, Lamanite are often described as "dark, filthy, and a loathsome people," "lazy," "idolatrous," and "full of idleness and all manner of abominations."[44] These views of American Indians as Lamanites made it easier for Mormon settlers to dissociate their role in introducing and using violence to wrest land from Indigenous peoples despite their promises not to use their weapons against them.[45] The Book of Mormon captures settler violence, whether in the use of physical violence or in racist, violent language to give meaning to the Lamanite subject position. Mormon settlers ignore these violent acts because they do not fit into the Mormon settler fantasy of Lamanites as violent. The Mormon settler fantasy reimagines Indigenous peoples as Lamanites using religious ideologies and texts that mark them as the racialized Other. Indigenous peoples do not exist on their terms but instead exist within the Mormon infrastructures as Lamanites. Mormon settlers became invested in converting American Indians because this gave meaning to their settler subject position and connection to land. Mormon settlers needed Indigenous peoples to become Lamanites, because this justified their racialized views of Indigenous peoples and LDS Church policies and infrastructures designed to save them from their fallen state. These views persisted into the twentieth century. For example, Melvin Ballard, an LDS Church apostle, continued to invoke these racist views of Indigenous peoples to justify ongoing missionary efforts to Lamanites. During the October 1926 semiannual General Conference, Ballard asserted that only the "gospel of the Lord Jesus Christ" would bring Indigenous peoples out of the darkness because they live in "ignorance and poverty in the midst of the ruins of great and glorious cities their fathers built[,] . . . evidence of their past wonderful civilization. . . . I looked up these poor wretched souls who have reached their state of degradation, poverty and misery, through sin, transgression and oppression."[46] Ballard's speech highlights the persistence of Lamanite discourse into the twentieth century whereby Indigenous peoples remain a racialized, fallen people. There is no regard to how settler colonialism, including Mormon settler colonialism, has impacted the lives of Indigenous peoples living in displaced homelands.

CONCLUSION

Since 1830, the LDS Church has claimed that the Book of Mormon is a history of this continent, meaning that the Book of Mormon is Indigenous history. In 1981, the LDS Church published a formal introduction to the Book of Mormon. According to this introduction, the Book of Mormon is " a volume of holy scripture. . . . [I]t is a record of God's dealings with the ancient inhabitants of the Americas" written by prophets.[47] The 1981 introduction connects American Indian peoples to their Lamanite ancestors, who survived ongoing conflicts with other Tribal Nations. Eventually Lamanites survived, and "they are the principal ancestors of American Indians." Mormon, a Book of Mormon prophet and a direct descendant of Nephi, records and preserves his people's history in the Book of Mormon for his descendants. Eventually Mormon delivers the Book of Mormon to his son, Moroni, who edits the entire text onto gold plates that Joseph Smith is shown in a vision in 1828.

The context for the Book of Mormon becomes essential in establishing early Lamanite discourse: Mormon's account of Nephites and Lamanites becomes the authoritative historical and religious account of this continent, especially Lamanite history. In reality, the Book of Mormon is primarily a Nephite or settler narrative of Mormon settlers' interactions with Lamanites, in which ongoing conflict occurs over notions of righteousness and land. This record becomes a way to control and manage a historical narrative that suits settler desires, first Nephites and later Mormons. Those who did not follow the right(eous) path became a people marked by their historical and spiritual otherness. The Book of Mormon becomes a code to decipher righteous claims to land, history, and subject position. The settler text also becomes another settler colonial tool to continue to write a narrative that benefits a settler narrative of removal and dispossession of Lamanites, a Mormon settler fantasy.

The removal and disappearance of Indigenous peoples continued when leaders in the LDS Church asked Doubleday, an American publisher, to make a minor change in the introduction to the Book of Mormon. According to Doubleday senior editor Andrew Corbin, the new 2006 revised edition "would be in accordance with future editions the church is printing." The introduction would modify previous claims of American Indians as the "principal" ancestors of Lamanites, changing from "they are the principal ancestors of the American Indians" to "they are *among* the ancestors of the American Indians."[48] While the change from "principal" to "among" may appear minor, this change signaled a significant difference regarding the ongoing discussion and claims by the LDS Church about American Indians as Lamanites. It was not until the following year that the public become alerted to the change via local reporting by the *Salt Lake Tribune* and the *Deseret News*, the two most widely circulated newspapers in the region. Carrie A. Moore, a journalist for the *Deseret News*, wrote that this change "re-ignited discussion among some Latter-day Saints about the book's historicity, geography, and the descendants of those chronicled within its pages."[49] Many members of the LDS Church believed the Book of Mormon to be a literal and religious history of an ancient civilization and American Indian peoples to be direct descendants of Lamanites. Despite these changes, the popular sentiment among members was to hold onto the belief of American Indians as Lamanites; the small textual change did little to sway or shift from this perspective. The change allows all previous claims by the LDS Church and its prophets, leaders, and religious texts about Lamanite discourse and subject position to be true, even when fluid and broad. Ultimately, the Book of Mormon, including changes made to the introduction, remains a Mormon settler text perpetuating Lamanite discourse and settler ideologies that secure their ties to the land. The Book of Mormon and the Doctrine and Covenants played a crucial role in creating, producing, and disseminating a Lamanite subject position and discourse about belonging to the land. The use of the term "Lamanite" was pivotal in shaping early LDS Church policies, especially those under the leadership of Joseph Smith, regarding American Indians and how Mormon settlers positioned and understood their subject position. Lamanite subject position and discourse gave meaning to Mormon settler ideologies that advanced their claims to land.

The Book of Mormon is the foundation of Mormon settler colonialism. The text marks Indigenous peoples as cursed and pushed them to the periphery of settler society as the racialized, spiritual Other. Being viewed as Lamanites continues to mark American Indians as foreign interlopers, the first immigrants on this continent. The Lamanite savage state and American Indians' inability to recognize their true historical and religious past justified their removal and possession by Mormon settlers. The fluidity of Mormon settler colonialism, like US settler colonialism, was deliberate, especially as Mormon settler desires changed, as evident by the discourse and fluidity around Lamanites. Lamanites will always remain on the periphery of Mormon settler society because their presence unsettles Mormon settler claims to land. This Lamanite discourse becomes the foundation for how Mormon settlers build empire.

In chapter 2, I examine how Smith and other leaders in the LDS Church developed Lamanite and Mormon settler ideologies as they promoted discourse around Mormon place on the periphery of US settler society. I examine how at these moments, US and Mormon settler colonial interests intersect and how Mormon settlers accessed their whiteness to build empire in Nauvoo, Illinois, in order to make visible Mormon settler colonial processes on the border of the United States and on the frontier.

2 COUNCIL OF FIFTY

OPERATIONALIZING MORMON SETTLER AND LAMANITE IDEOLOGIES ONTO THE LAND

There is an almost boundless extent of territory on the west and south...
where exists little or no organization of protective government[;] ... the
lands thus unknown, unowned, or unoccupied, are among some of
the richest and most fertile of the continent.... [M]any of the inhabitants
of the union would gladly embrace the opportunity of extending their
researches, and acquirements, so soon as they can receive protection in
their enterprize [sic]; thereby adding strength, durability and wealth to the
nation.... [T]he red man, the robber, and the *desparado* [sic] have frequently
interrupted such research and acquisition without justifiable cause... [t]o
open the vast regions of the unpeopled west and South to our enlightened
and enterprising yeomanry.

COUNCIL OF FIFTY PETITION
TO CONGRESS

Joseph Smith utilized religious texts to construct a category of race, the Lamanite
subject position, and discourse around Indigenous peoples as Lamanites. Mormon
settler ideologies about the racialized, religious Other informed Mormon settler
policies and embedded this discourse into infrastructures and narratives about
land and belonging. Using religious ideologies, Mormon settlers developed their
brand of manifest destiny to justify and legitimize their claims to land. In this
chapter, I explore another manifestation of Mormon settler colonialism, including how Mormon settlers asserted their sovereignty to establish a Mormon center,
infrastructures, and narratives about the land at various moments in their search
for belonging. I examine how their religious and political interests converge in
their bid to create Mormon empire on the periphery of US geopolitical boundaries
and eventually in the American West. While I focus on Nauvoo, Illinois, and the
Council of Fifty, I also include Mormon settlers in the Wisconsin Territory and

interest in the Republic of Texas to highlight the fluidity of Mormon manifest destiny and the various attempts to locate land and resources outside the critical eye of the US government. It is in Nauvoo where Mormon settlers began to carve out settler space and belonging and move to innocence as targets of non-Mormon settler violence. These experiences form their Mormon settler subject position and ultimately justify their desires to secure and claim land as Mormon. When Mormon settlers moved to Nauvoo, they did so to escape non-Mormon settler violence but also because they wanted to create a Mormon empire. Upon their arrival to Nauvoo, Mormon settlers immediately began building structures on the land to make visible Mormon presence. In addition to marking land as distinctly Mormon, the narrative surrounding their expulsion from Missouri becomes pivotal to creating community and belonging to the land. Despite Mormon settler fears of removal, this did not stop them from claiming lands. At this moment, the status of Mormon settlers meant that they could claim land, and in doing so they contributed to and benefited from US policies of Indian removal. Despite being on the periphery of the United States, Mormon settlers secured their belonging, easing their anxieties of expulsion within the larger US settler colonial project. Mormon settlers were quintessentially settlers; they relied on the US government to recognize their sovereignty and right to claim land. Even when critical of the US nation-state and other non-Mormon settlers, Mormon settlers relied on their whiteness to secure their claims to land. Their desires to build Zion on the periphery of the United States were supported by Mormon settler and religious ideologies.

Nauvoo and the Council of Fifty were a manifestation of Mormon settlers' desires to claim and belong to a specific place. Mormon ideologies shaped their views and relationships to the land, which were vital to Mormon narratives around belonging. As Mormon settlers carved out Nauvoo as the center of Mormon empire, it becomes evident that Mormon settlers saw themselves as a racialized, marginalized Other. Yet when their ideologies and experiences are placed within the framework of Mormon settler colonialism, their status as white settlers becomes more obvious. Mormon settlers were in fact white, and it is because of their whiteness that they had the ability to claim and develop distinctively Mormon spaces. Their interests in land and belonging aligned with US manifest destiny, the only difference being the use of Mormon religious ideologies to frame land and relationships to it. Manifest destiny, this right to land, the right to be *of* the land, advanced notions of civilization. Mormon migration brought civilization through conversion and acceptance of the Book of Mormon to Indigenous peoples and the western lands they occupied.

The Church of Jesus Christ of Latter-day Saints (LDS) Church originated in New York, and then Mormon settlers began to move to various locales, driven by religious ideologies to locate and build new sites for the Mormon settler center. At each new place, including Nauvoo, Mormon settlers began to build Mormon infrastructures to mark land that simultaneously supported their religious ideologies about their claims to land and settler presence. Interestingly, Mormon manifest destiny meant that Mormon settler claims to land were even more exceptional, so much so that their claims to land should supersede all other settler claims. Again, Mormon exceptionalism was not different from US claims of exceptionalism other than that Mormon settlers used specific religious ideologies to code their claims to land. The belief that God set aside land for their explicit use was not unique; in fact, it was very American. Mormon settlers carried their sovereignty with them from New York to Missouri to Illinois and eventually the Salt Lake Valley. Each place was meant to be Mormon, even as the Mormon settlers were being pushed from one place to another and non-Mormon settlers using violence secured their righteous claims to land. The violence experienced by Mormon settlers gave them a chance to create community based on their experiences and desire to belong to the land. Other scholars of Mormon history have used the racialization of Mormon settlers as nonwhite to argue and claim a marginalized status that reinforces claims of Mormon exceptionalism. However, I argue that Mormon settlers experienced violence because their presence was an affront to other settlers' claims as they challenged the sovereignty of the United States, especially when they challenged or rejected US settler sovereignty. When Mormon settlers don't diverge from the US settler colonial project, other settlers don't take issue with them claiming land, which is a very American tradition. Unangax̂ scholar Eve Tuck and settler scholar Wayne Yang write about the "absence of experience" in their article "Decolonization Is Not a Metaphor," which is useful for understanding the positioning of Mormon settlers as white. Tuck and Yang describe the "absence of experience" as the "self-positioning of white people as simultaneously the oppressed and never an oppressor, and as having an *absence of experience* of oppressive power relations."[1] This is useful when examining Mormon settlers' experiences in the nineteenth century and how this positioning allowed for Mormon settlers to make a move toward innocence, because as victims they are not the perpetrators of violence leading to Indigenous dispossession and disappearance from the land. In this chapter I use the Nauvoo experience, including the Council of Fifty, as a way to explore how Mormon settlers claim and mark land, a very American settler tradition, while using their religious persecution to create narratives around Mormon belonging as a means to justify their presence in Indigenous places. There are also moments when the interests of the LDS Church intersect with Indigenous people's interests, and in these moments, Mormon settlers rely on their religious ideologies to justify their desires to create empire. Even in Nauvoo, the location is symbolically on the frontier between the United States and Indigenous territories. This position was symbolic of how the LDS Church bridges and relies on this divide to stake claim to land. Much like Lamanite discourse, Mormon religious ideologies were necessary to carve out Mormon manifest destiny. Mormon settlers continue to use Indigenous peoples to advance their claims to land. My intention is to make clear Mormon manifest destiny and how the Mormon settler colonial project serves the US settler colonial project even when they diverge from one another at specific moments and places.

THE NEW CENTER OF MORMON SETTLER COLONIAL POWER: NAUVOO, ILLINOIS

Mormon settlers began looking for a new Mormon center when they faced violence and pressure to leave Independence, Missouri, the former Mormon empire. Mormon settlers had been violently expelled from Kirtland, Ohio, and Independence, Missouri, by non-Mormon settlers in 1838. Despite the military campaign to expel Mormon settlers, they had been instructed to not engage in violence but instead learn obedience and "wait for a little season for the redemption of Zion. That they themselves may be prepared, and that my people may be taught more perfectly and have experience and know more perfectly concerning their duty."[2] Missouri governor Lilburn Boggs issued an extermination order against Mormon settlers on October 27, 1838. Three days later, non-Mormon settlers attacked Mormon settlers at Hawn's Mill in Caldwell County, Missouri. Joseph Smith, his brother Hyrum, Sidney Rigdon, Lyman Wight, Caleb Baldwin, and Alexander McRae were later imprisoned on December 1, 1838, in Liberty, Missouri, for crimes committed against other Missourians. Brigham Young led over eight thousand Mormon settlers from Missouri to Illinois during the incarceration of Smith and the others.[3] Six months later, the guards released the men while they were being transported to another city for a fair trial. Smith, Hyrum, Lyman, Caleb, and Alexander escaped while in transit and traveled to Quincy, Illinois, arriving on April 22, 1839.[4]

Shortly thereafter, Joseph Smith and other members started to look for sanctuary and settled near Quincy, Illinois, a small town along the Mississippi River. Mormon leaders, including Smith, began negotiating with Isaac Galland, a "local editor, purported doctor, and land dealer" who owned vast tracts of land in Lee

County, Iowa.[5] Galland offered to sell Mormon settlers twenty thousand acres for two dollars per acre to be paid over the next twenty years. Of course, this offer was exciting to Smith and other Mormon leaders, who had no money or assets to purchase vast tracts of land. However, contestations over land arose, including who had the right to sell land, and the issue was eventually settled by the US Supreme Court in 1850.[6] Smith looked for another site and bought five hundred acres of highly priced land in another small town upriver, Commerce City, Illinois, later named Nauvoo.[7] Nauvoo symbolized refuge to Smith and other Mormon settlers escaping non-Mormon settler harassment and violence. Nauvoo also represents the intersection of Mormon and US settler colonial projects as Mormon settlers claimed land on the edge of the United States. The selection of Nauvoo was strategic, as the city overlooks and is surrounded on three sides by the Mississippi River, forming a protective barrier from other settlers. Nauvoo was the center of the Mormon settler colonial project and future Mormon empire.

Mormon settlers immediately began to build structures that would mark Nauvoo as Mormon. In 1841 construction on the Nauvoo Temple began; the physical and religious structure would mark Nauvoo as distinctly Mormon. The temple represented the spiritual and political power and presence of the LDS Church, which was why Mormon settlers prioritized the building of this structure. The rapid influx of Mormon settlers and the population growth in Nauvoo outpaced infrastructures in place to sustain this growing settler population. As a result, Mormon settlers needed to extract resources outside of Nauvoo to keep up with the need for additional infrastructures. The location of Nauvoo was strategic because of its proximity to the Mississippi River. The LDS Church used the river to navigate and travel to other places to extract resources necessary to build and sustain the settler society. In this context, Mormon settlers participated in settler colonial systems that extracted resources from the land once occupied by Indigenous peoples. Mormon settlers contributed to the dispossession of Indigenous peoples because they could not exist without extracting resources from the very lands in which Indigenous peoples have been relegated to or removed from. The fact that Mormon settlers could build Nauvoo and, under the guidance of the Council of Fifty, send a group of Mormon settlers to live in Wisconsin Territory in 1841 for the sole purpose of extracting timber for the Mormon settler center was an exercise of Mormon settler sovereignty. This early group of Mormon settlers found prime locations near the Black and Wisconsin Rivers, feeding into the Mississippi River, to directly transport timber to Nauvoo. The history of the Mormon pineries was important; however, this chapter focuses on how Mormon settler colonialism functioned at the periphery of US and Mormon settler societies in Nauvoo. Nauvoo and the Council of Fifty were the manifestations of Mormon manifest destiny, especially as the council developed Mormon settler colonial policies based on religious ideologies to fulfill Mormon settler desires for land and empire. I am also interested in the way the council functioned and how its policies contributed to the dispossession of Indigenous peoples, including how Mormon settler colonial policies could only be realized at the expense of Indigenous dispossession and disappearance from the land and narratives, especially those written by Mormon settlers. Indigenous peoples exist only when their presence intersects with the realization of Mormon settler goals.[8] I utilize Nauvoo to demonstrate how Mormon settlers have benefited from US settler colonial policies that pushed for the removal of Indigenous peoples. The removal of Indigenous peoples onto reservations made it possible for Mormon settlers to build Nauvoo.

A BRIEF HISTORY OF THE COUNCIL OF FIFTY AS A TECHNOLOGY OF MORMON SETTLER COLONIALISM

Joseph Smith organized the Council of Fifty on March 11, 1844, in Nauvoo to ensure the "safety and salvation of the saints by protecting them in their religious rights and worship."[9] Non-Mormon settlers targeted Mormon settlers and used violent tactics to expel them from Missouri and later Nauvoo. Governor Lilburn Boggs sanctioned Missouri citizens' violence against Mormon settlers by formally expelling them from the state.[10] The US military did not intervene in violent conflicts against Mormon settlers seeking military intervention to protect their religious rights. This violence prompted Smith to create the Council of Fifty to protect the settlers' constitutional right to freedom of religion, or "the rights of unpopular religious minorities."[11] Nauvoo would "provide protections the Latter-day Saints had lacked during the 1830s."[12] Smith also created a local militia, the Nauvoo Legion, to protect Mormon citizens from non-Mormon violence. The establishment of Nauvoo, a Mormon settler colonial outpost, was a manifestation of Mormon and US settler colonialisms. Mormon and US settler colonialisms converge at Nauvoo around settler desire for land and empire. Despite religious persecution by non-Mormon settlers, Smith and his followers could purchase tracts of land to establish this Mormon settler outpost because their presence did not directly challenge US settler sovereignty. Mormon settlers benefited from and relied on US settler colonial policies that required Indigenous removal to make land available for settlers.

The Council of Fifty operationalized theocratic policies to create a Mormon empire, or "the beginning of the literal kingdom of God on earth."[13] Mormon settlers would build their kingdom in Nauvoo, once Indigenous land. The council addressed issues through a Mormon religious and settler lens, such as the redemption of Lamanites, while simultaneously extracting resources from and occupying Indigenous land. Smith attempted to separate the civil affairs of Nauvoo from the religious needs of the LDS Church, yet the political and religious desires could not be separated; in fact, they were intimately intertwined, especially since Smith was the religious and political leader of the LDS Church. His dual roles as prophet of the LDS Church and chair of the council further blurred the lines between these two organizations. He was the "Prophet, Priest & King," and the council would "uphold him in that capacity in which God ha[d] anointed him."[14] In this position of authority, Smith became the authoritative figure of the LDS Church and the Council of Fifty. The separation of church and state was impossible, because Smith, with his ecclesiastical and political power, was the center of Mormon settler colonial power. The Council of Fifty and LDS Church leadership also mirrored one another; many of the men participated in both institutions. Many council members served in the LDS Church in the highest-ranking leadership organizations, including the First Presidency, the Quorum of the Twelve Apostles, and the Nauvoo High Council. It was nearly impossible to separate these two organizations due to their shared religious and political goals of Mormon empire.

These individuals, along with Smith, drove Mormon settler colonial ideologies and structures while reinforcing patriarchal and paternalistic power because white Mormon male settlers made up the entire leadership. Initially, the First Presidency included Joseph Smith, and the second-ranking leadership body was the Quorum of the Twelve Apostles chaired by Brigham Young, who would later become the second prophet of the LDS Church and chair of the Council of Fifty after Smith's death. Eventually twenty-two other men were added as council members, including Willard Richards as recorder and William Clayton as a clerk. Council members sat "according to their ages[,] the oldest member being seated at the right hand of the chairman and forming a semicircle in front of the chair [and] the youngest member seated at the left of the chairman" during their meetings.[15] The meetings began with prayer. Parliamentary order was used to facilitate meetings, and the reading of previous meeting minutes was read and accepted. Committees would report to the council, and any new business had to be "submitted to the chair."[16] Under Smith's leadership, the council focused on theocratic issues, such as Smith's presidential campaign, a Mormon constitution, and Lamanites, all related to the creation of a Mormon settler empire. The council relied on committees to explore specific issues ranging from petitions to Congress, exploration of southern and western territories, the legitimacy of the Nauvoo Legion, and preparations to migrate west. These committees reflect the purpose of the council: to locate a place for Mormon empire outside the purview of the United States.

The last Council of Fifty meeting under the leadership of Smith was held on May 31, 1844, before his death on June 27, 1844, while imprisoned in Carthage, Illinois. After Smith's death, Brigham Young, then president of the Quorum of the Twelve Apostles, assumed leadership of the council, which did not meet again until February 4, 1845, to identify a new site for Mormon settlers. The only administrative records of the council that remain are from March 1844 to January 1846 and any "additional contemporaneous records of this council that were kept separately."[17] William Clayton, council clerk, recorded the meetings in Nauvoo on loose sheets of paper that he later transcribed into bound records, which were then published and made public for the first time in 2016. The council's administrative records capture "early Mormon thought on earthly and heavenly governments and constitutions. While illuminating Latter-day Saint ideas regarding settlement in areas on the geographic [US] periphery, the minutes provide an unparalleled view of decision making at the center of what participants viewed as the nascent kingdom of God."[18] Thus, these minutes reveal the Mormon settler colonial processes.

The Council of Fifty created settler policies to protect and advance Mormon settler rights. The council's settler policies sought to create a Mormon theocratic, settler society. First, the council's missionary efforts to convert Lamanites coincided with groups of Mormon settlers sent to explore and identify potential sites for future Mormon settler society. The council sent out settlers to explore Texas, Oregon, California, and the Great Basin as possible sites of future Mormon settlement. Despite wanting to escape from the territorial boundaries of the United States, Mormon settlers' gaze looked west to realize their desires for land, which supported and aligned with US desires to claim land in the West. Like other settlers, Mormon settlers also saw the West as a place of refuge not only for religious freedom but also to realize their goals to build a theocratic empire. This goal of Mormon empire could not be realized without advancing US expansionist goals and further dispossessing Indigenous peoples. Mormon settlers capitalized on this opportunity to claim land because their desires, or Mormon manifest destiny, were more important than Indigenous people's rights to land, even if this contradicted Mormon religious beliefs about the civilization of Indigenous peoples via conversion to Mormonism. The LDS Church and the Council of Fifty benefited and relied on US government Indigenous removal and assimilationist policies to realize Mormon empire. Mormon religious ideologies influenced the council's resolutions, including the notion of American Indians as Lamanites in need of Mormon civilizing. Council meeting minutes highlight widely held paternalistic attitudes toward Lamanites in need of Mormon redemption. The redemption of Indigenous peoples coincided with the expansion and movement of Mormon settler empire into Indigenous lands. Again, Lamanite missions were about land and exploration of land for Mormon use. This missionary fervor and empire building continued under the council. Smith and the council developed Mormon settler policies to claim and extract Indigenous resources. Council policies did not always explicitly target Lamanites, despite the necessity of Indigenous dispossession and disappearance to build and carry out the infrastructures of Mormon settler colonialism. Mormon settlers framed their intrusion onto Indigenous lands as efforts to convert and save Lamanites while expanding the LDS Church, thus opening access to land and resources for Mormon settlers.

Nauvoo serves as an example that Mormon settlers claimed and built Mormon settler infrastructures onto the land to delineate land as part of their Mormon settler empire. Even as Mormon settlers first began to build in Nauvoo, they acknowledged that "there are the remains of the Indians here, [and] we did not slay them. Let it be to the disgrace of the government."[19] Even in this declaration, Mormon settlers place blame on the United States for killing Indigenous peoples, yet Mormon settlers had no problem claiming the land as their own. The Council of Fifty acknowledged in its minutes that Nauvoo was situated on Indigenous burial grounds. Joseph Smith's store, "where the council frequently met, was built on top of one such mound, and some of the recovered artifacts were even used in its construction." Even if Mormon settlers did not violently expel or kill Indigenous peoples, they still directly benefited from their removal and disappearance from the land. The fact that Mormons unearthed the remains of Indigenous peoples did little to halt their desires to build Mormon infrastructures onto the land. There was no mention of what happened to the remains of Indigenous peoples. Did they leave them? Did they rebury them? Where did the remains go? This is how Indigenous peoples disappear literally and figuratively, especially in the Mormon settler narrative. Mormon settlers also secured their innocence in the US settler colonial project and in the narratives they produced about Nauvoo and about their belonging to Mormon places. Like Tuck and Yang's "absence of experience," Mormon settlers can separate themselves from settler violence toward Indigenous peoples. Mormon settlers literally built their city on the bodies of Indigenous peoples. Council minutes reinforce Lamanite removal, as manifested by the burial mounds in and around Nauvoo, as an act of God, a literal manifestation of Mormon manifest destiny, as God made way for Mormon settlers. Mormon empire could not be realized if Mormon settlers could not claim land and resources, even as they asserted their innocence in Indigenous violence and dispossession.

THE COUNCIL OF FIFTY: DEVELOPING THE MORMON SETTLER COLONIAL PROJECT

During a March 21, 1844, meeting, the Council of Fifty appointed Willard Richards, Hyrum Smith (brother to Joseph Smith), and William W. Phelps to draft a petition to Congress.[20] The petition, about the "boundless extent of territory on the west," was later approved by the council on March 26, 1844. The petition pleaded with Congress to make Joseph Smith a member of the US Army. As a member of the army, Smith would have the authority to take volunteers, most likely other Mormon settlers, into the western borderlands of the United States to protect Texas and Oregon from other foreign settlers. The council's petition illustrates how Smith and the LDS Church, as a settler colonial structure, began to develop Mormon settler colonial policies around land. The interest in making a Mormon empire coincides with efforts to colonize and claim land. Smith, the LDS Church, and the Council of Fifty developed formal policies and infrastructures to aid in their exploration of new lands as God's chosen people. The council, a political organization within the LDS Church, played a vital role in forming early Mormon settler colonial policies centered on and driven by Mormon ideologies rooted in the land. During these formative years, the council's minutes "capture the principles, protocols, and activities" while in Nauvoo.[21] The council was also crucial to understanding the views of early LDS Church leaders toward land and their desires to claim and build infrastructures onto the land to demarcate as Mormon.

The Council of Fifty governed the political affairs of the LDS Church, yet its efforts intersected with the religious needs of the faith. For example, the council oversaw Smith's presidential campaign bid that catapulted the LDS Church onto the national political stage. Interestingly enough, his desire to become president was driven by Mormon settler desires of belonging, to be able to practice their religion without government interference. Yet they also desired interference from the government to protect their right to practice their religion freely. The *Times and Seasons*, a newspaper published in Nauvoo, wrote that Smith's presidential desires were because "we [Mormons] have no other alternative."[22] Smith believed that he needed to protect the rights of his "friends [so they] could have the privilege of enjoying our religious & civel [sic] rights. . . . I feel it to be my right & privilege to obtain what influence & power I can lawfully in the United States for the protection of injured innocence."[23] He felt compelled to run to protect Mormon settlers from non-Mormon violence, especially after experiencing violence in Missouri and having been banned from the state. While critical of the US government, Smith and Mormon settlers expected their constitutional right to freedom of religion to be protected, and when Smith felt as though their rights had been violated, he was put forth as the Mormon settlers' presidential candidate of choice. Smith's presidential campaign and platform reveal that Mormon settlers will engage with the US nation-state when their interests intersect, especially in regard to the potential to protect Mormon settler interests.

The Council of Fifty was interested in establishing a settler society, distinct and separate from the United States, since they wanted to create a theocratic nation-state. But at the same time, they relied on the US government to recognize and substantiate their land claims. This chapter explores the Nauvoo period, 1839–1846, during which Smith relocated the headquarters of the LDS Church and began to build a Mormon settler city in Nauvoo. Nauvoo became this place and space where Mormon settlers began operationalizing their Mormon settler colonial project of empire. Smith charged the Council of Fifty to "locate a new site for Latter-day Saint settlement, to promote Joseph Smith's 1844 campaign for the presidency of the United States, and to cultivate relations with American Indians."[24] Mormon settler colonial ideologies about land intersect at Nauvoo, the Mormon settler colonial center. Mormon settlers sought to convert Indigenous peoples and, while on these missions, scouted out potential sites that could sustain the center of Mormon settler society as a fulfillment of Mormon manifest destiny and their views of Indigenous peoples as a people in need of redemption. However, these goals were at odds with one another because Mormon settlers were interested in Indigenous peoples only as they related to Mormon settler desires to build Zion. Indigenous peoples could live in Zion only as Lamanites, and if they rejected this subject position, Mormon settlers could claim land for their sole use. The Council of Fifty sent various expeditions into Wisconsin Territory, Oregon, and even the Republic of Texas to scout potential Mormon settler sites. This goal intersects Mormon and US goals to expand the boundaries of the United States into the West. I use the council's minutes to capture how Mormon settler colonial desires and religious ideologies converged as they developed LDS Church settler colonial policies, including Mormon manifest destiny, that were rooted in and of the land. Council minutes also highlight the fluidity and complexity of Mormon settler colonial infrastructures as Mormon settlers developed religious and political ideologies around their presence and claims to land. The structures of Mormon settler colonialism are ongoing. The Council of Fifty played an important role in Mormon settler claims to land and built infrastructures and narratives onto the land that persist into the modern era and naturalize Mormon settler belonging.

THE COUNCIL AND MORMON SETTLER IDEOLOGIES ABOUT LAMANITES AND LAND: MORMON SETTLERS IN WISCONSIN TERRITORY

Under Council of Fifty directions, a group of Mormon settlers had been sent into Wisconsin Territory to extract timber to build Nauvoo. Mormon settlers joined other settlers, a constant influx into Wisconsin Territory, exacerbating tensions between Indigenous peoples, settlers, and the US government. The unsatiated settler desire for Indigenous land remained unabated, and Indigenous peoples were continually pushed to the periphery, often being relegated to reservations. Settlers pressured the US government to open lands reserved for Indigenous peoples, despite various Tribal Nations having already ceded millions of acres of land to the United States in various peace treaties. For example, the Ojibwes had signed one of the first treaties in this region in the 1825 Treaty of Prairie du Chien, intended to end the intertribal conflict by establishing boundaries between the "Sioux and Chippewa, Sacs and Fox, Menominie [sic], Ioway, Sioux, Winnebago, and a portion of the Ottawa, Chippewa, and Potawattomie" Tribes and to open up land for settler purchase.[25] The US government sought to establish physical "boundaries among them and the other tribes who live in their vicinity, and thereby to remove all causes of future difficulty," so these nations met at Prairie du Chien in the "spirit of mutual conciliation." These treaty negotiations aimed to delineate clear boundaries between Tribal Nations, settlers, and the United States. These intertribal conflicts existed because settlers encroached onto Indigenous lands, pushing tribes west into the traditional homelands of other nations and peoples as they competed over resources and lands. Wisconsin Territory became contested terrain as Indigenous nations, such as the Menominee Nation, relied on treaties to maintain and protect their land and resources from settler encroachment.

Wisconsin Territory became another site where US and Mormon settler desires intersected and converged. The US settler project of empire required the elimination and dispossession of Indigenous peoples from their lands, thus opening vast tracts of land and resources for settlers, including Mormon settlers. Mormon settlers looked to the rich forests in Wisconsin Territory to extract "virtually" free timber to build the center of Mormon empire in Nauvoo.[26] This timber was not free. Indigenous peoples had paid the price through land cessions to the US government in treaties that recognized Indigenous sovereignty. Indigenous peoples managed to keep title to land, including resources, that the US government was obligated to protect even if at times it did not uphold treaty agreements. Nauvoo existed because of Indigenous dispossession and removal. The location was marked as a distinctly Mormon settler space and place, a direct result of Indigenous dispossession and the ability of settlers to then purchase tracts of land that had once belonged to Indigenous peoples.

Indigenous peoples living in Wisconsin Territory fought against continual pressure from settlers to give up their lands and resources as they moved to small tracts of land within the political boundaries of the United States. Mormon settlers arrived in the early 1840s to extract timber as they joined other settlers in this region, further complicating already tenuous relationships between the US government and Tribal Nations. For example, Ohio, Indiana, and Illinois "had already been freed of Indian title in a succession of treaties between Indian groups and the United States government. What remained in these states were enclaves of natives, subsisting on agriculture and government annuities, surrounded by whites."[27] Settlers continued to pressure to open even more Indigenous lands, since they believed that Indigenous peoples failed to make their land profitable, thus halting settler society. In Michigan and Wisconsin, settlers had been limited to the "southern and central tiers of counties" after the Erie Canal opened in 1825. Although the Potawatomies had ceded vast tracts of land beginning in 1789, they managed to keep a "single large tract in northeastern Illinois and southeastern Wisconsin" by 1833. The US government pushed to remove the final Potawatomies onto small tracts of individually allotted land, ceding the remaining lands to the United States. In two treaties in 1834 and 1836, Potawatomies ceded lands in exchange for "considerations of goods, money, payment of debts, and annuities" and moved to Indian territory west of the Mississippi.[28]

Like the Potawatomies, the Sac and Fox Tribes faced settler intrusion onto their lands. The Sac and Fox Tribes signed an 1804 treaty in which they ceded lands in western Illinois and southwestern Wisconsin. Yet Black Hawk, a treaty signatory, refused to leave his village, Saukenuk. At the same time, Keokuk, another leader, "began to establish new villages along the Iowa River" and "preached acquiescence in the demands of the United States."[29] Black Hawk's resistance to removal was primarily due to illegal settler encroachment, a violation of the treaty with the

United States. Eventually, Black Hawk and his supporters surrendered and negotiated peace, and narratives characterized the Black Hawk War as "'an unprovoked war upon unsuspecting and defenseless citizens of the United States, sparing neither age nor sex'" by "'certain lawless and desperate leaders, a formidable band, constituting a large portion of the Sac and Fox nation.'"[30] This narrative was not accurate. Black Hawk and many other Indigenous leaders tried to protect their way of life, including their right to exist in traditional homelands. Instead, the US government retaliated and demanded a large cession of territory along the Mississippi River, along the boundaries of what would become Iowa. The Sac and Fox Tribes would be expected to leave their homelands by July 1, 1833, and would not be allowed to hunt, fish, or plant crops on these ceded lands.

These histories are vital to understanding Nauvoo and Mormon settler narratives about this region. Mormons settled on ceded land, and that history is important to frame Mormon settler presence in Nauvoo. The complicated history between settlers and Indigenous peoples in this region paved the way for Mormon settlers in Nauvoo and Black River Falls in Wisconsin Territory. Indigenous peoples ceded their homelands and moved west of the Mississippi River to open land for settlers, and Mormon settlers could purchase land and build structures because they benefited from the US settler colonial project. Mormon settlers left Nauvoo in 1841 to extract and mill enough timber to build necessary structures and sustain the Mormon settler center. LDS Church leaders sought to establish sawmills and transport timber directly to Nauvoo. Leaders established two committees and appointed two converts, Lyman Wight and George Miller, to raise funds to construct the temple and the hotel in Nauvoo. These men labored for four years in Wisconsin Territory extracting the necessary lumber to build these infrastructures, including the temple in Nauvoo. Once this Black River Falls expedition fulfilled its mandate to build a temple and hotel, members in Black River Falls formed a committee—Lyman Wight, George Miller, Pierce Hawly, Phineas R. Bird, and John Young—to write two letters to the LDS Church leadership in Nauvoo regarding the future purpose of members in Wisconsin Territory. In essence, the letters conveyed a shift in purpose from procuring lumber for Mormon settler infrastructures in Nauvoo to harvesting lumber for profit and converting Indigenous peoples to the faith. Smith received these two letters and convened a meeting with the Quorum of the Twelve Apostles. LDS leadership discussed and debated the various issues communicated in the letters from church leadership at the Black River Falls site. The Council of Fifty was formed in response to these letters, a request that aided in the formalization of Mormon settler policies around land, assimilation, and removal of Indigenous peoples. In a letter dated February 15, 1844, a small committee of Mormon members from the Black River Falls church wrote to Smith and other leaders to share the "views and feelings, temporal and spiritual prospects as they now exist."[31] According to the letter, the Menominees agreed to move once the federal government "remove[d] all strange Indians and trespassing white men off their lands—consequently the Agent and Superintendent of Indian affairs are taking such steps as will stop all further trespassing on the Indian lands, on the Wisconsin, Black, and Chippewa Rivers under the penalties of the laws relative to the case."[32] The Menominees asserted their sovereignty and challenged Mormon settlers' presence and extraction of resources by invoking US sovereignty to uphold these nation-to-nation agreements, as articulated in the 1825 Treaty of Prairie du Chien.

Black River Falls Mormon settlers fulfilled their primary purpose of supplying enough timber for Nauvoo, but now they wanted to start a private enterprise that could be turned into a lucrative lumber business to fund other Mormon settler enterprises, including missionary efforts to other Lamanite tribes in the area.[33] Mormon settlers shifted their focus from timber to potential Lamanite missionary efforts three years after their arrival. Again, the primary interest of Mormon settlers in this region was not to establish a Lamanite mission but instead to extract valuable timber for their use. And once that was accomplished, their settler desires shifted to missionary efforts among the Lamanites. In one letter written to LDS Church leadership, Black River Falls members described the "apparent prospects of the introduction & spread of the Gospel among the Chippewa & Menomanee [Menominee] Indians."[34] Before this letter, interest in Lamanites was limited to Indigenous timber. Mormon settlers engaged in Lamanite missionary efforts when it fulfilled their settler desires and fantasies to claim and mark land as Mormon. In addition to their missionary efforts, Black River Falls Mormon settlers saw the private timber enterprise as a means to enrich the Mormon settler colonial center. In fact, timber could sustain Mormon settler infrastructures if the Menominees would support this capitalist venture.

The Menominees interrupted the Mormon timber enterprise when they visited the Black River Falls Mormon settlers to demand that they pay for timber. The Menominees believed that the treaty they signed with the US government guaranteed that they could keep land "from Fort Winnebago to Black River falls; thence to Chippewa falls; & thence to the Big Bull falls upon the Wiskansan, &c. to the place of beginning."[35] Even with the most precise interpretation of boundaries, treaties would not stop settler encroachment onto Menominee land. Contestation over these lands reflects the ongoing tensions between settlers, the US governments, and Indigenous peoples. The Menominees faced continual pressure by settlers and other tribes in the region to move west of the Mississippi, thus opening up even more land and resources for settlers, including Mormon settlers. Mormon settlers trespassed into Indigenous lands and extracted resources without proper permits from federal Indian agents. There was no recourse against settlers who trespassed and violated federal law, and the US government did little to prosecute or remove settlers off Indigenous land. Instead, the US government often acquiesced to settler pressure to open up even more land.

Since the Doctrine of Discovery, Indigenous sovereignty had been weakened and limited by settler nations and later encoded into federal law that did not fully recognize Indigenous sovereignty.[36] For example, the first Trade and Intercourse Act of 1790 regulated trade and the cession of land by recognizing the United States as a sovereign nation that had power over Indigenous peoples. Settlers had to obtain a license issued by the US government before entering into Indigenous land to trade.[37] US settler law supersedes Indigenous sovereignty. The Trade and Intercourse Act of 1790 failed to provide real safeguards to protect Indigenous peoples and further eroded Indigenous sovereignty because this legislation failed to uphold treaties that restricted and regulated settlers on Indigenous lands. The weakness of US settler law did little to stop or punish settler claims to land, especially in Wisconsin Territory over the illegal theft of timber.[38] There were minimal laws and infrastructure to ensure that settlers would be prosecuted; instead, many settlers remained illegally on Indigenous land as they extracted valuable resources.[39] The Black River Falls Mormon members sent representatives to meet with the Menominee chief Oshkosh to discuss access to timber. After talking to Chief Oshkosh, Mormon settlers obtained permission to operate their logging business. Oshkosh gave Mormon settlers the right to lumber because the "timber 'was all his, and . . . the agent and United States had no business to interfere in the matter . . . he had come to attend to his timber himself.'"[40] Mormon settlers would have the exclusive right to cut timber if they fed "his people in their passing" in the Black River Falls region. In a letter to James D. Doty, Wisconsin territorial governor, in February 1844, David Jones, Indian agent to the Menominees, believed that "every White Man engaged in the Lumbering Business" was a trespasser on Indian lands.[41] As a result, Jones opposed this agreement and was "determined to stop all trespassing on Indian land."[42] Despite federal laws put in place to prevent trespassing and regulate commerce with Indigenous nations, little was done to enforce and remove settlers living illegally on tribal lands and halt the extraction of Indigenous resources. This moment highlights the tensions between the Menominees, Mormon settlers, and the US government. At times, their interests overlapped or were at odds with one another in this period.

The Menominee and Indian agent interests intersect in their desire to expel settlers, while at other times Chief Oshkosh wanted to assert Menominee sovereignty and negotiate with settlers over the extraction of timber. In its letter, the Black River Falls group wrote that "three different tribes of Lamanites [Winnebago, Menominee, and Chippewa] upon the most friendly terms, receiving us as their councilors both temporal and spiritual [visited in January 1844]."[43] The Black Falls River Mormon settlers shifted their focus from timber to the conversion of Indigenous peoples to fulfill their two-pronged approach in Wisconsin Territory. In its letter to LDS Church leader, the Black River Falls group claimed that Indigenous peoples from Wisconsin Territory to the Gulf of Mexico wanted to learn about the LDS Church and its teachings, going as far as to claim that they preferred the missionaries of the LDS Church because of their "righteousness" and because the "feasts and attendant ceremonies are precisely like ours."[44] Yet this account from a Mormon settler narrative uses Indigenous voices to support Mormon settler ideologies about Indigenous peoples as Lamanites and the acceptance of the Book of Mormon and the LDS Church because of the similarities, further reinforcing Smith's claims about the Book of Mormon as authentic, containing Lamanite traditions. This letter illuminates how Mormon settler colonialism functions at the margins, especially when Mormon settlers interact and engage with Indigenous peoples. Indigenous peoples were meant to legitimize Mormon settler ideologies, especially when they supported Lamanite discourse. This letter makes that shift from Mormon settler colonial extraction to religious conversion, both of which support Mormon settler ideologies about the land, especially Mormon claims to land. Mormon settlers needed Indigenous peoples to subscribe to the center of Mormon settler colonial power so as to legitimize their presence and belonging to the land. These letters and Council of Fifty minutes reinforce the Mormon settler narrative of Lamanite acceptance of Mormonism, thus justifying Mormon colonizing actions. According to one letter, Lamanites wanted to be converted, but this does not negate Mormon settler desires to civilize and assimilate Lamanites into Mormon society. The motives of Mormon settlers, such as resource extraction to build and sustain Mormon settler colonial efforts, become invisible when the narrative shifts to Lamanite conversion, a cover for Mormon settler desires to be of the land.

There was no record in council minutes about mass conversion of Lamanites from Wisconsin Territory to the Gulf of Mexico. Mormon settlers recognized the difficulty of introducing Mormonism to Menominees, and it would take "more exertion to all appearances to check the enthusiastic ardor of these our red brethren until the full principles of faith in our *Lord* and *Saviour Jesus Christ* shall be reasoned into their minds than to urge them on to receive it."[45] Menominee conversion was a consequence of Mormon settler goals. While Chief Oshkosh expressed interest in Mormonism, he would not make the decision for his people and instead proposed to bring it back to his people to "consider the whole matter, and act upon it in national council, and in that case their change of religion would be national and permanent."[46] Chief Oshkosh sought consensus among his people, and he was also politically astute; conversion to Mormonism could strengthen Menominee political power in the region by aligning with Mormon settlers. The Menominees, like many other Indigenous peoples, were strategic in their relations with settlers in their bid to retain sovereignty and connection to place.

While Mormon settlers in Black River Falls interacted with the Menominees as an extension of the LDS Church in Wisconsin Territory, the LDS Church and the Council of Fifty also interacted with Indigenous peoples at Nauvoo, the center of Mormon settler power. On April 18, 1843, the Potawatomies visited Nauvoo and Mormon leadership to secure "assistance and advice in their struggles with white Americans."[47] The Potawatomies visited Smith in hopes of leveraging his position of power to stop the increasing number of settlers on their lands. They wanted Smith's help because he could communicate with the "Great Spirit."[48] Potawatomies asserted their sovereignty and sought assistance from Mormon settlers who successfully claimed land while pushing back against non-Mormon settlement. Nauvoo was meant to be a safe Mormon settler space. The Potawatomies looked toward Smith and the LDS Church as a potential ally even if they were considered a religious minority by other settlers. Yet this did not entice Smith and, by extension, the LDS Church to support Potawatomi resistance to the US government, and instead Smith informed the Potawatomi delegation that "he could give them no assistance, that his hands were tied by the US but that he could sympathize with them." Smith recognized that they could not side with Indigenous nations because that would be seen as a direct challenge to US sovereignty and could also make them targets. Mormon settlers understood that in this moment they could not exert their settler sovereignty against the United States, especially as their settler gaze turned to new lands for potential settlement. Another Potawatomi group showed up on July 2, 1843, and met with Smith. According to the Mormon settler record, this Potawatomi group asked for support because the "white man has hated us and shed our blood" until Indigenous peoples no longer existed. Smith was "much affected and shed tears" but urged the Potawatomies to get along with other settlers and Indians and gave them a copy of the Book of Mormon, food, and horses for their return home. The last group of Potawatomies visited Smith in August 25, 1843, when they returned to Nauvoo and asked Smith to advise them on selling their land. Smith informed this delegation that they should not sell any more land to the US government and to find peace with other settlers and Tribal Nations. Smith understood his precarious position between the Potawatomies and the US government and knew he could not upset this tenuous balance between Tribes, settlers, and the government. In sending a delegation, the Potawatomies recognized Mormon settler sovereignty as they tried to negotiate with Smith. The Potawatomies strategically approached and sent delegations to Nauvoo as they attempted to leverage one settler power against another.

The Council of Fifty met with Potawatomi Indians who wanted their help to "avoid losing their land" on April 4, 1844.[49] The eleven Potawatomi representatives came with their French interpreter and met at the meeting house in Nauvoo with the council. In council meeting notes, Potawatomies were described as "friendly" and sought Mormon assistance to resist US pressure to sell even more lands, as they "did not want to sell them any more land."[50] Potawatomies continued to fight against the US government over land, and while they sought support from Mormon settlers, Smith and the council did not have the political power to protect Potawatomies from the United States. Mormon settlers and Potawatomies had been targeted as the Other by the US government for different reasons. Mormon settlers, because of their religious beliefs of Indigenous peoples as Lamanites, including Potawatomies, and their practice of polygamy had marked themselves as the Other, not because they had been racialized and marginalized like Indigenous peoples as the Other. Mormon settlers stood in the way of the US settler colonial project, a homogenized settler society that did not practice polygamy, while Potawatomies also stood in the way of civilizing policies, especially when they refused to cede even more lands to the US government to build a settler nation. Mormon settler colonial powers could not advocate for Potawatomi land because they were not a sovereign nation like the United States but instead directly benefited from the very policies the Potawatomi delegation sought to halt. Smith's paternalistic response did little to end conflict; rather, he counseled the Potawatomies to "cease their wars with each other & be at peace." Smith and the Council of Fifty failed to recognize how their presence at and settlement of Nauvoo also contributed to this conflict between the US government and Potawatomies, and Mormon settlers did little to alleviate these conflicts. In fact, their presence exacerbated existing tensions between the US government and Potawatomies.

Smith's negotiations with the Potawatomies highlight nuanced ways in which US and Mormon settler colonialism can be both at odds and align when there are contestations over land. Smith's sentiments echo US settler colonial desires around the civilization and assimilation of Indigenous peoples. In these moments with the Menominees and the Potawatomies, the nuances of Mormon settler colonial processes became more visible. While in Nauvoo, Mormon settlers used this settler colonial outpost to leverage their access to lands and resources. Indigenous peoples mattered only when they could be in service to Mormon settler colonial power, including attempts made to convert Indigenous peoples. In general, Mormon settlers were vested in the spread of Mormonism, yet when it came to Indigenous peoples, the rejection of Mormonism served the Mormon settler colonial center because Mormon settlers could justify their presence and claims to land. This rejection became the catalyst for Mormon settlers to develop and hone settler colonial ideologies around land and settler belonging. Mormon religious ideologies drove Mormon settler exploration to other potential sites of Mormon settler society.

LOOKING SOUTH TO THE REPUBLIC OF TEXAS: THE COUNCIL OF FIFTY AND THE SEARCH FOR FUTURE MORMON EMPIRE

Mormons served the settler colonial center, and once Mormon settlers in Black River Falls decided that this site would not be promising for future Mormon settlement, they looked toward the Republic of Texas. The Republic of Texas offered the possibility to purchase lands to build and sustain a Mormon empire and exist outside the periphery of the United States. Joseph Smith's views about Texas annexation reflect national discussions and tensions over slavery and the use of this region as a buffer from other settler powers.[51] The annexation of Texas would protect and advance the US and Mormon settler colonial projects centered around claiming land to realize their manifest destiny dreams. However, there were concerns over slavery and Texas as a slave state if it became part of the United States. Smith put forth a proposal whereby Texas could enter the union as a slave state and that maintaining a balance between slave and free states could be achieved by either emancipating slaves or acquiring additional land. Although Mormon settlers desired to create a Mormon theocracy, separate and free from the United States, the annexation of Texas would serve both US and Mormon settlers' interests in the purchase and settling of land. Once Black River Falls Mormon settlers and the Council of Fifty determined that the lumbering operation could never become a lucrative private business or, at the very least, that Black River Falls could not be a Mormon settler site that served the center, Nauvoo, the LDS Church shifted its gaze to territories outside the United States, such as the Republic of Texas, Oregon Territory, and the Great Basin. Their interest aligned with US settler colonial goals of expansion to the West Coast, but Mormon settlers wanted to still build their sovereign Mormon empire. Mormon settlers, including the Council of Fifty, aligned Mormon settler interests with the US settler colonial project because their exploration of these territories fulfilled their religious ideologies about land even if they established a new Mormon settler center outside of Nauvoo.

In the Black River Falls letters to Smith and the Quorum of the Twelve Apostles dated February 15, 1844, Mormon settlers wrote about their lumbering operations in Wisconsin Territory and their desire to begin missionary work in Texas. In these letters, Wisconsin Mormon settlers petitioned Smith and other LDS Church leaders to consider their request to pivot in purpose and meet the needs of their larger Mormon settler community: finding land and resources to expand and sustain a sovereign Mormon settler society. Smith and other leaders could adapt their political and religious agenda to suit their needs, including the establishment of a "theocracy either in Texas or Oregon or somewhere in California."[52] These two letters became the catalyst for the creation of the Council of Fifty and were important to the overall development of Mormon religious and settler ideologies about land and belonging. Manifest destiny shifted to serve Mormons' ever-changing settler desires, whether from Nauvoo to the Black River Hills site in Wisconsin Territory and now to the Republic of Texas. Quite simply, Wisconsin Territory was no longer ideal for Mormon settlers. They described the place as a "dreary cold region" with little value beyond the land they occupied.[53] Unable to secure an agreement with the Menominees over timber, Mormon settlers proposed a move to the Republic of Texas because no other resources could be developed, so they looked toward other regions to share the "Gospel [which] has not been fully opened in all the South and South Western States, as also Texas, Mexico, Brazil &c, together with the West Indian Islands." Again, these letters align manifest destiny with the Mormon missionary efforts to convert Indigenous peoples. Black River Falls Mormon settlers tied land, including resource extraction, to their desire to proselytize.

These missions became the conduit for Mormon settlers to explore possible sites for future Mormon settlement. Their attention shifted to Texas's "table lands" in hopes of finding "eligible" land for a future "place of gathering for all of the South."[54] Black River Falls Mormon settlers wanted to sell their mills and instead focus on their missionary efforts in the South and sought approval from Smith and the

Council of Fifty to build a sustainable Mormon empire. Mormon settlers looked to the "Colorado [sic] River with all its beautiful hills and vallies [sic] and fertile soil with deep regret" because there were so many people "without the knowledge of God or the doctrine of the Church of Jesus Christ of Latter Day Saints."[55] Unlike their Wisconsin pinery operations, Mormon settlers in Texas would rely on their members' labors to sustain missionary efforts for LDS Church enterprises. Mormon settlers in Black River Falls wanted Indigenous peoples to sell their lands and join their efforts to convert other Indigenous peoples in Texas.[56] The Five Civilized Tribes and other nations had been forcibly removed west, outside established state boundaries, which meant that Indigenous people could no longer obstruct settler society. However, Indigenous peoples would never be safe as settlers continued to encroach onto these lands as the US government fulfilled its expansionist goals of empire.

Mormon settlers' interest in expanding into the Republic of Texas was so great that the Council of Fifty decided in its March 14, 1844, meeting to send Lucien Woodworth on a mission to explore the possibility of purchasing land for the LDS Church in the Republic of Texas.[57] In its March 21, 1844, meeting, the council decided to petition Congress to protect US citizens immigrating into other territories as they explored "lands thus unknown, unowned, or unoccupied, [and] are among some of the richest and most fertile of the continent."[58] The council also appealed to Congress to make Smith a member of the US Army to help protect the United States from "from foreign invasion."[59] The council's interest in militarizing members was meant to protect the LDS Church from anti-Mormon sentiment and violence, especially when the US government failed to intervene and protect Mormon settlers. Mormon settlers were more than willing to serve on behalf of the United States because their service would directly benefit their settler goals. Smith and other leaders in the LDS Church negotiated this balance between becoming an extension of the US settler colonial project and acting on their own settler desires, revealing the fluidity in which Mormons exercised their whiteness. Mormon settlers were more than willing to claim and use their whiteness to demand access to land under the guise of religious liberties and protecting land on behalf of the US government even as they claimed a religious, minoritized status.

The LDS Church, through the Council of Fifty, wanted to advance the US settler colonial project to suit its needs. In a council meeting on March 26, 1844, members drafted a petition to Congress regarding Mormon settler involvement in westward expansion. In its petition to Congress, the council sought permission to interfere in Republic of Texas and Oregon politics, writing "Texas has declared herself free and independent, without the necessary power to protect her rights and liberties. . . .

oregon [*sic*] is without any organized government, and those who emigrate thither are exposed to foreign invasion, and domestic feuds . . . [and] by geographic location, and discovery more right . . . fully belongs to these United States, than to any other general government."[60] The council's attempts to position itself as a protector of Oregon and the Republic of Texas was a very paternalistic view similar to the US relationship with Indigenous peoples. Smith and council members believed that these lands belonged to the United States, a very US-centric settler perspective, only because their interference served their desires to explore, extract resources, and establish missions to fulfill Mormon settler colonial ideologies about land and Lamanites. Smith and his followers wanted to extend the boundaries of the United States not because they were truly loyal citizens but because these expansionist efforts served a larger settler desire of creating a Mormon theocratic nation in these newly claimed lands.

The Council of Fifty in Nauvoo shaped the political and theological discourse as Mormon settler expeditions left to explore future sites of Mormon settlement. Council leadership, including Lyman Wight and Lucien Woodworth, was entangled in the religious and political affairs of the LDS Church; there was no separation of the LDS Church and the council. Smith and the council instructed Wight and Woodworth to return to Nauvoo, and both arrived in early May. Wight traveled from Wisconsin Territory on May 1, 1844, and the following day Woodworth arrived after his brief mission to the Republic of Texas in hopes of securing land for a Mormon settlement.[61] The council convened a special meeting on May 3, 1844, with twenty-four members present due to the last-minute request. During their meeting, Woodworth gave a thorough report of his negotiations with Sam Houston, the governor of Texas. In his report, Woodworth recounts his travels to Galveston, Texas, to negotiate with Houston for land. Initially, Woodworth tried to convince Houston to sell or gift land to Mormon settlers, but Houston was not entirely convinced that the contentious political parties and the Texas Congress would grant or sell land due to tensions over annexation. Houston could no longer authorize land grants to attract settlers due to the fear of Texas becoming an antislavery state.

Woodworth's mission to Texas was entirely political. He did not "come to treat with him [Houston] on religion. I told him if he did agree to give us a tract on which we might institute a government, we might try to get some other grant and assist them in their government."[62] Woodworth's Texas mission highlights the nuanced ways in which Mormon settler colonialism functions. In this instance, Mormon settlers' desires were at the forefront in their search for Mormon lands in Texas. Mormon settlers could create a settler society in Texas as long as their theocratic, settler government did not interfere with Texas settler sovereignty. In fact, Houston and other allies hoped that Mormon settlers could be utilized to defend Texas from Mexico as they sought to claim even more Mexican land. Texas and Mormon settler interests converge but were also at odds with US settler sovereignty. This scenario was much like the Menominees and Potawatomies reaching out to Smith and Mormon settlers to advocate for their sovereignty, but at the same time, Mormon settlers had a vested interest in dismantling Indigenous sovereignty. Texas also wanted to use Mormon settlers to maintain their sovereign status from the United States, yet Mormon settlers wanted to infringe on Texas sovereignty for the purpose of locating a site for Mormon empire. During the Council of Fifty's afternoon session on May 6, 1844, Woodworth was authorized to return to Texas to lobby at the next congressional session that would occur later that year. Woodworth would continue negotiating with Texas to confer title to land along the Texas-Mexico border to Mormon settlers.[63] Despite Woodworth's best efforts, the death of Smith on June 27, 1844, halted any further negotiations. At the same meeting, the council discussed the return from Wisconsin Territory of twenty-five men working there in the pineries to Nauvoo with no monies or home. Council member George Miller proposed that these men, including Lyman Wight, Lucien Woodworth, and George Miller, continue onto Texas "near Nachitoches [Nacogdoces] . . . to commence farming."[64] Ultimately, the council granted the Wisconsin Mormon settlers' petition to move to Texas to focus on missionary work because this mission fulfilled Mormon settler desires of conversion so members' labor could be used to serve the LDS Church's settler center. Nauvoo simply did not have the resources to sustain their growing population, and this small band of Mormon settlers on a mission to Texas served three purposes: exploration and expansion into Texas, expanding missionary efforts, and building up a self-sustaining Mormon settler outpost.

While Woodworth was negotiating in Texas with Sam Houston, Orson Hyde went to Washington, D.C., to represent the Council of Fifty and Smith. In his April 25, 1844, letter, Hyde advised that Mormon settlers needed to take decisive action in settling either Oregon or Texas because their settler power would not protected by the US government. Hyde urged Smith to send "wise" and "efficient" settlers to teach and civilize Lamanites via "religion—to cultivate the soil—to live in peace with one another and with all men."[65] Hyde provided recommendations about settling in Texas but concluded with his views on the potential settlement of Oregon by Mormons by arguing that Mormon settlers had to become the majority; if not, other settlers would not tolerate them. Hyde's letters triangulates Mormon settler colonialism to US settler colonialism and Lamanites as the Other. At times,

Mormon and US settler colonial goals align: civilize Indigenous peoples via religious conversion, farming, and claiming land. Their settler impulses mirror one another in their attempts to claim and mark lands as settler space by building structures onto the land. Yet Mormon settlers became the Other only when their presence became an obstacle to US settler infrastructures, much like Indigenous peoples. Once Mormon settlers became an impediment to the US settler colonial project, other settlers utilized violence to expel them from settler society, but they were not the racialized Other.

The dispossession of Indigenous peoples was also predicated on settler violence. Mormon settlers enacted violence against Indigenous peoples to construct Mormon empire. Nauvoo became pivotal to the expansion of Mormon empire into the West. Hyde further reinforced the importance of Nauvoo in his discussion of Mormon migration to Oregon and said that if Mormon settlers were removed "to that country, Nauvoo is the place of general rendezvous" to strategically make their way "to the best portions of Oregon," where "no government shall be established" there.[66] While in Washington, D.C., Illinois Supreme Court associate justice and US congressman Stephen A. Douglas gave Hyde a map and John C. Fremont's *Report on an Exploration of the Country Lying between the Missouri River and the Rocky Mountains, on the Line of the Kanzas [sic] and Great Platte Rivers*, which contained valuable information about westward migration. Fremont's report, maps, and other notes supplied invaluable information about the West, including travel routes and possible settlement sites for the council to consider regarding a future Mormon Zion. When Mormon settlers looked west, it was not just because of God's desires for Mormon settlers to claim land and to build a Mormon Zion, but their efforts at these different places demonstrate that they had knowledge of specific lands in the West that could be claimed as Mormon. They relied on the labor and knowledge of other settlers to make informed decisions about the land where they chose to build a Mormon empire. In this instance, Hyde was in possession of valuable knowledge and resources that would benefit Mormon expeditions into the West. The production of a narrative about Mormon settlement of the West becomes naturalized when placed within a framework of Mormon settler ideologies, such as Mormon manifest destiny, rather than acknowledging that Mormon settlers made informed decisions about their migration west.

The Council of Fifty would later discuss these materials during a March 18, 1845, meeting when Orson Spencer, chairman of the "committee on the geography of the Western Country," verbally updated the council.[67] The materials discussed by the committee would be published the following day in the *Nauvoo Neighbor* and, based on the reports, identified northern California as a region with moderate temperature and rich soils. Oregon appeared less ideal because there was no harbor along the coast, and the Columbia River was also not an ideal location to build a port. During these discussions, Brigham Young interjected that a company of settlers should be sent out in the spring to "find a location not far distant, where we can stay a year or two as circumstances may require, [and] we will soon have a company on the way."[68] Young asserted that Mormon settlers would benefit economically and militarily from living along a coast surrounded by mountains. As the LDS Church became a more global institution, the port could "bring the saints in from all parts of the world," and Mormon settlers could arm themselves against settler violence and secure a place to build their sovereign settler society. According to Young, Smith found California to be the most advantageous site for Mormon empire; "that was his mind." The council wanted to settle in northern California but would build "stopping places all through the journey" where other Mormon settlers could follow the path to Mormon Zion. The first Mormon settler expedition would pave the way for other Mormon settlers; however, they were not the first settlers in the region. Mormon settlers benefited from other settler excursions into this region; they simply marked these places as Mormon in the narratives about their migration. Thes council's discussion about westward expansion illustrates how Mormon settlers navigated between settler sovereignties to realize their goal of a Mormon Zion. The council needed the approval of either the US government or state governors to purchase vast tracts of land. Yet Mormon settlers wanted to receive US protection from "foreign foes" and simultaneously "make their own laws" until they were strong enough on their own.[69]

The Council of Fifty's discussion makes visible the moments in which Mormon settler colonialism served as an extension of US settler colonialism, despite desires to remain sovereign from the United States, or exist "one hundred miles beyond . . . the jurisdiction of the United States [where] we are safe, for the present, and that is all we ask."[70] Their movement would displace Indigenous peoples as Mormon settlers, and others claimed lands and resources along these settler trails. Young later commented that there was little purpose in sending out an expedition party for two years when they "will not be able to bring more information" than they already possessed.[71] The council's exploratory missions to California and Oregon capitalized on the maps and notes already documented by other settlers; Mormon settlers identified vast areas rich in resources that could sustain a growing settler empire in the region.

The increasing movement and presence of settlers would exacerbate tensions with and between Indigenous nations and settlers. Unlike US-Indian relations,

Young and the Council of Fifty viewed Mormon-Lamanite relations much more favorably and believed that they could have good, mutually beneficial relationships with Lamanites. During the council's March 22, 1845, meeting, the focus and purpose of the western mission shifted from settlement to exploring and securing land to establishing a potential refuge site and meeting with Tribal Nations gathering in June organized by the Creek Nation in response to Pawnee and Comanche violence.[72] Orson Spencer and Jonathon Dunham encouraged the council to view this gathering of Tribal Nations as an opportunity to secure relations with Lamanites, although Mormon settlers did not attend in case they needed allies against non-Mormon settler attacks. The council continued to perpetuate paternalistic views of Lamanites, and there was little recognition that conflicts between Tribal Nations were due to settler disruption. With Indigenous peoples forced onto increasingly smaller land bases often far from traditional territories, their lifeways changed dramatically. Settlers, including Mormon settlers, disrupted Indigenous lives and connection to lands. The council's shift to the Republic of Texas signals how Mormon settlers operated at the margin of US settler society so long as their settler sovereignty acquiesced to US settler authority.

CONCLUSION

On June 17, 1844, in Carthage, Illinois, Joseph and Hyrum Smith were killed by violent non-Mormon settlers. The death of Joseph Smith caused turmoil in the LDS Church, including the Council of Fifty, as members jockeyed for power to shape the trajectory and future of the LDS Church and a Mormon settler society. The council advanced the Mormon settler center of power, particularly as it sent exploratory groups to scope out potential sites of Mormon settlement while also trying to expand the Mormon missionary efforts at these sites, especially to convert Indigenous peoples. Mormon settler views of the West echoed widely held sentiments about Indigenous peoples and lands. A key feature of US and Mormon settler colonialism was the "*dispensability* of the indigenous person" in pursuit of land.[73] Council policies and petitions to the US Congress centered on and around land, a feature of Mormon settler colonial ideologies and processes. Mormon settler colonialism was premised on the "systematic disavowal of any indigenous presence, recurrently representing 'colonialism' as something done by someone else and 'colonisation' as an act that is exercised exclusively over the land and sustains fantasies of the 'pristine wilderness' and innocent pioneering effort."[74] Mormon settlers' narratives about the West as a pristine wilderness meant that Indigenous peoples were simultaneously not present or were obstacles to settlers' efforts to tame the land. Mormon settlers absolve their participation in dispossessing Indigenous peoples from the narrative and land in council discussions because they exist within a Mormon religious framework. Mormon settlers claimed "unknown, unowned, or unoccupied" lands in the West and the South, a deliberate attempt to shape the narrative to erase Mormon settlers' participation in the theft of Indigenous lands. Indigenous peoples had a relationship to the land that was disregarded and ignored by settlers. Mormon settlers asserted their right to the land by framing their claims using religious ideologies about land. The council shaped early LDS Church policies around Mormon settlers' claims to land. Mormon settlers created a Mormon settler outpost in Nauvoo, the periphery of US settler society. Despite attempts to extricate themselves from the United States, the council's efforts often overlapped and aligned with US settler colonial goals in places like Wisconsin Territory and the Republic of Texas.

The Council of Fifty wanted to create a distinct Mormon settler society, yet its settler desires reflected and advanced US settlers' desires of empire. As much as the council, Smith, and the followers of the LDS Church wanted to create a distinct Mormon settler society, the council had been influenced by US political ideology. For example, in a council meeting on April 18, 1844, members drafted a Mormon Constitution that began much like the US Constitution: "We, the people of the Kingdom of God, knowing that all power emanates from God, that the earth is his possession, and he alone has the right to govern the nations and set in order the kingdoms of this world; that he only has a right to institute laws and establish decrees for the government of the human family."[75] Their ideas reinforced US notions of democracy and the right to "life, liberty, possession of property, and pursuit of happiness" but placed these ideals within Mormon religious ideologies, especially the right to exist as Mormon settlers. Despite efforts to establish Mormon sovereign authority, the council replicated the very systems that the LDS Church tried to escape.

On April 11, 1845, in one of the final meetings of the Council of Fifty under the leadership of Brigham Young, LDS Church members Lewis Dana (Mormon Oneida member), Jonathan Dunham, and Charles Shumway were assigned to the western mission to convert Lamanites and locate a new Mormon settler site. The future site would be "on this side of the rocky mountains, where we can be safe & have a suitable place to locate" their families and be received by the Indians, and be permitted to settle amongst Indigenous peoples to "instruct them."[76] The council met in the final months of 1845 and early 1846 to organize their move west. Mormon settlers had the ultimate authority given to them by God, and the council's explorations into the Salt Lake Valley would become a reality as Mormon settlers experienced increasing non-Mormon settler violence. With the death of Joseph and Hyrum Smith and increasing anti-Mormon violence in Nauvoo, Mormon settlers looked west once more to claim and make Mormon space.

The Mormon move west was simply a fulfillment of Mormon settler logic, justified by religious ideologies. Mormon settlers used their experiences in Nauvoo to establish a Mormon settler center in the Salt Lake Valley. Mormon settlers fled Nauvoo and the violence they experienced by other settlers became the foundations of their Mormon pioneer subject position and their desire to belong and be of the land. Mormon manifest destiny was realized in their migration to the West, where their religious ideologies converged with their settler desires for land. Mormon settlers' desire to mark space as Mormon, much like the infrastructures and narratives they wrote onto the landscape of Nauvoo, continued to mark land and build structures in the Salt Lake Valley to secure their belonging. Nauvoo became the foundation for the development of Mormon settler colonial technologies, particularly discourse around land, missions, and Lamanites. The Mormon settler subject position was fluid, ever changing to suit the needs of the Mormon settler colonial center as Mormon settlers explored Wisconsin Territory, the Republic of Texas, and eventually the Great Basin.

The center of Mormon settler colonial power and empire changed once more as Mormon settlers looked to the West to secure a new home and used narratives and infrastructures to secure their belonging to land while moving Indigenous peoples to the margins of Mormon settler society. The Mormons' move west was representative of how their settler colonial project functioned, especially as Mormon settlers relied on their whiteness to migrate and claim Indigenous lands while also naturalizing their presence and their Mormon settler subject position as they marked land once more as distinctly Mormon settler land.

3 THE MORMON PIONEER SETTLER LANDSCAPE

EMBEDDING MORMON IDENTITY ONTO THE LAND

We'll find the place which God for us prepared,
Far away in the West,
Where none shall come to hurt or make afraid;
There the Saints will be blessed.
We'll make the air with music ring,
Shout praises to our God and King;
Above the rest these we'll tell—
All is well! All is Well!

WILLIAM CLAYTON,
"COME, COME, YE SAINTS"

Pioneer Day is an official state holiday in Utah that commemorates and honors the arrival of the first Mormon settlers traveling through Emigration Canyon into the Salt Lake Valley on July 24, 1847. Utah state government and many private businesses shut down to celebrate Pioneer Day. Throughout the state, various towns and cities celebrate "with parades, fireworks, and music—and, for some, pie and beer."[1] Of Utah's almost 3.4 million residents, around 42 percent are Mormon, yet Mormon history and settler subject position, often expressed in the form of pioneer, not only dominate the state's built landscape and infrastructures but also serve to center the subject position as *the* normative identity in Utah.[2] Since the first official celebration of Pioneer Day on July 24, 1849, the Church of Jesus Christ of Latter-day Saints (LDS Church) has tried to become more inclusive of Mormons and non-Mormons alike, but one theme remains constant: the celebration of a distinct Mormon settler subject position, or pioneer status, grounded in whiteness and made invisible in the annual celebration of Mormon settlers that marks and reifies Mormon whiteness onto the land, including Mormon settler monuments.

The Mormon settlement of the Salt Lake Valley and the surrounding region in the dominant historical narratives has depicted Mormon settlers as pioneers seeking refuge from religious persecution. The dominant narrative about Mormon settlers moving west focuses on the physical and religious sacrifices they made during the move. In their migration west, they exercised their settler sovereignty to claim land as they dispossessed Indigenous peoples from their homelands because the Mormon vision of Zion required Indigenous peoples to be moved to the periphery of Mormon settler society. As Mormon settlers moved west, they imagined living outside the periphery of US geopolitical boundaries. Mormon settlers refused to fully acquiesce their settler sovereignty to the US nation-state even as they relied on the US settler colonial project to settle the West. Thus, Mormon empire and settler desires became an extension of the US settler colonial project. Mormon manifest destiny and Mormon exceptionalism mimicked US manifest destiny and settler desires to claim Indigenous land, and, in the Mormon context, Mormon settler claims to land were even more exceptional, which meant that their claims to land superseded all others. Mormon settlers carried their sovereignty with them as they established a new center of Mormon settler colonial power in the Salt Lake Valley. This chapter seeks to make visible the processes of Mormon settler colonialism using Mormon settler texts around their migration to the West as God's chosen people, or Mormon manifest destiny. These historical and religious narratives were important in constructing Mormon pioneer as a subject position written onto the land as a state holiday and with infrastructures, including This Is the Place Heritage Park. These infrastructures mark space as distinctly Mormon. In Joanne Barker's *Native Acts: Law, Recognition, and Cultural Authenticity*, these narratives about "national progress, civilization, democracy, freedom, liberty, and equality" sanction settlers' power to move beyond their "roles in Native genocide, dispossession, and exploitation to embody an ever-present multicultural humanism."[3] Mormon settlers utilize these "discursive maneuvers" to reinvent indigeneity and belonging because they have "historically benefited from histories of Native oppression—especially including genocidal violence and land dispossession—[and] can now perceive their positions of power and legal entitlements as somehow inevitable," since Lamanites, or Indigenous peoples, have proved unworthy of being on and claiming land. In this iteration of Indigenous dispossession, Mormon settlers' status was secured as natural, a fulfillment of Mormon religious ideologies that prophesied their place and possession of Indigenous lands. The dispossession of Indigenous peoples and the making of Mormon place went hand in hand. The Mormon settler colonial project was reliant on the possession of Indigenous lands. Since the beginning of the LDS Church, leaders such as Joseph Smith and Brigham Young utilized their settler status to explore possible sites of Mormon empire in the West. These settler impulses coincided with US settler desires of expansion and could only happen because Mormon settlers accessed and wielded their status as settlers and, in doing so, secured their access to and possession of Indigenous lands.

In this chapter, I focus on the arrival of the first Mormon pioneer company as the origins of a Mormon pioneer subject position used to claim and demarcate space as Mormon settler space. An official state holiday, narratives, and monuments such as This Is the Place Heritage Park reinforced the Mormon pioneer/settler subject position, pushing Indigenous peoples to the periphery of the Mormon settler colonial imaginary through historical and religious narratives that required Indigenous peoples to exist at the border of Mormon settler empire. Tom Lynch argues in *Outback and Out West: The Settler-Colonial Environmental Imaginary* that the settler-colonial imaginary "envisions its relationship to the world in a particular way and generates a hegemonic discourse and symbolic system to enforce that perspective."[4] Mormon settlers constructed their relationship to land, Indigenous peoples, and other systems using Mormon religious ideologies to establish their hegemonic power in the Salt Lake Valley, the center of Mormon settler colonial power. Mormon and religious texts became central to Mormon hegemonic discourse as they went about their business of claiming land through symbolic systems such as a state holiday, parade pageantry, and monuments, meant to reinforce Mormon settler presence as natural. Mormon settlers also moved beyond the symbolic hegemonic discourse and built Mormon infrastructures onto the land.

Contemporary contestations have occurred in the United States over monuments that reinforce specific violent hegemonic discourses, such as Confederate monuments that have been targeted for removal because they silence and erase the perspective of so-called Others. Mormon settler colonialism persists as Mormon settler structures that continue to mark the land as Mormon. I focus on the Mormon settler/pioneer subject position, Pioneer Day, and Mormon settler colonial infrastructures to make visible the enduring structures of Mormon settler colonialism. Historical and religious narratives about Mormon settler belonging and place-making become the foundations for Mormon pioneer/settler subject position.

I make visible Mormon settler belonging by placing the Mormon migration, settlement, and creation of a Mormon empire within a larger discourse of US settler colonialism. The production of Pioneer Day and the Mormon settler subject position were tied to land as Mormon settlers justified their place on Indigenous lands. Patrick Wolfe's logic of elimination points to the structures of settler colonialism and as Unangax̂ scholar Eve Tuck and settler scholar Wayne Yang articulate, in "the process of settler colonialism, land is remade into property[,] and human relationships to land are restricted to the relationship of the owner to his property."[5] Tuck and Yang point to the processes of settler colonialism, and in Mormon settler colonialism, Mormon settlers have remade land as part of Mormon empire and subject position, thus changing Indigenous and non-Indigenous relationships to land. As Mormon settlers went about claiming and settling the land, Indigenous and Mormon settler relationships to land and one another dramatically changed. Indigenous peoples could no longer exist on their homelands and live as they had since time immemorial. Instead, Mormon settlers made "a place their home" as they "destroy[ed] and disappear[ed] the Indigenous peoples that live[d] there."[6] While the state of Utah and the LDS Church celebrate Pioneer Day, the processes of Mormon settler colonialism extend beyond Mormon settler arrival into the Salt Lake Valley on July 24, 1847, and extends into the modern period as Mormon structures continue to mark land as Mormon settler land. Mormons' claims to exceptionalism were supported by their safe arrival into the Salt Lake Valley, this land set aside by God for their explicit use. Mormon settlers believe their settler status to be exceptional, with their religious beliefs marking them as special even as other settlers saw them as a threat to settler sovereignty as Mormons sought out land for their empire. However, Mormon settlers were simply settlers of a "different religion." Mormon settlers exercised their right to land framed within and justified by Mormon religious ideologies. They made their home on Indigenous lands, and their migration into the Salt Lake Valley signaled Mormon settlers' move to innocence. As Mormon settlers built their homes, they participated in or benefited from the dispossession and removal of Indigenous peoples. Indigenous peoples were considered to be "in the way" as Mormon settlers destroyed Indigenous peoples and communities while they established Mormon settler empire. Indigenous peoples "must be erased, must be made into ghosts." Indigenous peoples and communities were erased from the land as Mormon settlers ritualized their claim to land through Pioneer Day and the Mormon built environment, including This Is the Place Heritage Park. The annual repetition becomes a "structuring force . . . that shapes collective memory. It nurtures narratives of peaceful colonization and Indigenous acquiescence. . . . [These] calendrical commemorations reproduce the political temporality of settler colonialism."[7] Pioneer Day continues to shape the collective memory and experience of Mormon settlers in which Indigenous peoples exist within the Mormon settler temporality and settler colonial imaginary as Lamanites.

Mormons are a religious minority in the United States but a majority in Utah. However, despite Mormon settler colonial structures shaping and governing public and private spaces in Utah, the processes of Mormon settler colonialism and the production of Mormon settler fantasies via structures, such as monuments and the built environment, have been naturalized, made invisible, because Mormon settler presence has largely been excluded from settler colonial studies and within Mormon history and studies. Mormon settler narratives about Mormon pioneers and empire ignore how Mormon settler colonialism functions, especially how land, memory, and history became structures to normalize the "everyday enactments of place, personhood, and belonging."[8] Adria L. Imada argues that the production of colonial nostalgia is just one aspect of settler colonialism: "Settler colonialism—the displacement of Indigenous peoples through the expropriation of land and institutions by foreign settlers—relies on and produces an investment in uncomplicated, ahistorical fantasies."[9] Imada's work is useful in understanding how the Mormon historical and religious narrative is a production "in uncomplicated, ahistorical fantasies." The use of "pioneer" implies that the first wave of Mormon settlers were in fact the first peoples into this region. This is simply not true. Indigenous peoples have existed since time immemorial from and on this land, even as their ties to land were being severed and destroyed. The Mormon settler move to belonging as legitimate is secured by the elimination of Indigenous peoples. Indigenous peoples, in the Mormon settler colonial imaginary, exist only to sanction Mormon settler claims to Indigenous lands and resources. Jared Farmer's *On Zion's Mount: Mormons, Indians, and the American Landscape* explores how Mormons created their homelands using Indigenous place-names to mythologize and nostalgically infuse indigeneity onto the land and historical narrative to serve the Mormon settler colonial project.[10] Indigenous peoples exist to give meaning to the Mormon pioneer subject position, another function of Mormon settler colonialism. Imada's and Farmer's works demonstrate how the production of colonial nostalgia and Indigenous place-names were central to Mormon settler narratives about this land. Pioneer Day, in all its pageantry, is not just about the celebration of Mormon settlers; it is also about the enacting of Mormon settler nostalgia, or pioneer nostalgia, for a past that never existed, which is why the curation of Mormon pioneer narrative, identity, and holiday becomes even more important to understanding the naturalization of Mormon settler colonialism processes. The trek west by Mormon settlers and the commemoration of their ancestors' sacrifices signaled the production of a celebratory narrative and nostalgic holiday to reenact and further embed this collective experience in the mundane everyday of all citizens, whether Mormon settler, non-Mormon settler, or Indigenous.

The Mormon migration west must also be placed within a larger conversation about US settler colonialism and expansion that dispossessed and subjugated Indigenous peoples throughout the nineteenth and twentieth centuries. This dispossession and disappearance of Indigenous peoples continues today. This chapter explores the manner in which the LDS Church and Mormon settlers have understood, interpreted, and (re)created their past through the creation of a pioneer subject position to cement their belonging to place. Finally, this chapter highlights the various manifestations of Mormon settler/pioneer subject position and the use of structures to mark Mormon settler space.

THE ORIGINS OF A MORMON PIONEER IDENTITY AND THE MOVE TO INNOCENCE

Increasing religious persecution served as a catalyst for the Mormon migration west. The West became a symbol of refuge to Mormon settlers. Mormon expeditions disguised as missions had been sent by LDS Church leaders, such as Joseph Smith and the Council of Fifty, to explore potential options for future Mormon settlement long before 1847. As discussed in chapter 2, Smith and the Council of Fifty charged a group of members to explore potential sites for a future Mormon Zion. Eventually, the Great Basin region was identified as an ideal location. This region appealed to Mormon settlers because there was not a large non-Mormon settler presence; the region was isolated, naturally demarcated boundaries by various mountain ranges, and there were sizable tracts of fertile land for farming. Once Mormon settlers located this potential site to build a Mormon empire, a space they could claim and transform without external interference from the US government and other settlers. This move west had been planned long before the death of Smith, and once Brigham Young became the next prophet of the LDS Church after Smith's death, Mormon settlers continued to organize their move west.

The Mormon settler migration west was highly organized and reflected the religious, patriarchal authority of the LDS Church leadership. Young served as leader of the first pioneer company. God commanded Young to lead members of the LDS Church west. His religious authority was also secured by modern revelation and established settler male authority in LDS Church leadership. The manner in which Young and others organized their migration west supported their claims of Mormon exceptionalism. According to "The Word and Will of the Lord Concerning the Camp of Israel in Their Journeyings to the West," Mormon settlers were expected to be organized in their travel, signaling their divine status.[11] Mormon leaders were meticulous in their organization of each company, and all settler groups moving west had to be led by Mormon settler men. In addition to installing a theocratic governing body in each pioneer company, Young expected settlers to be prepared with adequate supplies for their migration west. Everyone was expected to assist and provide for one another; "the poor, the widows, the fatherless, and the families of those who have gone into the army" were not to be left behind. Mormon settlers created community, a shared experience central to the construction of their pioneer subject position. The migration west was necessary for Mormon settlers' sense of self, securing their right to claim Indigenous lands. Brigham Young led the first pioneer company from Winter Quarters, Nebraska, on April 16, 1846. His company was composed of 142 men, 3 women, and 2 children. Mormon settlers leaned into their status as pioneers despite not being the first settlers to migrate west. Mormon settlers used established trails when possible, and their migration to the Salt Lake Valley often paralleled other settler trails, such as the Oregon Trail and the California Trail.

Eventually Brigham Young and his company made their way across the plains, and on July 13, 1847, he sent out a group to scout the area ahead to mark the path that the remaining party would follow. Orson Pratt, a member of the Quorum of the Twelve Apostles, followed the "Reed-Donner Trail, which they improved and followed over big and little mountains through Emigration Canyon into the valley[,] . . . sav[ing] more than two week's travel."[12] The first Mormon scouts reached the valley before Young and had arrived on July 21, 1847. Orson Pratt and John Brown, captain and LDS Church member from Mississippi, saw the Salt Lake Valley and descended down Emigration Canyon. Orson Pratt recalled, "[We] beheld in a moment such an extensive scenery open before us [that] we could not refrain from a shout of joy which almost involuntarily escaped from our lips the moment this good and lovely scenery was within our view. Although we had only one horse between us, we traversed a circuit of about 12 miles." Several days later, seven other men led by Pratt and George A. Smith, member of the company, rode into the valley on July 22, 1847, to scout out places for future crops. Sixty wagons and their accompanying party also entered the valley on the same day under the leadership of Willard Richard, an apostle in Young's First Presidency. Young arrived lying sick with mountain fever in the back of Wilford Woodruff's wagon on July 24, 1847.[13] Woodruff, a prolific diarist, wrote,

This is an important day in the History of my life and the History of the church of JESUS CHRIST of Latter-Day Saints. On this important day after trave[ling] from our encampment 6 miles ... we came in full view of the great valley or Basin [of] the Salt Lake and land of promise, held in reserve by the hand of GOD for a resting place for the Saints upon which A portion of the Zion of GOD will be built. We gazed with wonder and admiration upon the vast rich fertile valley which lay for about 25 miles in length & 16 miles in width Clothed with the Heaviest garb of green vegetation in the midst of which lay a large lake of Salt water.[14]

Woodruff characterized this day as "an important day in [his] life and history of the church of JESUS CHRIST of Latter-day Saints."[15] His account describes the Salt Lake Valley as a Mormon garden of Eden, ready to be claimed by Mormon settlers. His account echoes other settler tropes about the American continent as empty, fertile, and in need of civilization. The expansive views of rich tracts of land, set aside by God for Mormon settlers to build Zion, echo and align with other US settler narratives that justify the conquest of land. Mormon settlers, including Woodruff, relied on these settler tropes depicting land as empty, thus justifying their presence and claims to land. Mormon settlers, like other settlers, used their religious beliefs to justify their claims to land. Much like John Gast's 1872 painting *American Progress*, Mormon manifest destiny was also led by Mormon settlers migrating west, bringing Mormon religious enlightenment to the West. However, Mormon settlers wanted to create a Mormon Zion outside the political boundaries of the United States, yet at the same time their movement west advanced US goals of expansion. Wilford Woodruff's account of this moment when Young first sees the valley becomes the origins of a pioneer subject position, an expression of Mormon settler subject position. Woodruff wrote, "When we came out of the canyon in full view of the valley, I turned the side of my carriage around, open to the West, and President Young arose from his bed and took a survey of the country. While gazing on the scene, he was enwrapped in vision for several minutes. When the vision passed he said, 'This is the right place, drive on.'"[16]

Woodruff's account of Young's vision that this was the right place marks land as Mormon and echoes into the modern era. Young later designated what would become Salt Lake City as the center of Mormon empire, and settlers began to plant crops and prepare for the influx of other Mormon settlers. Young's company marked the first wave of Mormon settlers into the region. Mormon settlers migrated west to secure refuge and to create home, a sense of belonging to a specific place. This origin story about Mormon pioneers is part of the settler colonial process to justify Mormon settler presence and the dispossession of Indigenous lands. These types of narratives surrounding Mormon settler migration become part of the hegemonic discourses surrounding Mormon settler presence. Mormon settler industriousness, such as immediately taming the land, planting crops, and building Mormon settler infrastructures, proved that Indigenous peoples had not lived on these lands. Mormon religious ideologies justified Mormon settler migration and signals Mormon settler exceptionalism.

This first migration, a historic and pivotal moment in Mormon history, became the foundation of a pioneer subject position. Woodruff's documentation of the Mormon settler arrival to Shoshone, Paiute, Goshute, and Ute lands reinforces the notion that Mormon settler history is the *only* history of this land. Yet his account "recirculate[s] everyday modes of settlement" even as he and other settlers existed and produced these narratives on Indigenous lands.[17] At the time of this writing, Woodruff's journal was on display in the LDS Church Library in Salt Lake City, Utah, part of the exhibit *Foundations of Faith: Treasures from the Historical Collections of The Church of Jesus Christ of Latter-day Saints*"[18] The location of Woodruff's journal and the manner in which it was displayed legitimizes Young's declaration and claims to land. The journal itself becomes evidence of Mormon settler discovery and conquest of the region. Woodruff's account reifies the presence and legitimacy of Mormon settlers and Pioneer Day and secures their contemporary claims to land. This first migration into the Salt Lake Valley, a historic and pivotal moment in Mormon history, became the foundation to the Mormon settler narrative of discovery in which land was vacant and virile, chosen by God for Mormon settlers to build Zion, thus civilizing the land. This narrative of discovery and civilization becomes vital to the Mormon settler colonial process whereby Mormon settlers' claims to land are legitimized by the production of materials and ritual practices meant to naturalize Mormon settler presence and belonging.

THE MAKING OF A STATE HOLIDAY: PIONEER DAY

The first year after Mormon settlers arrived in the Salt Lake Valley, they began celebrating their successful colonization of the land. The first official Pioneer Day celebration began in Salt Lake City the following year on July 24, 1849. Mormon settlers survived the first year and gave thanks on August 10, 1848, with a harvest feast featuring crops they had raised. Their celebration demonstrates their industriousness in taming land that was terra nullius, although the land in fact had sustained various Indigenous nations prior to Mormon settlers' arrival. These celebrations justify their claims to land, evidence of their exceptionalism and the roots of their pioneer origin story. Pioneer Day would be established as a legal state holiday along with the ratification of the Utah Constitution in 1895.[19]

One of the LDS Church's official publications, *The Improvement Era*, described the events of the first annual Pioneer Day and noted that the day of celebration began with "nine rounds of artillery accompanied by martial music."[20] The parade procession was led by Horace S. Eldridge, marshal on horseback, twelve bishops carrying flags to represent their respective Mormon congregations, and "twenty-four men in white, with white scarfs on their right shoulders and coronets on their heads, each carrying in their right hands the Declaration of Independence of the United States and swords sheathed in their left hands, one of them carrying a beautiful banner with 'The Lion of the Lord.'" Twenty-four women then followed "dressed in white, with white scarfs on their right shoulders and a wreath of white roses on their heads, each carrying the Bible and Book of Mormon and one bearing a very neat banner blazoned with 'Hail to our Chieftain.'" The LDS Church's general authorities, high-ranking religious leaders, followed the men and women dressed in white, and after them were twenty-four men over the age of fifty who had been part of the Nauvoo Legion (a state-authorized militia for the city of Nauvoo, Illinois), each carrying a red painted staff with "a white ribbon fastened at the top, one of them carrying a flag and the inscription, 'Liberty and Truth.'"

Historian Laurel Thatcher Ulrich asserts that "men were defenders of liberty, women custodians of faith. Yet both groups carried banners affirming the union of the secular and religious authority in the person of their prophet."[21] Eventually, President Young was presented with copies of Declaration of Independence and the US Constitution. In his speech, Young acknowledged and venerated the sacrifice made by Mormon pioneers who first entered the valley in 1847. His speech recalled his arrival just two years earlier and Mormon settler labor that created a trail for other Mormon settlers to follow. The speech also highlighted how Mormon settlers used these pioneer experiences to create a Mormon community rooted in this subject position. Interestingly, at the same time, Mormons draw upon US iconography throughout Pioneer Day pageantry to legitimize their place. The pageantry and symbolic use of white represent purity, righteousness, and the divine that secure Mormon pioneer whiteness. The first annual celebration of Pioneer Day became a ritual reenactment in which Mormon settler presence became normalized while Indigenous peoples were removed from the central narrative despite being on Indigenous lands.

The first celebration of Pioneer Day is significant because Mormon settlers used these public celebrations to give meaning to their settler subject position and to secure their move toward innocence. The public commemoration absolves Mormon settler guilt as Mormon settlers assert their right to land, a fulfillment of their religious beliefs. Mormon settlers used Pioneer Day to align with other settlers seeking religious freedom in the United States. Parade participants carried both the Bible and the Book of Mormon. Mormon settlers used the parade to stake a claim to space, both literally and figuratively, in the American West outside of the legal boundaries of the United States, which would eventually extend the American empire. Mormon settlers asserted Mormon settler sovereignty in which Mormon and US settler sovereignties were equal to one another, evident in the religious texts as symbols of settler power. Young's speech recalled how young men "carried the flag of the United States through states of Mexico." The American flag was symbolic of US and Mormon colonialism, a deliberate, ritual act in which these young men used the flag as a way to performatively claim land. The parade and use of the flag highlights how Mormon settlers occupied and existed in the borderlands between two separate sovereigns. On one end, Mormon settlers advanced the US settler colonial project to claim land from coast to coast, yet at the same time their mere presence was a challenge to US and Mexico settler sovereignty.

Mormon settlers' eventually aligned with US settler desires to carve out vast tracts of land for Mormon settlement. Rather than celebrate American independence, Young reminded other Mormon settlers that "we choose this day that we might have a little bread on our tables."[22] Pioneer Day was a celebration and exercise of Mormon sovereignty as Indigenous people's presence secured Mormon settler belonging. For example, while there were "Indians" present at this first celebration, they were merely mentioned as being present at the day's celebration. Little information is given on the number of Indigenous peoples present, representation from Tribal Nations, and where they lived or even acknowledgment that Indigenous peoples had lived in this region before the arrival of Mormon settlers. There were no other identifiers included or recognition of Indigenous land. Pioneer Day secured Mormon settler presence and access to land. The ritualization of Pioneer Day plays a more significant role as Mormon settlers moved toward a more cohesive, shared pioneer subject position. According to geographer D. W. Meinig, these experiences were based on "defeat, displacement, martyrdom, and alienation" as well as "a shared history, a sense of grievance, a people apart, and a determination to transform exile into nationhood" by which "Mormons create[d] a cohesive identity," or subject position.[23] The fear expressed by Mormon settlers became the foundations of their settler anxieties over the land, their fear of being the settler Other. This fear became the catalyst for Mormon settlers to manufacture an origin story to justify their belonging. Pioneer Day served a specific purpose: to ease Mormon settlers' anxiety about potential expulsion. Mormon settlers utilized religious ideologies, especially those pertaining to Lamanites and land, to prevent future expulsion or invasion. Just like the disappearance or dispossession of Indigenous peoples from Pioneer Day reenactments, Mormon settler presence required Indigenous dispossession from their lands. Mormon settler culture is tied to the land, and Pioneer Day reinforces the processes of Mormon settler colonialism in which Indigenous peoples exist only to serve Mormon settler empire. The narratives manufactured by Mormon settlers embed narratives onto the land and into Mormon settler structures, such as Pioneer Day.

Mormons and US pioneer subject positions hide the violence of conquest and settler colonial processes in the migration west because settler narratives focus on the settlement of "uninhabited" lands rather than the conflicts and tensions between Mormon settlers and Indigenous peoples. The perpetuation of a pioneer identity hides Mormon colonization of Indigenous peoples and lands. Young's speech highlights the importance of Mormon pioneers to the creation of a religious empire and the taming of the land. Mormon settler efforts made the land livable and productive, all markers of US and Mormon civilization. Other settlers did the same as they claimed land, an expression of US settler colonialism. As historian W. Paul Reeve has argued, "Mormons were agents of civilization and progress, in other words, the carriers of the agrarian dream into the driest region in the continental United States, and as such deserved respect."[24] The prophet Brigham Young did not see Mormons wholly outside the jurisdiction of the US government; instead, Mormons were "agents of American empire. They served the vital interests of the United States, taming an inhospitable and undesirable desert in the face of hostile Indians. It was difficult frontier service which in the Mormon view should have garnered praise from a thankful nation rather than derision and scorn." Reeve's argument places Mormon settlers on the peripheries of American society, racialized by other white settlers, but the move west and the claiming of land not only marks Mormon settlers as white; they could migrate because of their access to whiteness. Mormon settlers accessed their whiteness to fulfill their settler desires. For example, Mormon settlers could migrate outside the political boundaries of the United States and lay claim to Indigenous land because of their whiteness. The celebration of Pioneer Day was not just about the commemoration of the first Mormon settlers in Salt Lake Valley but was also the celebration of both American and Mormon empire building in the American West.

The first Pioneer Day celebration captured the ongoing process of Mormon settlers becoming pioneers. Mormon settlers occupied a physical and metaphorical space that privileged their religious beliefs. Mormons could not fully escape their status as settlers despite attempts to affirm their religious identity as their primary identity. The utilization of historical memory to reminisce about the Mormon migration west made it possible to create a cohesive religious and historical narrative that perpetuates a narrative of hardship and persecution. Ultimately, nostalgia about Mormons' pioneer past justifies their settler presence. Mormon settlers understood, interpreted, and constructed their settler past, present, and future.

The Mormon settler narrative positioned Indigenous peoples as antagonists to Mormon westward progress and civilization as a means to secure their presence on Indigenous lands. In LDS Church manuals and discourse, references to Indigenous peoples serve the Mormon settler narrative. In the *Essentials in Church History*, a section titled "Dangers on the Way" produced a narrative about Indigenous violence in the Mormon settler move to innocence, or native status to secure rights to land. The emphasis on Indigenous violence serves a purpose, Mormon settlers were "constantly on the alert to protect themselves from attacks by Indians," yet there was no mention of how Mormon settlers migrated into Indigenous territories and claimed land and resources for their own exclusive use.[25] Indigenous peoples were protecting their way of life from increasing settler presence, including that of Mormons.

Narratives produced by the LDS Church also erased Indigenous presence from the land by making claims that "the Indians enjoyed relatively free run of the American Plains. . . . Scouting reports confirmed that they inhabited or hunted areas to the north and south of the Great Salt Lake."[26] This narrative infers that Indigenous people did not live in the Salt Lake Valley region but instead existed north and south of this space reserved solely for Mormon settlers by God. The narrative also implies that Mormon settlement and colonization of the region did not impact Indigenous people. Mormon settlers relied on the narrative of land as terra nullius, meaning they did not impact Indigenous lives or land. Indigenous peoples could continue to live on their traditional lands unaffected and undisturbed by Mormon settlers because they lived just north and south of Mormon settlement, which is simply not true or accurate.

BUILDING MORMON SETTLER INFRASTRUCTURES: THIS IS THE PLACE MONUMENT AND PARK

The processes of Mormon settler colonialism included building infrastructures onto the land to mark and name space as Mormon settler land. This Is the Place Heritage Park, located in Salt Lake City, Utah, demonstrates how Mormon settlers claimed and demarcated land as distinctly Mormon. This Is the Place Heritage Park also illustrates various Mormon settler colonial processes at play, including how Indigenous peoples were written out of the historical narrative of a place and the erection of monuments venerating Mormon settlers. The very presence of This Is the Place Heritage Park reinforces this space as Mormon, as park signage and structures reconstruct the past to naturalize the presence of Mormon settlers while Indigenous peoples and their histories exist on the periphery or in support of Mormon settler claims to land. These Mormon settler structures work in tandem to give meaning to the pioneer subject position by using these experiences to sustain their ties to land. Mormon settler structures commemorated Mormon pioneer colonizing efforts, entrenching Mormon settler colonialism onto the land. The center of Mormon settler colonial power became evident in the built environment in downtown Salt Lake City, the heart of LDS Church headquarters located within Temple Square. The LDS Church owns an area of five square blocks around the Salt Lake City Temple, the spiritual center of the LDS Church. There are many infrastructures, including the Salt Lake City Temple, that are uniquely Mormon.

An important monument was unveiled during Pioneer Day on July 24, 1947, the centennial celebration of the arrival of the first Mormon settlers, to "record the unequaled achievements of these men and women" who made the first trek west.[27] The monument itself was to be located in a park, once part of the Fort Douglas Military Reservation located at the mouth of Emigration Canyon, where Young's pioneer company first entered the valley. The monument was to face "slightly north of west and will look toward Temple Square" four miles in the distance.[28] The site commemorates the place where Brigham Young declared, "This is the Place." The location of the monument offers a panoramic view of the valley where Young and his followers entered the valley. The monument, titled "This Is the right place," has 60-foot-high center pylon atop of which is a 12.25-foot statue of Brigham Young, Wilford Woodruff, and Heber C. Kimball.[29] This monument used the same granite found in Little Cottonwood Canyon that was used to construct the LDS Salt Lake Temple downtown, symbolically linking the spiritual center of the LDS Church to this sacred place. In essence, the use of the same rock to construct these Mormon settler infrastructures links Mormon settlers and narratives to the land. Mormon infrastructures tie them to the land; they are *of* the land, much like Indigenous peoples.

At the top of the monument, Brigham Young is flanked by Wilford Woodruff and Heber C. Kimball as they overlook the valley. The monument physically claims and delineates the vista and land as Mormon settler space; the structure cannot be missed. The statue of Young takes on mythical proportions because the artist who designed it, Mahonri Young, a descendant of Brigham Young, "assured the Committee that while the impression created by the model was not historically accurate (Brigham Young had first looked over Salt Lake Valley from Wilford Woodruff's wagon), it expressed the spirit of the occasion."[30] The monument dominates the entrance to the park and surrounding landscape. As one follows the signs toward This Is the Place Heritage Park from downtown Salt Lake City, the This Is the Place Monument looms in the distance as you drive toward the mouth of the canyon, becoming more visible upon approach.

Historian Cynthia Prescott argues that Mahonri Young's design "represented a return to the statuomania, social Darwinism, and culture of famous white men that had been common in the late nineteenth century."[31] The statue (re)imagines the land using structures and narratives of a mythical settler past, justifying their bid to belong to the land. The monument reflects how Mormon settlers understood and constructed their history using these infrastructures, including signage. The reliefs and plaques located at the base of the monument also retell a story of mythical proportions or "ahistorical fantasies" designed to create Mormon settlers' belonging and justify their presence on Indigenous lands. For example, the monument "epitomizes dramatic chapters in the opening of the western United States and commemorates the arrival of the pioneers in Utah Territory.[32] At the base of this monument, a portion of the plaque reads "'This Is the Place' Monument, dedicated July 24, 1947, commemorates the arrival of the Mormon pioneers into the Valley of the Great Salt Lake one hundred years before, and also the role of others—Spanish Catholic Fathers, Trappers and Fur Traders, official government explorers and California immigrants, who contributed of the successful founding of an empire in 'the mountains.' Driven from their homes in Missouri and Illinois because of political and religious prejudice, the Mormons began their historic fifteen hundred mile trek from Nauvoo to the Rocky Mountains."

This plaque focuses on the presence of Mormon settlers and produced a narrative centered around the settler experience. The structure and narrative pay homage to other settlers and Mormon empire yet make no mention of Indigenous peoples.

Several key figures and groups "are exemplified by the various bronze group statues which are a part of the monument structure. These include Father Escalante and Dominiquez, Trappers and Fur Traders William H. Ashley, Jim Bridger, Jedediah S. Smith, Peter Skene Ogden, Capt. Bonneville, John C. Fremont, Chief Washakie, Etienne Provost and dozens of others."[33] Mormon structures and narratives work in tandem to (re)imagine the land as settler land. Other settlers paved the way for Mormon empire as early as 1813 and also serve the Mormon settler colonial project. These Mormon settler structures and narratives serve a purpose: to construct, define, and sustain the Mormon settler subject into the present. Mormon settler origins in the Salt Lake Valley become naturalized through the narration throughout the park's infrastructures, including signage. The monument, including the base, reinforces Mormon settler presence while naturalizing settler narratives of the land. The granite base of the monument "convey[s] a more extensive history of Utah exploration and settlement, laying a sound foundation for the central pillar's genealogy of Mormonism[,] . . . [and] depicts an orderly progression within the Great Basin from American Indians to Spanish padres, mountain men to white settlers, and finally Mormon leaders."[34] Prescott argues that this historical interpretation "traces an evolution from Indian savagery to Christian faith, and from untamed mountain men and doomed Anglo migrants to devoted Mormon leaders. . . . *This is the Place* emphasizes famous individuals rather than a generic class of pioneers."[35] While the park is celebratory of individual settlers, these individuals represent the settler experience in the American West, especially as they led other Mormon settlers to civilize and tame the land. However, this progression of civilization centers the Mormon settler experience as Indigenous peoples were pushed from the land to make way for Mormon settlers. The processes of making Mormon place and belonging uses structures and narratives to justify Mormon settler claims to land.

Mormon settler colonialism required the dispossession and erasure of Indigenous peoples, yet Indigenous peoples must also give legitimacy to Mormon settlers. Indigenous peoples get to be included in Mormon structures only when they serve the Mormon settler subject position. Thus, Indigenous peoples sanction Mormon settlers, especially their claims to land. The only "famous" American Indian man to be included at the base of the This Is the Place Monument is a statue of Chief Washakie, Shoshone leader and Mormon convert, holding a peace pipe. The use of Chief Washakie was purposeful. He was a "good" Indian and supported Brigham Young and Mormon settlers. Mormon settlers considered Chief Washakie to be a "great Warrior, wise leader of this people, known all over western country as one of the most intelligent and able Indian chiefs"; he was a "close friend of Brigham Young and the Mormon people."[36] Yet, Washakie's people, the Shoshones, would fight to preserve their way of life and claims to land. Mormon settler society required land and built Mormon structures onto Indigenous lands. The primary reason why Chief Washakie was included is that he was a "friendly" Indian and therefore a safe Indian, worthy of inclusion. The image of Chief Washakie becomes part of the Mormon settler narrative because he was "friendly" to Mormon settlers, meaning he welcomed them. Chief Washakie holding a peace pipe is meant to reaffirm his friendliness to Mormon settlers and implies that he and his people accepted and sanctioned Mormon settler presence and settlement of the region. Chief Washakie's religious conversion to the Mormon faith is also another important feature of Mormon settler colonialism.[37] Mormon settlers used Chief Washakie to legitimize and support their claims to land, his baptism a literal fulfillment of Mormon religious doctrine about Lamanites. Chief Washakie exists in the Mormon settler narrative and monument because he welcomed Mormon settlers, ultimately justifying their existence.

In addition to the main plaque, other settlers were honored as part of a larger settler narrative of the region that had paved the way for Mormon settlers. On the small north pylon, early trappers from 1825–1845 were also included. "The beaver hat rage created a tremendous market for fur, causing the west to abound in trappers and mountain men, who were the real pathfinders of the American West."[38] The Donner-Reed party, perhaps the most infamous group of settlers who had passed through Utah one year before Mormon settlers, traveled a "mile-a-day . . . through these mountains [and] saved the Mormon pioneers several days of hard work a year later." But the journey proved to be fatal to the Donner-Reed party. Only fifty-one of eighty-seven party members survived the early October snow in the Sierra Nevada mountains in California. The Donner-Reed party is notable because it relates to Mormon settlers and the Mormon settler narrative and served to make Mormon settlers a home, in doing so destroying and "disappear[ing] the Indigenous peoples that live[d] there."[39]

The disappearance of Indigenous peoples continues in the narrative found on the park's website, which notes that "with several notable exceptions, relations between the Native Americans and the settlers were relatively cordial during the settlement era."[40] These "notable exceptions" range from the Bear River Massacre to Black Hawk's War.[41] The park makes no mention of these "notable exceptions," including the Bear River Massacre, which occurred about 114 miles from This Is the Place Heritage Park. Darren Perry, a descendant of survivors, a citizen of the Northwestern Band of the Shoshone Nation, and a Mormon member, has written extensively about the Bear River Massacre. The contrast between how Mormon settlers treat the memory of Chief Washakie and the Bear River Massacre reflects the insidious nature of Mormon settler colonialism. Indigenous peoples exist only in service to Mormon settlers, especially as Mormon settlers created a narrative of belonging to land that necessitated Indigenous complicity. Chief Washakie is considered to be a willing participant of Mormon settler colonial desires, while the Bear River Massacre challenges claims made by Mormon settlers about land. Shoshone peoples pushed back against Mormons' settlement and the claiming of Indigenous lands and resources. Mormon settlers literally disappeared Shoshone peoples, including the most vulnerable, to assert their righteous claims to land. In doing so, Mormon settlers' narrative of hardship legitimizes their claims to land as Indigenous peoples were dispossessed of their land.

(RE)MAKING MORMON PIONEER SPACE AND NARRATIVE AT THIS IS THE PLACE HERITAGE PARK

The Mormon subject position relied on the (re)production of a Mormon settler narrative that cemented Mormons' belonging to the land, or the Salt Lake Valley. Mormon settlers celebrated their civilizing and taming of land set aside by God for their explicit use by building Mormon infrastructures and narratives onto the land. Every year, Mormon settlers and the State of Utah celebrate this imposed, shared past on Pioneer Day. Yet Mormon settler structures, such as This Is the Place Heritage Park, reinforce Mormon settler narratives of the land permanently.

The one hundred–year anniversary of President Brigham Young and the first Mormon settlers who entered Emigration Canyon and colonized the Salt Lake Valley became an opportunity to commemorate and reinforce Mormon settler colonial structures and settler subject position tied to the land. This celebration would contribute to the making of Mormon space and the institutionalization of a pioneer subject position in public and private spaces in Utah. The LDS Church and the State of Utah worked together to purchase land necessary to build Mormon settler structures that would reinforce Mormon settler belonging to land. The This Is the Place Monument and Heritage Village overlook the Salt Lake Valley at the mouth of Emigration Canyon on 283.16 acres of land.[42] The State of Utah contributed $145,100, the public donated $251,240.20, and the LDS Church contributed "the balance of the funds necessary to complete the Monument and its surroundings, the exact amount at this date not having been determined," which was about $50,000.[43] The LDS Church was the driving force behind the monument and the park. LDS Church president George Albert Smith stated during its dedication that it was " the realization of a personal dream of many years standing."[44] Smith recalls,

> This monument is the culmination of a dream of many years on the part of a large group of people of all denominations throughout Utah and the West. Its completion marks a fitting climax to 100 years of western history. While the Mormon Pioneers are particularly honored on this, the occasion of the Centennial of their arrival into the Salt Lake Valley. The "This is the Place" Monument, from the very first of its preparation, has been designed to be a highlight history in granite and bronze of the exploration and development of Utah from the time of the coming of the first white man into the Great Basin.[45]

Smith's dedication highlights the importance of ancestry and history in the LDS Church. His grandfather by the same name had been a leader in the LDS Church and an early settler of the region. His family's history is representative of many other Mormon settlers who migrated west. The monument was a celebration of Mormon settlers taming the land and harnessing the region's natural resources. For example, Smith's dedication focused on the arrival of Mormon settlers to the region but also that that moment should be celebrated using "granite and bronze," symbolic of enduring Mormon settler presence. Smith also connects Mormon colonization to the larger history of the American West that began with the "coming of the first white man into the Great Basin." Even at this celebratory moment, American and Mormon colonization of the American West became markers of civilization, legitimizing settlers' land claims and exploitation of resources.

During his dedication, Smith effectively erased Indigenous peoples and histories from the historical narrative. Chief Washakie's son, Charles Washakie, and his wife, Ellen, and granddaughter were all present at the unveiling of his father's statue.[46] Yet Charles Washakie was not an integral part of the celebration despite Mormon settlers praising his father's support of Mormon settlement. Paradoxically, Jubilee Celebration organizers reached out to "Don Napier, husky Cherokee now residing in North Hollywood, [who] will arrive with his war bonnet and other regalia to present his 'medicine show' and supervise Salt Lake's Indian Village, in operation for the Celebration."[47] Napier's presence was acceptable because he performs indigeneity for non-Indigenous peoples that fits into their settler colonial imaginary of Indigenous peoples. His presence and, by extension, that of Indigenous peoples only supports and justifies Mormon settler presence. For example, other Mormon settler communities throughout Utah were interested in having American Indians participate and invited them to feasts or to "march in the parade in 'Indian regalia,'

and participate in historical recreations."[48] Interestingly enough, several communities even had non-Indian members who would dress up as Indians and abduct
parade watchers, or real Indigenous peoples would play along and abduct parade
participants. Again, this type of (re)enactment serves Mormon settler presence
and moves Indigenous peoples to the margins. Indigenous peoples are depicted as
violent, attacking Mormon settlers. In these scenarios, Indigenous peoples do not
belong; they are the Others on their homelands.

Much like the first Pioneer Day celebration, during the 1947 Pioneer Day the
LDS Church and US interests intersected once more as Mormon members sought
to preserve the moment in a time capsule. Some of the items placed in the time
capsule were the entire edition of the June 6, 1947, *Salt Lake Tribune* newspaper
(the day when the time capsule items were gathered); *The Improvement Era Semi-
Centennial Year Book* for 1846–1847 campaign; brochures for the This Is the Place
Monument; the Utah Centennial booklet; a list of contributors; an American Pioneer
Trails Association membership card; coins; and various poems. The Daughters of
Utah Pioneers even donated a Utah state flag, an American Flag, a Bible, the Book
of Mormon, and Pearl of Great Price, another Mormon religious text. The time
capsule included an interesting mix of both religious and secular items that were
identifiably Mormon and American. Despite Pioneer Day and Mormon settler
structures centering the Mormon settler, Mormon settler members want to place
Mormon history within the larger " state, regional, or national historical story."[49]
At these moments, Mormon and US settlers' colonial projects and interests intersect, and in the time capsule these symbols of settler power get preserved, further
legitimizing their presence and claims to land. During the weeklong celebration of
Mormon settlers entering the Salt Lake Valley, the performance and pageantry of
their belonging was vital to their colonial processes to mark land as Mormon. The
Sons of Utah Pioneers (re)enacted the infamous trek from Nauvoo, Illinois, into
downtown Salt Lake City and would be part of a parade led by various state and
LDS Church leaders. The first car carried the parade's marshal, J. Wallace West.
The second car carried the governor of Utah, Herbert B. Maw. and the president of
the LDS Church, George Albert Smith. Spencer W. Kimball, apostle and advocate
of Lamanite members, accompanied the "trekkers" and believed that this reenactment would foster a "higher regard for Utah and her people as a result of this trip."
Speaking next to the This Is the Place Monument, featuring Young, Kimball, and
Woodruff, the mayor of Salt Lake City, Earl J. Glade, believed the trekkers' reenactment of Mormon settlers to be the largest that has ever occurred. "You sought to
exemplify the heroism of the pioneers, who were living symbols of looking to the

future." During the centennial celebration in Sugarhouse, a neighborhood in Salt Lake City, "the Sugarhouse American Legion drum and bugle corps[,] garbed as Indians, reenacted an Indian war dance and other features both on Main St. and in Sugarhouse." The "Indians" were also played by over 250 Aaronic priesthood members of the Granite LDS Stake, also located in Sugarhouse, and were "prepared to 'ambush' the trekkers" as they passed through the parade route. Much like the first Pioneer Day celebration and other Pioneer Day celebrations, Indians had been included when their presence supported Mormon settler narratives. Mormon settlers "played Indian" because Indian violence gave meaning to their subject position as settlers and secured their right to land. As Dakota descendant and historian Philip Deloria articulated in his groundbreaking work *Playing Indian*, settlers performing as Indian give meaning to an authentic American identity. In the Mormon context, Mormon settlers participated in a very American tradition, "playing Indian," as they moved toward solidifying their subject position as white settlers, as Indigenous peoples remained uncivilized, violent, and obstacles to the Mormon settler project of empire.

In addition to the unveiling of the This Is the Place Monument at the mouth of Emigration Canyon and plans to celebrate the centennial arrival of Mormon settlers in the Salt Lake Valley, the State of Utah, along with the LDS Church, began to collaborate to shape Mormon settler narratives and infrastructures onto the land. The Division of Parks and Recreation, in consultation with the Division of State History, wrote a preliminary master development plan in February 1971 to commemorate the arrival of prophet Brigham Young, the first company of Mormon settlers, and other settlers to the Salt Lake Valley. These local efforts to preserve aspects of the Mormon Trail echoed and supported the National Park Service's larger preservation goals to protect sites that played a pivotal role in the development of the American West.[50] An amendment to the National Trails Systems Act was passed on November 10, 1978, to "include a category of national historic trails," which would include the Mormon Trail, now known as the Mormon Pioneer National Historic Trail.[51] As part of this amendment, a comprehensive study and an environmental assessment draft were prepared by the Heritage Conservation and Recreation Service with the assistance of the LDS Church, the Mormon Pioneer Trail Foundation, various historical societies, and individuals. These groups believed that the Mormon migration was significant and "unique by contrast to other migrations because [of] its purpose, organization and cultural impact."[52] Mormon settler claims to exceptionalism become evident in their efforts to memorialize and shape the narrative about Mormon settlers. The Mormon settler narrative pushes a story of industrious people paving the way for other settlers, including other Mormon settlers, by improving the trail; they "measur[ed] distances and set up mileposts; noted good locations for camping, wood, water and forage; and generally became the guide for the thousands of emigrants who later followed this trail."

However, it must be noted that Mormon settlers had not cut this trail entirely on their own; they relied on other settlers' efforts that made the trek west and through this region successful. While Mormon settlers had been organized in their migration west, the display of Mormon exceptionalism becomes evident in their claims of importance, particularly in regard to their "purpose, organization and cultural impact" on the making of the American West. Mormon settlers were unique because they framed their migration west within a specific religious ideological framework, but their claims to land were no different than those of other settlers. In the preliminary master development plan, "This is the Place Monument and Village" were to "remain the dominant feature at this site, and the great pioneer-frontier heritage is to be depicted by the recreation of a pioneer village."[53] This village was to replicate other Utah settlements from the period 1847–1869 portraying the real "pioneer way of life[,] . . . reflecting all types of early Utah art, crafts and culture." The master development plan, like the LDS Church's centennial celebration, emphasized 1847 as the beginning of not just a "pioneer way of life" but also the region's history that had to be preserved and commemorated. The history of this region began in 1847 with the arrival of Mormon settlers, and plans around the park focused on them.

As construction on the park began, the project faced challenges to ensure that the park represented both non-Mormon and Mormon settlers. In a March 21, 1975, a memorandum by Vincent P. Foley, superintendent of the Pioneer Trail Development Project, to the Pioneer Trail Advisory Council updated the advisory board on the first six months of the project. One important detail that the these organizations tackled was finding a suitable name for the village so it would not be perceived as a "Church project," that "[the] proper choice of name, we believe, could preserve the identification of the uniqueness of the Utah Experience without adding fuel to the feelings of some possibly hyper-sensitive Gentiles [non-Mormons]."[54] The planning around the village recognized that "the park [had to] represent a broad cross section of Utah pioneer life; care [had to] be taken not to build a miniature Salt Lake" and to mimic as close as possible the development of a real settlement, with "essential structures" built first.[55] The village would be able to support three hundred to five hundred settlers. This is interesting because the park itself is an intersection of State of Utah and LDS Church interests. The criticisms by non-Mormons highlight how lines blur between state and church. Many Mormon members worked in the LDS Church and for the state and were part of the advisory group, which is why there were efforts to present a generic settler experience, one that would be unifying to park visitors. There was no mention of Indigenous peoples as central to the park experience. Once "essential structures" were built, additional structures would be built to create a pioneer village replica to provide park visitors with the "most unique recreational and educational experience."[56] The Division of Parks and Recreation wanted to create an experience in which tourists could consume the "pioneer life" because it was part of the "living historical museum."[57] The living historical museum also enforced necessary processes to maintain the historical memory of place because the individual is able to participate in a (re)enactment of pioneer life, which reinforce a particular narrative about Mormon pioneers and frontier experiences. The park was designed to be an educational experience where visitors can "step back in time" to a historic settler village filled with actors who provide an "authentic" experience of Mormon settler life on the frontier. There are over fifty buildings in the park, complete with livestock, a blacksmith, a tinsmith, a craftsman, and a saddle maker who use their skills to act out "how the West was built." These original buildings were relocated to the park so that visitors could not only reimagine the past but also play Mormon pioneer. These claims of authenticity further legitimize white settler claims to Indigenous lands.

In the midst of building the pioneer village, the committee also worked to build an Indian encampment. In an interim report, Vincent P. Foley discussed the complicated nature around potentially competing goals of the Indian encampment. The report referenced tensions between the committee and the five Tribes in Utah. The Division of Parks and Recreation had been concerned that the construction of an Indian encampment would be construed as cession of land to the five Utah Tribes because they would be erecting a "formal encampment on 'indian land' where they could 'do their thing.'"[58] The Tribes saw this Indian encampment as a way to reclaim land and space on their homelands as they presented their history on their terms. Foley understood these potential conflicts but assured the Pioneer Trail Advisory Council that he had made clear to the Tribes that the cession of any land on Mormon Flat lands would not be possible. Mormon settlers and, by extension, the state, controlled access to land, including building the Indian encampment.

As discussions continued regarding the construction of an Indian encampment. the Pioneer Trail Advisory Council wanted structures to be authentic. Unlike the pioneer village that had a specific date or starting point in 1847, the Indian encampment had to work with all Tribes in region to determine the "beginning" of tribal history. Tribes had chosen the year 1776, presumably to align with the founding of the United States. The committee believed that Indigenous peoples were not familiar with their traditions. "[They] are dim as to how their forefathers lived at that time, much less as to the kind of structures in which they dwelt."[59] There was no evidence to support Foley's claim. Instead, Foley and the committee perpetuate the notion that Indigenous peoples do not know or have not documented their history, including knowledge about traditional lodgings, simply because they were not documented in written western sources. However, many Indigenous peoples still used traditional structures. Foley began collecting "pictorial documents" from his colleagues at "various institutions and the Smithsonian Institute" to ensure authenticity.[60] Foley begun "accumula[ting] drawings and photographs of early travelers through the native areas of each of the tribes." The second issue regarding the Indian encampment was due to the "lack of valid tradition[;] some method would have to be framed that would allow us to guide them towards authenticity without opening ourselves to any critisism [sic] of constructing a white man's impression of indian history."[61] Settler colonialism, including Mormon settler colonialism, necessitates the possession of Indigenous peoples, yet Indigenous peoples must also sustain Mormon settler presence. Despite Foley's efforts to prevent a "white man's impression of indian history," the Indian encampment became a production of "indian history" by this council. The issue was not just about finding the most "accurate" structure but also how these settler institutions control Indigenous peoples in the production of the past.[62] The Division of Parks and Recreation would have "ultimate authority in the encampment village," with the possibility of having "an advisory committee to act as liaison between the Division and the tribes." Initially, Indigenous peoples would not have complete control over how the council would construct the Indian encampment based on a historical narrative they created.

Foley was clear that the park was meant to provide "an authentic, functioning indian encampment, displaying proper aboriginal dwellings, customs, crafts, clothing and economic base of each tribe involved."[63] The Five Tribes in Utah expressed similar wants: "a) A place to meet where indians can be 'indian.' b) A place to market crafts. c) A Place and monument to indian history and their contribution to the country and world. d) If not *owned* by indians, the place should be under indian control."[64] Foley understood the tensions between Tribal Nations and the state and contestations over representation and land. These Tribal Nations exercised tribal sovereignty by wanting access to the park for their purposes, which was not just about performing "Indian" for non-Indian park visitors. There was a desire for programming to be authentic that "would encourage Indian use of the amphitheatre" and that "any Indian craftsmen be assured of a 'fair shake' as to any sales of their products in the park."[65] Foley also acknowledged that the Pioneer Trail Advisory Council would operate in the best interest of the park and did not intend to be experts on American Indian peoples or their culture. As such, the council created a subcommittee that had representation from all five Utah Tribes: Ute, Navajo, Paiute, Goshute, and Shoshone. The Pioneer Trail Advisory Council was working on creating an amphitheater where "dances and ceremonies, including the commemoration of the role of the Indian in Utah history," can take place along with the "additional developments and structures in the amphitheater vicinity to intensify the visitor's opportunity to learn more of the history and culture of Utah's Indian Groups."[66] The state committed to the construction of an amphitheater that would allow for shows and dancing, a restaurant, and a museum for "exclusive" use by Indian peoples and communities.[67] Utah's Tribal Nations wanted to control how they were being represented to the general public and park visitors so they could understand that Indigenous people belonged to the region.

On July 29, 1976, James Moyle of the Utah State Bicentennial Commission facilitated the dedication of the new Indian amphitheater at the Pioneer Trail State Park. Both "state and Indian dignitaries . . . gathered in a grassy, tree-studded bowl for the dedication of the Bicentennial Amphitheater for Indian Activities."[68] The amphitheater was designed to hold over "5,000 spectators and will feature a dressing room" and "an Indian Village depicting hogans, tepees and other items of the 1880s." The five Tribes in Utah had been part of the amphitheater project. Dorothea Livingston, Indian representative on the Utah State Bicentennial Commission, believed "[the] new amphitheater [would] be the perfect place for Indian pow-wows and represents a long Indian dream that is going to come true."

From the beginning of the park, Indigenous presence would be included as long as it did not contradict the main purpose of the park: an opportunity to experience pioneer life. Indigenous peoples have been relegated to the "Native American village nestled against the mountains." The Native American Village is located within the 450-acre park, along the eastern bench of the Wasatch Mountains. As visitors wander the park, they can visit the Native American Village, located far away from the center of the settler village, literally on the periphery. The Native American Village describes Indigenous peoples and lands as a "world long since gone."[69] This narrative reinforces the notion that Indigenous peoples are a people of the past despite still existing as a people and sovereign nations today. The physical placement of the village is also important. Indigenous peoples were not included in any meaningful way in the "Heritage Village," with the Native American Village having been pushed to the edge of the park. The relegation to the past and the literal periphery of the park is an expression of Mormon settler power. The narrative and structures around pioneers, especially Mormon settlers, reinforce their claims to land, especially because their structures have been preserved and used throughout the park. The physical placement of the Native American Village on the periphery also serves to strengthen the narrative that Indigenous peoples did not exist on the land prior to Mormon settlement. Indigenous peoples did not interfere with Mormon settlement; the park includes the Native American Village but excludes the rich histories of these five Indigenous nations—Shoshone, Paiute, Ute, Goshute, and Navajo—from the historical narrative and the park.

The current Native American Village focuses on two Tribal Nations: Shoshone and Navajo. The two primary dwellings—the Shoshone tipi and the Navajo hogan— were included as permanent structures within the park. The park used authentic materials in the construction of the tipi and included both female and male Navajo hogans. The park selected Indigenous dwellings that were recognizably Indigenous, including the tipi. These dwellings further romanticize Indigenous peoples as a nomadic people of the past. Park visitors consume Indigenous culture without having to confront the Mormon settler colonial past or how the park exists on Indigenous lands. These traditional dwellings have been constructed in a way that positions Indigenous peoples as extinct, a people of the past. Park visitors can enter into the dwellings, grind corn, and make arrowhead necklaces and sand drawings. Visitors get to "play Indian" and consume Indianness without any meaningful educational engagement about the genocide and dispossession of Indigenous peoples of their lands and resources. Today, the park has a permanent tipi structure, "the largest in America," that can hold just over one hundred people and is constructed of man-made materials.[70] The Native American Village and the Heritage Village can be contrasted with one another to show how the later became the marker of civilization. The park (re)imagines a past, a fantasy about Mormon presence at the expense of Indigenous peoples who disappeared from Mormon settler narratives about place.

CONCLUSION

The LDS Church used the establishment of Pioneer Day, a state holiday, as well as the centennial celebration of Pioneer Day and This Is the Place Heritage Park to give meaning to the pioneer subject position and used infrastructures to mark land as Mormon. Alongside these infrastructures, Mormon settlers also utilized narratives to tie themselves to the land, to move from settler status to the status of belonging to the land. The history of the Salt Lake Valley begins with Mormon settler arrival in 1847. Mormon settlers reoriented history to legitimize their belonging to the land by excluding Indigenous history that predated their arrival. Indigenous peoples are of the land, and their stories reaffirm their connection since time immemorial. Yet the infrastructures and built environment of the Salt Lake Valley dominate and shape the land. Temple Square, the center of Salt Lake City, carves out a secular space reflecting Mormon settler ideologies and structures, such as the Salt Lake City Temple and various settler structures and monuments. At the intersection of Main Street and North Temple Street, on the north side of the sidewalk on property owned by the LDS Church, is another Brigham Young Monument that commemorates his colonizing efforts and the first Mormon settlers in the region. At the base, a statue of an Indigenous man bears no name. Yet this Indigenous man sits at the base of the monument, a nod to Indigenous peoples as he symbolically supports Mormon colonizing and settler presence. This Young monument on LDS Church property downtown is one more structure that upholds Mormon settler colonial power as it possesses and marks Indigenous lands.

Mormon settlers escaped Nauvoo, Illinois, and arrived in the Salt Lake Valley as sovereign settlers. As Mormon settlers migrated west, they did so with intentions to create a Mormon empire and used the built environment and infrastructures to mark the land as Mormon. Mormon settlers accessed their whiteness to lay claim to Indigenous land. When Mormon settlers moved west, Brigham Young proclaimed "This is the right place!," naturalizing their presence and claiming title to the land, a fulfillment of Mormon manifest destiny that this land was explicitly for Mormon settlers. This pivotal moment in Mormon history laid the foundation for the creation of a pioneer subject identity in their move to becoming white, a manifestation of Mormon settler colonialism. The Mormon pioneer, or settler, subject position could only exist when Indigenous peoples disappeared from their lands and the historical narrative so that Mormon settlers could assert their belonging and right to Indigenous space. Their subjugation of Indigenous peoples and lands further demonstrated Mormon settlers' willingness to become American by taking on mainstream values and replicating a racialized hierarchy in the American West.

Indigenous peoples resisted Mormon settler colonialism, especially in resisting Mormon settler desires to claim land and assimilate Indigenous peoples into Mormon settler society. The American Indian Movement (AIM) resisted and pushed back on Mormon settler colonial efforts by also using Mormon spaces to reclaim indigeneity and assert Indigenous sovereignty. AIM leadership from Utah and the national organization gathered at Pioneer Trail State Park in Salt Lake

City on April 11, 1974, and used the media to draw attention to their criticisms of the LDS Church and its treatment of Indigenous peoples. AIM leaders David Hill (Utah State Director), George Redstone (Utah Assistant State Director), John Trudell (National Chairman), and Vernon Bellecourt (National Field Director) gathered at this site and made demands to the LDS Church. In the "Declaration to the Mormon Church," they wrote that they

> met in prayer and ceremony and have come to mind. The Great Spirit has spoken to our hearts and minds. Because of your insensitivity to our religion and traditions in keeping the remains of our forefathers on display, and from the mother earth. Because of your racist attitudes regarding our skin color. Because of your divisive practices of pitting Indian against Indian. Because of your attempts at cultural and religious genocide. Because Native Americans have approached you . . . to resolve these matters and you have turned them away. You are hereby ordered to recall all your missionaries from the reservations and the areas where Native Americans frequent. You are hereby ordered to return all traditional Indian land and property to Indian people, which the Church has in possession of and forfeit all improvements of said lands.[71]

AIM and other Indigenous peoples attempted to (re)appropriate Indigenous land and confront Mormon settler infrastructures to assert Indigenous presence and claims to land. AIM's statement is significant in its demands and recognition of how the LDS Church has sought to assimilate Indigenous peoples. AIM connected the LDS Church to the larger US settler colonial project in which Indigenous peoples have been dispossessed from their land, spiritual practices, and culture. AIM uses important Mormon symbols and monuments to confront the LDS Church and Mormon settler colonial structures in which Indigenous peoples became the racialized and religious Other, with their skin marking their otherness. AIM also commanded the LDS Church to stop all "pageants. . . . If any attempts are made in the future, depicting Indians, in the Book of Mormon by the white race of the Mormon Church; ther [sic] will be direct confrontations upon your people by the Landlords of this Continent."[72] AIM utilized language by the LDS Church to confront the invisibility of Mormon settler colonialism, especially in the Mormons' use of Indigenous imaginary in texts and pageants to legitimize Mormon settler presence and belonging as they racialized Indigenous peoples.

The construction of an ethnic and religious pioneer subject position lends itself to the interrogation of race in the American West. To be a Mormon pioneer meant being a white settler, exercising the right to claim land, and dispossessing Indigenous peoples. Mormon manifest destiny is coconstituted with US manifest destiny in that all settlers believed they had a right to land, yet Mormon settlers differed in their exceptionalism in that their status superseded other white settlers because somehow their religious persecution marked them as special when in fact they were no different than other settlers. In fact, Mormon pioneers have largely been excluded from critique because the use and connotation of pioneer status is benign rather than recognizing how Mormon settlers and settler colonial processes have actively shaped what is now the American West. The processes of Mormon settler colonialism remain invisible, and in this chapter I highlight how Pioneer Day, various (re)enactments, annual celebrations, and This Is the Place Heritage Park all serve the Mormon settler colonial center.

The Mormon settler and Lamanite subject positions exist in contrast to one another. Lamanites give meaning to Mormon settler status and serve to justify Mormon settler colonial ideologies that mark them as the religious and racialized Other. Both subject positions—pioneer and Lamanite—simultaneously exist alongside one another; pioneers cannot exist without Indigenous peoples. This pioneer subject position as well as monuments and This Is the Place Heritage Park were all necessary for the claiming and (re)making of Indigenous space and place as distinctly Mormon settler space. Mormon settler colonial infrastructures marked Indigenous peoples as inferior; thus, religious and educational assimilation was necessary to hopes of saving Indigenous peoples.

In chapter 4, I use the Indian Student Placement Program as a settler colonial infrastructure to possess Indigenous children as they were (re)made into Lamanites. The program was a fulfillment of Mormon religious identities designed to redeem Indigenous children. The Mormon settler colonial project shifted in the late nineteenth and early twentieth centuries from Mormon settler ideologies and infrastructures tied to the land, to the LDS Church relying on missionary impetus to redeem Lamanites by using educational infrastructures meant to assimilate Indigenous peoples into the LDS Church. Mormon settler colonial ideologies and discourse about Lamanites converged in the production of the Indian Student Placement Program, Lamanite missions, civilization, and Mormon settler belonging that could be realized if Indigenous peoples (re)claimed their Lamanite identity.

4 "THE LAMANITES SHALL BLOSSOM AS A ROSE"

THE INDIAN STUDENT PLACEMENT PROGRAM AND REDEMPTION OF LAMANITE CHILDREN

Go my son, go and climb the ladder
Go my son, go and earn your feather
Go my son, make your people proud of you
Work, my son, get an education
Work, my son, learn a good vocation.
Climb my son, go and take a lofty view
From on the ladder of an education you can see
to help your Indian nation
then reach, my son, and lift your people up with you.

"GO MY SON," CARNES BURSON AND
ARLENE NOFCHISSEY WILLIAMS

Mormon and US settler colonial goals of empire shifted from possessing Indigenous people's land and civilizing a people using religion. Mormon settler colonialism in the twentieth century coincided with efforts made by the US government to civilize and assimilate Indigenous peoples. Like the US government, the Church of Jesus Christ of Latter-day Saints (LDS Church) shifted Mormon settler and Lamanite ideologies to claim stewardship over Indigenous peoples and targeted their children for assimilation using religious programs and ideologies. Mormon settlers continued to develop nuanced forms and expressions of Mormon settler colonialism by creating formal educational and religious programs centered around the assimilation of Indigenous children. These programs ultimately removed aspects of indigeneity by removing Indigenous children, or Lamanite children, and placed them into Mormon foster homes. The racialized ideologies of Indigenous peoples as Lamanites became the necessary justification for this educational program. Only through their baptism, or conversion to the LDS Church, could Indigenous children and, by extension,

Indigenous peoples discard this racialized cursed past and subject position as they regained their status as a promised people. Mormon-Indian policies, like federal Indian policies, attempted to address the "Indian problem" through a civilizing project achieved by Indian child removal policies, Mormonization/Christianization, and Western education. In the LDS Church context, it would be the creation of the Indian Student Placement Program (ISPP), which utilized a more intimate form of settler colonialism: the homes of Mormon settler foster families to serve as a civilizing tool of Indigenous children. The LDS Church's goal of religious and secular assimilation echoed federal Indian policies in the mid-twentieth century.

This chapter is not meant to be a comprehensive history of the ISPP; rather, it is meant to make visible Mormon settler colonialism and how Mormon settler desires to assimilate Indigenous children and peoples are not unlike US settler colonial desires. I use the ISPP as a means to illustrate how LDS Church leaders and members implemented Lamanite policies, embedding the Mormon settler colonial project within the infrastructure of the church. Indigenous peoples as Lamanites would always exist as a subject position within the LDS Church, evident in the framing of the ISPP as an expression of Mormon settler colonialism. Indigenous peoples became and remained Lamanites in the ISPP and as members of the LDS Church. This chapter situates the ISPP within the larger context of US settler colonialism to make visible the ways in which Indigenous children became Lamanites through the Mormon civilizing mission of educational, spiritual, and cultural assimilation.[1] Mormon settler colonialism is not exceptional and in fact relies on and uses ideologies around US exceptionalism. The difference was that Mormons' settler colonialism couches their brand of exceptionalism using specific religious rhetoric. The narrative of religious persecution and violence perpetuated by other settlers surrounding the Mormon settler experience has rendered Mormon settler colonialism invisible, because the LDS Church has largely escaped critique as an institution that actively participated in the assimilation and removal of Indigenous children in the twentieth century due to the church's historical narrative of religious persecution. The intersection of Mormon and Indigenous history highlights the absence of the LDS Church in the literature regarding Indigenous child removal policies such as foster care and education. The ISPP replicated and relied on US-Indian policies around boarding schools and child removal as a means to possess, define, and give meaning to Indigenous peoples.[2] Mormon settler colonialism provides a framework to understand how the LDS Church and its settler members engaged in the construction and understanding of indigeneity in the twentieth century.

I briefly begin this chapter with a history of the ISPP and the connection between the program, US settler boarding schools, and child removal policies. The purpose of these infrastructures was to assimilate Indigenous children using education and settler colonial infrastructures. Mormon settlers' assimilationist desires were driven by their religious beliefs about the salvation and racial uplift of Lamanites. The ISPP as a structure served the same purpose as American Indian boarding schools in the United States, yet the program has been overlooked in the literature about boarding schools because assimilation happened within individual Mormon settler foster homes and, unlike boarding schools, makes the Mormon settler colonial project less visible. This chapter connects the ISPP to US Indigenous child removal policies driven by settler colonial ideologies of racial uplift to remove and remake indigeneity in the twentieth century. Indigenous children were sent to Mormon settler foster families to become "white and delightsome," a realization of the Mormon settler colonial project.[3] The LDS Church wanted Indigenous peoples to become Lamanites, which meant embracing Mormonism, or simply put, Indigenous peoples would become settlers, or Mormons. Mormon settler foster homes, like Indian boarding schools, became physical sites of American and Mormon colonization designed to remove all markers of Indigenous identity. Indigenous children were removed from their homes on the reservation and placed into individual Mormon foster homes to make them not just religiously Mormon but also culturally white. The ISPP was also similar in purpose and process to US boarding schools, foster care, and adoption in the twentieth century. The program would be a secular solution to a religious mandate that required Mormons to save the Lamanites. The ISPP also had an impact on the social and religious construction of a Lamanite subject position by American Indian foster children as children negotiated being Mormon and Lamanite.

The US government, like the LDS Church, assumed an authoritative role over the lives of Indigenous peoples through its civilization policies. In both cases, attitudes regarding Indigenous people as "savage," in need of religious, educational, and cultural salvation, provided the necessary justification that became the foundation for Indigenous child removal policies by the LDS Church in the twentieth century. Civilization and assimilation of Indigenous peoples would be achieved through their most valuable resource, their children. Western education became a tool of cultural genocide wielded against Indigenous children. The civilization mission of Indigenous children is predicated on the dispossession of Indigenous lands.[4] Indigenous child removal policies and education were intimately connected to Indigenous dispossession not just of their lands but also their ability to remain Indigenous. Mormon settler colonialism, including the ISPP, was not just about the education of Indigenous children; it was also about remaking indigeneity to suit Mormon settler desires about Lamanites. Indigenous children's connections to land, language, culture, and community became the target of Mormon and American settler colonial projects. Education would not just civilize but would also remake indigeneity.

Mormon settler colonial policies, much like US settler colonial policies, utilized infrastructures to implement assimilationist policies to address the "Indian problem." While the US government used relocation and termination to destroy tribal sovereignty in the 1950s and 1960s, the LDS Church used Mormon foster homes to facilitate the assimilation process, a characteristic of the Lamanite subject position. Mormon and US settler colonial projects intersect and converge in their desires to define the status of Indigenous peoples and nations through the operationalization of educational and removal policies.

The US government and the LDS Church viewed Indigenous peoples and nations as deficient, whether it be education, culture, or socioeconomic status, to name just a few. The center of Mormon settler colonial power was predicated on the notion of Indigenous peoples as Lamanites, a deficient people in need of salvation or, really, assimilation. The Mormon settler colonial project aligned with these larger US settler colonial policies of termination and relocation, which were designed to remove Indigenous peoples from their families and communities and assimilate them into American society. The very nature of the ISPP supports US assimilationist goals using education as the vehicle to implement assimilation. The ISPP, like the federal Urban Relocation Program, was an individual approach to a structural problem in which Mormon settler homes became the structure for assimilation. Rather than assimilate Indigenous children into mainstream American society, the LDS Church wanted them to become distinctly Mormon, a specific expression of whiteness.

The US government utilized education to assimilate and civilize Indigenous children, hoping to "kill the Indian in him, and save the man," a phrase coined by Richard Henry Pratt, who founded the Carlisle Indian Industrial School in 1879, the first boarding school, located in Carlisle, Pennsylvania.[5] More than a century later, the LDS Church utilized similar settler civilizing ideologies to create the ISPP. The historian David Wallace Adams examines ideas around education and civilization in *Education for Extinction*, where he articulates that the US government operated on one definition of civilization.[6] Indigenous children had to be removed from their family and communities to sever the tie with their tribal communities.

The physical distance from their traditional homelands was deliberate and essential to the civilizing process. If Indigenous children could be removed far from their family homes, communities, cultures, and land, this would minimize their ability to run away and be surrounded by perceived negative influences of their families and communities. Mormon settlers also subscribed to this ideology of civilization but used religious ideologies about Lamanites to justify the need for civilization efforts, using the ISPP as a structure to define and enforce assimilation.[7] These educational institutions, including the ISPP, "were established as laboratories for a grand experiment in ethnic cleansing" of Indigenous children.[8] The LDS Church used a more intimate form of civilizing: Mormon settler homes, which became sites to operationalize the Mormon settler colonial project to uplift and civilize Lamanites.

HELEN JOHN AND MORMON SETTLER IDEOLOGIES: THE ORIGINS OF THE INDIAN STUDENT PLACEMENT PROGRAM

The LDS Church credits a young Diné woman, Helen John, for the creation in 1947 of a pilot program that would become the ISPP. Helen pushed to stay with the Mormon settler family who owned the beet farm where her family had worked as laborers. Rather than move with her family, she wanted to stay to finish her Western education. The ISPP was initially designed to provide off-reservation educational opportunities to American Indian children living in the United States who were or became members of the LDS Church.[9] American Indian children were removed from their families who lived on various reservations in the United States and reserves in Canada and then placed in predominantly white middle-class Mormon settler foster homes. Once the ISPP became an officially recognized program by the LDS Church, its lay clergy and LDS Church employees worked with appropriate state officials for official state licensing. In their bid to become a licensed foster care program, the state became complicit in the illegal removal of American Indian children across state lines, since the majority of the ISPP Indian foster children were placed with Mormon settler families in Utah. Mormon settler foster families believed they were fulfilling a religious mandate to "save" Indigenous people by fostering their children. Mormon settler foster homes became physical, intimate spaces of assimilation in which Indigenous children's bodies became sites of Mormon settler colonial practices. The ISPP was not just about an individual Diné woman's desire for an education but was also the justification needed to create an institution rooted in settler colonial desires of Indigenous civilization. While Helen and the Averys, a Mormon settler family, were at the center of the origins of the ISPP, this Mormon settler colonial narrative centers the lives of Mormon settlers and Indigenous peoples and remains interwoven and interconnected, a characteristic of Mormon settler colonialism.

Helen's story began when her life intersected with the Avery family, who owned their agricultural land and had hired and transported Diné peoples, such as the John family, to work in their beet fields.[10] The Johns had completed their work in the fields and began preparations to leave at the end of beet season. Helen did not want to leave with her family and was unwilling to leave the Avery farm. Her father had her removed from school after the sixth grade so she could participate in Diné traditions. Helen and her younger sister, Ruth, had previously attended the Tuba City Boarding School until the fifth grade. Both sisters had stayed there for nine months before returning home for the summer. This practice would also be utilized by the ISPP. Lamanite children would live for nine months with a Mormon settler foster family during the academic year and return to their family for the duration of the summer. Rather than letting his daughters return to school in the fall for sixth grade, Mr. John decided to keep them at home because he was afraid they would lose their Diné language. Mr. John wanted his daughters to learn how "to make rugs and learn ways of the Navajo rather than follow the white man's way so he kept me home until I was about 16," Helen recalled. Mr. John understood the importance of education. He valued Diné lifeways and wanted to ensure that his children did not lose them.

Initially Helen had complied with her father's wishes, but she wanted to finish her education and sought assistance from Amy Avery, the farmer's wife. Helen pleaded with Amy to let her stay in Richfield, Utah, to finish her education. Helen had told Amy that she "would be no trouble to her if she would just let her pitch a tent in the back yard and live there so she could go to school."[11] Although Amy was supportive of Helen's desire to continue her education, she did not feel as though she could care for Helen because she had three daughters of her own. Although the Avery family would not be able to accommodate Helen's wishes, Amy introduced Helen to Golden R. Buchanan, president of the Sevier Stake (a group of local LDS Church congregations). Buchanan became an avid supporter of not just Helen but also education for other Indian children.[12] After visiting Helen in camp, he reached out to Spencer Woolley Kimball, an apostle in the LDS Church's Quorum of the Seventy, for guidance regarding Helen John's request to stay with the Buchanan family and get an education. Kimball visited the Buchanan family and informed Golden that he wanted Helen to stay with them. Kimball had specific instructions for the Buchanans. Kimball expected Buchanan to treat Helen "as your girl, and treat her in every way as you would your own daughter."[13] But the effort required to treat American Indian foster children as family members was in this case and other cases too much for many Mormon settler families.[14] Mrs. Thelma Buchanan responded to Kimball's request bluntly: "Brother Kimball, I can't do it. . . . I've never liked the Indians."[15] Despite pleas by high-ranking LDS Church leaders, Mrs. Buchanan did not believe she could have a young Indian child in her home without a racist or prejudicial attitude. Thelma Buchanan's reaction was not unique and reflected widely held opinions by other Mormon settlers about Indigenous peoples. Thelma Buchanan stated,

> No one would want dirty Indians in their home. I think we have to go back on that[;] if we're going into that I think you have to go back to the Black Hawk War times. Most people looked at the Indians as enemies. The Indians had killed some of their loved ones. There was very few of the old pioneer families that hadn't had a brother or a father or an uncle or maybe even an aunt that hadn't been killed by an Indian in some raids. The Indians were uncivilized. They didn't know how to take care of themselves. The way they lived was atrocious. You couldn't be friends with an Indian and keep your self respect. It just wasn't done. At least in our part of the country that's true.[16]

Thelma Buchanan's attitude reflects multiple issues at once. The use of terms such as "we" and "us" denote how Mormon settlers viewed themselves in relation to Indian peoples. Indigenous peoples are not part of the collective "we." Even as members of the LDS Church, they are viewed as the Other, as Lamanites. Indian peoples were considered dirty, unholy, and "uncivilized." Buchanan's sentiments also highlight the intergenerational anger toward Indigenous peoples based on conflict that her settler ancestors had with Indigenous peoples. Her comments also highlight how Mormon settlers' move to innocence was reliant on the narrative of Indigenous violence. Indigenous peoples were the perpetrators of violence despite the influx of settlers claiming Indigenous land and resources. The violence becomes one-sided, initiated by Indigenous peoples, and their uncivilized responses cement the Mormon settler move to innocence. Thelma Buchanan's use of "pioneer" was also telling and supportive of this Mormon settler move to innocence, which is necessary to justify the presence of Mormon settlers, including the Buchanan family.

The arrival of Mormon settlers into the Great Basin region in the nineteenth and twentieth centuries had an impact on the environment and on Indigenous peoples. These two groups had very different worldviews, and their presence in the same region put them in direct conflict with one another over land and resources. Western Shoshone historian Ned Blackhawk writes in *Violence over the Land: Indians and Empires in the Early American West* about violence as both a "subject and a method" in regard to the history of the Great Basin region in the eighteenth and nineteenth centuries.[17] Blackhawk asserts that violence defined and shaped the relationship between Indigenous peoples and settlers, which was true for Mormon settlers and various Indigenous groups in the region. Rising tensions between the two groups led to the Black Hawk War of 1865–1872. Led by Black Hawk, Ute leader, Northern Utes and their allies attacked Mormon settlements throughout the region, oftentimes raiding cattle and other goods. In the Mormon historical narrative, Indigenous peoples were seen as the primary perpetrators of violence, and their living conditions were used as examples of their degraded status.[18] However, Mormon settlers had trespassed onto Indigenous land and claimed resources as their own. Thelma Buchanan's view highlights how these wounds between the two groups had yet to heal by 1947 but also highlight the lack of understanding about her family's role as settlers who had wrongfully claimed and occupied Indigenous lands.

Thelma Buchanan, like many other Mormon settlers and settler descendants, viewed Lamanites as the aggressor, or the perpetrators of violence inflicted on Mormon settlers. These views were also reflected in LDS Church doctrine, particularly the Book of Mormon, in which Lamanites were said to be "wild, and ferocious, and a blood-thirsty people, full of idolatry and filthiness."[19] Religious ideologies reinforced modern beliefs and attitudes toward Indigenous peoples as the perpetrators of violence, and Buchanan's perspective renders Mormon settlers as innocent, not the cause of conflict and war.[20] The past wars and ongoing tensions between the two groups shaped Mormon-Lamanite relationship into the twentieth century. This relationship reflected Mormon settler power to dispossess a people from their traditional lands and disrupt ways of living. Mormon settlers framed their interactions from their worldviews, which were shaped by decades of distrust and constant power struggles with other settlers and the US government to protect their way of living and religious ideologies that justified Mormon settler claims to land. Despite Thelma Buchanan's initial refusal to foster Helen, the Buchanan family changed their mind after Kimball pleaded with them to reconsider their initial reaction. Only with Kimball's intervention, including his high-ranking status and role in the LDS Church, did Thelma acquiesce.[21]

Helen John would become the first Indian child placed in a private Mormon foster placement in what would eventually become the ISPP.[22] In this private individual placement, the LDS Church did not seek state approval or proper licensing to Helen from her family to a Mormon settler foster family. In fact, Golden Buchanan and other local LDS Church leaders' efforts would not be recognized by the LDS Church, even as it was being organized and driven by LDS members and leaders.

Golden Buchanan remembers Kimball and Stephen L. Richards, a prominent LDS Church leader, telling him that they could not "approve your program, but we don't want you to stop. We want you to go ahead on an unofficial basis. We can't even recognize that it exists."[23] Kimball encouraged Buchanan's efforts: "Now we can't tell you do it. We can't give you any money for it or any traveling expense. We don't do one thing for you, but the Brethren are watching it. They don't want you to quit. I've talked with them in council in the temple. They don't want you to stop, but they can't tell you to go forward. You're on your own. You do whatever you think you ought to do and whatever you're inspired to do."[24]

Kimball's advice to Buchanan demonstrated that the early years of the ISPP were not only illegal but also that the LDS Church and its leaders would not acknowledge or sanction the existence of the program. The comments made by high-ranking LDS Church leaders and their refusal to recognize the early efforts to organize the ISPP meant that they understood the risks of Indian child removal and were more invested in providing institutional protection from potential external criticisms. Buchanan determined that a program run by the LDS Church could "literally [save] hundreds of Indian children [who] would have the privilege of living in LDS homes where they not only could be taught in school but they could be taught the principles of the gospel."[25] Yet the ISPP and Mormon settler foster families did not have any financial funding or support from the LDS Church. The program was not even acknowledged by church leadership in its early years.

From the very beginning, Belle Spafford, president of the Relief Society (an LDS Church auxiliary organization), believed the program to be unethical because the ISPP authorities did not have the necessary foster permits and interstate compact agreements or licenses to remove Indian children from reservations to Mormon settler foster homes. Spafford's professional recommendations and concerns were completely ignored. Miles Jensen, under the direction of Spencer W. Kimball and later the Relief Society, worked to organize and eventually oversee the ISPP for over twenty years. Jensen recalled, "Legally and technically I was working for the Relief Society, but you can realize that the Brethren were giving direction."[26] In the LDS Church, a gendered hierarchy exists in which men hold power and authority over women, even within a women's LDS auxiliary organization, because they have the priesthood, a religious mantle given to men to act with the power and authority of God. This authority was manifested in the organization of the ISPP. Kimball's influence and position as an LDS Church apostle convinced lower-ranking church leaders and members to create and oversee an illegal program that failed to put the interests and safety of Indigenous children first before Mormon settler civilizing desires. The First Presidency and Quorum of the Twelve Apostles, top LDS Church leadership units, did not officially approve the ISPP as an LDS Church program until July 1954 after the Indian Committee made the recommendation. They sent out formal letters on August 10, 1954, to signal their approval to stakes (a group of local congregations) in southern Utah soliciting Mormon families to host Indian children during the school year.[27] There had been legal concerns regarding the placement of Indian children. John Farr Larson, director of the Bureau of Services for Children for Utah, a component of the Utah Department of Public Welfare, had "expressed his concern" to Belle Spafford, LDS Church Relief Society president. The Relief Society was licensed by the state to "place minor children."[28] Even at this time, the state preferred to place foster Indian children in homes with the same racial background, yet there was recognition that the scale of the ISPP would make this nearly impossible. Therefore, the LDS Church and the Utah Department of Public Welfare decided that these placements would be overseen by the "Indian Committee and the Relief Society General Board" to ensure legal foster placements.[29] LDS Church members, like Golden R. Buchanan, would continue to assist in the placement of these Indian children once their parents gave voluntary consent to the Relief Society. Lauramay Nebeker, director of Relief Society Social Services, would supervise and approve all placements, including the evaluation of foster homes.[30] Kimball's words reflect the cautiousness of LDS Church leaders to develop formal Lamanite programs designed to assimilate Indigenous children and transport them from their families and communities into largely Mormon settler families across state boundaries. The gendered and racialized hierarchy behind the formation and oversight of the ISPP signals the influence of the LDS Church in the state and the removal and placement of LDS Indian children into Mormon settler homes as a larger Mormon settler colonial project.

The LDS Church and its lay leadership feared that the ISPP would incite internal and external criticisms of the church's assimilationist Lamanite policies. Buchanan continued his work with Indian children and encouraged other Mormon settler members to join and support the program, saying "Lamanite people are in need of the guidance, training, understanding, and love which Latter-day Saints can and should give."[31] Each month a meeting was held in Kimball's office, and as the program developed, Kimball wanted to name the program. The name was given by Rex Ashdown, who suggested "'The Indian Student Placement Program.' After all, each child is an Indian, each child will be a student, they will be in placement and it is a program."[32] The ISPP began to officially recruit Indigenous children to participate in the program, first using LDS Church missionaries serving in the Southwest Indian

Mission, an LDS mission with geographic boundaries that included primarily reservations in Arizona, Colorado, New Mexico, and Utah. Recruitment would later expand into other tribal reservations in the United States and Canada.

LDS CHURCH MISSIONARIES AS AGENTS OF THE MORMON SETTLER COLONIAL PROJECT

LDS missionaries were pivotal to the implementation of Mormon settler colonial policies, including the ISPP. Since the beginning of the LDS Church, leaders targeted Indigenous peoples for conversion to fulfill religious claims regarding their status as Lamanites. Mormon settler members, including missionaries, played a pivotal role in the Mormon settler colonial project. Joseph Smith, the first prophet and the founder of the LDS Church, sent the first LDS church missionaries to Tribal Nations in the West in the late nineteenth century. LDS Church missionaries were expected to live in tribal communities as they proselytized and converted Indigenous peoples. This missionary tradition continues in the modern era. The ISPP relied on the labor of LDS Church missionaries to simultaneously share church doctrine and recruit children to participate in the ISPP in the twentieth century. In this section, I highlight how LDS Church missionaries aligned the ISPP with US settler colonial policies of assimilation via education to convince Indigenous parents to send their children to Mormon settler homes. LDS Church missionaries as individuals exist within and perpetuate the structures of Mormon settler colonialism. I highlight the techniques utilized by LDS missionaries to make visible Mormon religious rhetoric and policies as a technology of Mormon settler colonialism. While Helen John became a poster child for the ISPP because of her desires for a Western education, other Indigenous foster children had to be actively recruited to participate in the ISPP. While other religious groups, federal, and state officials used aggressive tactics, such as coercion and even kidnapping, Mormon missionaries utilized a more benevolent approach. LDS Church missionaries went into the homes of Indigenous families to encourage parents to send their children to the ISPP by framing it as an educational opportunity, not a foster care program. Not only did LDS missionaries proselytize among and in Indigenous homes and communities, they also used the ISPP to generate interest in the LDS Church. A large number of Diné students had been recruited due to LDS Church missionaries' efforts in the Southwest. The LDS Church even developed bilingual missionary lessons written in English and Diné. These scripted dialogues in Diné taught missionaries how to introduce and talk about the ISPP with families. Ironically, the Diné language was utilized as a tool to aid in the religious colonization of Diné peoples because the very nature and purpose of the ISPP meant that children would lose their language. The ISPP settler foster homes, located far away from children's families, communities, and reservations, contributed to Indigenous language loss for the children. It would have been very difficult for most Diné children to learn or keep fluency in their first language because they often could not speak the language daily. These missionary lessons, written in both English and Diné, reveal the LDS Church's willingness and commitment to use the Diné language to expedite the recruiting process for the ISPP while increasing Diné, or Lamanite, membership.[33]

The LDS Church missionaries promoted the strengths of the ISPP to their Lamanite membership: Indian children could leave the reservation, stay with Mormon settler families who had been approved by social workers, speak English at home and school, and attend Utah's best public schools.[34] Again, the emphasis is placed on children leaving their families and reservations, implying that there was something inherently deficient in their communities or in their current living conditions. LDS missionaries rely on the rhetoric of civilization and use education as a means to enforce the notion that Mormon religious and secular education would offer opportunities that these young people would or could not experience if they stayed home. The use of education, Christianity, and proficiency in English became code for civilization, including Lamanite progress. Yet Indigenous children will always remain firmly cast in the racialized category of indigeneity and in the Mormon settler colonial context, Lamanite. The intimate tools of Mormon settler colonialism pushed the narrative of progress via the ISPP in hopes that their civilizing efforts would entice people to send their children. Indigenous children would be removed from reservations and transported into Mormon settler homes as they began their transition into civilized Lamanites. Once civilized, Lamanites would return to their communities and aid in the assimilation process by converting and civilizing their people. Even as good Lamanites, or graduates of the ISPP, Indigenous children remained on the margins of Mormon and American society and despite their education were expected to return home and perpetuate the cyclical nature of Mormon colonization.

LDS Church missionary recruitment tactics had been successful because many Diné parents wanted their children to get a Western education even if it meant sending them away from the reservation. LDS Church officials and members viewed the ISPP as a potential educational pipeline from reservation to Mormon settler foster homes.[35] Despite efforts to distinguish the ISPP from other US settler colonial educational structures, LDS Church missionaries simultaneously relied on their familiarity with federal boarding schools to convince Indigenous parents to send their children to participate in the ISPP because of the quality of education offered by Mormon settler families. For families looking for off-reservation education, federal boarding schools were often their only choice. The ISPP became an attractive alternative: foster placement would increase access to quality education both inside and outside the home. Literature produced by the LDS Church for missionary use highlighted the weaknesses of other non-Mormon educational programs available to Indian families so as to make the ISPP an unrivaled choice. For example, one criticism focused on the use of English to deliver curriculum while living at US government boarding schools, where Diné children could still use their language outside the classroom despite potential punishments. Diné children would never need to learn only English when they could communicate on a daily basis with other Diné speakers. Diné children who attended school on the reservation spent excessive time on the bus each day. Public schools on the reservation were also problematic from an assimilationist perspective because Diné children received instructions in English but lived at home where they could speak Diné with their families daily, all weaknesses of these educational programs.[36]

While recruiting for the ISPP, Mormon missionaries highlighted these flaws and offered up what they believed to be the best alternative: the ISPP. The ISPP was a fully immersive nine-month program that was supposed to prepare Indian children for postsecondary education. Mormon foster homes used only English, reinforcing the use of English by ISPP foster children to aid in their assimilation. The use of English became the centerpiece and selling point for the ISPP. Miles Jensen, second director of the ISPP, believed that there were immediate and extensive language benefits for ISPP children. He recalled, "Many of them didn't know the English language very well, so if they lived with a family, they would learn the English language so they could communicate and discuss in the language with confidence."[37] Jensen believed that Mormon Indian children could become fluent in the English language through their participation in the ISPP.

LDS missionaries placed additional pressure on Indigenous families already under pressure by the federal government to educate their children. Many Indian parents wanted their children to be educated as a fulfillment of US treaties that included provisions addressing compulsory education for Indian children. For example, in the Treaty with the Navajo, ratified on July 25, 1868, Article 6 states that in order to "insure the civilization of the Indians entering into this treaty" and the "necessity of admitted," education is essential, and Navajo citizens must "pledge themselves to compel their children, male and female, between the ages of six and sixteen years, to attend school."[38] Some Diné parents interpreted this specific article to mean that they should send their children off the reservation for education. Indian parents viewed the ISPP as a less intrusive alternative than government boarding schools on and off the reservation.[39] Both ISPP and US government off-reservation education required the removal of Indian children from their homes and tribal communities despite Indian children's protests. Julius Ray Chavez, Diné, recalled that despite his protests, his mother enrolled him in the ISPP. He remembered the traumatic experience of having to leave his grandmother, who had been teaching him about his people. He vividly recalled the time he spent with his grandmother learning the Diné language; his lineage; the history of Diné people, including the Long Walk; and spirituality. "I was surprised that I was even going. All I remember is that I had to go home one night. My stuff was packed, and I was on the bus the next day headed for Utah."[40] He was shocked and traumatized, but his grandmother told him, "You have to go. Remember what I told you of how our people were released from captivity. It was under the conditions that we send our children to school. That's written on paper to this day with the white man. Even if you don't want to go because it's written on paper."[41] Chavez's mother and grandmother both cited the 1868 treaty with the Navajo as the reason he had to leave his home on the Navajo Nation reservation and go on placement. It was because of the treaty, not their beliefs in Mormonism, that the Chavez family decided that Julius would participate in the ISPP. It is interesting to note that Julius's mother and grandmother saw his participation in the program as fulfillment of the 1868 treaty, yet Julius did not understand why he needed to leave his grandmother, who was teaching him about his people in the Diné language. The rigid interpretation of the treaty meant that only US settler education would satisfy this requirement, which would include the ISPP. As he recounted his experiences, Julius understood that he was being educated in Diné by his grandmother about his people's history, yet it was not enough for him to remain with his family. For the LDS Church and its missionaries, the definition of education was limited to their assimilationist views. There was little consideration given to the importance of oral histories, languages, traditions, culture, and community as integral components of one's education. American Indian children were expected to "live with these people [Mormon white foster families] and go to school, church and parties," Jensen said. "Then they come back home for three months' vacation [and] learn more Navaho. This is the best schooling any child can get."[42] This limited perception and professed authority is evident in how ISPP recruiters addressed the school year. The attitude that returning home would be a "vacation" ignored any issues Indian children might have about returning to their homes and communities, including language loss, a vital component of indigeneity and epistemology. Living in one's tribal community for only three months would prevent Indian children from achieving the level of first-language speaker fluency and, more importantly, maintaining connection to one's family, community, and traditions. The Chavez family's decision to participate in the ISPP does not legitimize the program or the LDS Church. Instead, their choice highlights how Diné families negotiated their place within these US and Mormon settler colonial structures, including the ISPP.

Indigenous families navigated US and Mormon settler colonial structures on their terms, but their participation does not always equate to complete religious conversion. During the formative years of the pilot program there was no specific age requirement for children; some as young as four years old joined the ISPP. LDS Church officials later decided that these children were much too young.[43] A minimum age requirement was instituted only after the ISPP was formally recognized and supervised in 1954. Mormon Indian students had to be at least eight years of age, the same minimum age for children to be baptized in the LDS Church. The ISPP children were also expected to remain in good standing as LDS members, have passing grades, and successfully adjust to their foster families to remain ISPP participants.[44] However, Indigenous families found ways to navigate around these requirements. Matthew West, second counselor in the Fort Hall Branch in Idaho in the Fort Hall Reservation, remembers several instances when Indian children were baptized for the sole purpose of being able to participate in the ISPP.[45] One student, Ray R. Mitchell, also remembers that on the Navajo Nation reservation there was pressure to enroll Indian children in the ISPP, often at the expense of signing up students who were not religiously committed to Mormonism. Mitchell believes that other Indian students wanted to simply go on placement to "see what it looks like living off the reservation with an Anglo family in a big city. After they came back, some of them never went back to church."[46] These recollections complicate the LDS Church's narrative about the ISPP and Indian students who participated as active, faithful members of the LDS Church. The accounts highlight how individuals, such as missionaries and potential converts, negotiated their place within the program, a structure within the Mormon settler colonial project.

MORMON SETTLER FOSTER HOMES: A TECHNOLOGY OF MORMON SETTLER COLONIALISM

LDS missionaries worked in Indigenous communities to solicit participation in the ISPP, while Mormon settler homes became the structures that enforced Mormon settler colonial ideologies. LDS missionaries solicited participation, and the Mormon settler home became a technology of Mormon settler colonialism, a structure designed to legitimize and enforce Mormon settler colonial ideologies about Indigenous peoples while strengthening the Mormon settler colonial center. The LDS Church relied on Mormon settler families, as it did with missionaries, to operationalize and embed Mormon settler ideologies within the home. The Mormon settler home became a structure of Mormon settler fantasy, as Mormon settlers believed that they were aiding in the salvation of Lamanites. The Mormon settler home as a physical structure of Mormon settler colonialism has largely been rendered invisible because the focus of the ISPP literature has been on the altruism of Mormon settler families and on active ISPP participants, not how these individual Mormon settlers carried out Mormon settler colonial ideologies. The ISPP was not solely about the education of Indigenous children; it was really about Mormon settler motive. The ISPP reinforced their views of Indigenous peoples, through their children, as an inferior people.

The ISPP as a structure of Mormon settler colonialism could only work if LDS Mormon settler families fostered and absorbed the cost of hosting Mormon Indian children in their homes. In addition to benevolent attitudes and misguided concern for the welfare of Mormon Indian children, Mormon settler families had been admonished to participate. James Lionel Lewis during a 1948 meeting with LDS Church officials recalled Golden Buchanan, ISPP director, as a featured speaker. Buchanan encouraged members to help Indians living in "adverse conditions."[47] Mormon members viewed Indians as a "primitive" people who lived in "poverty, their filth and in many instances, their indolence and ignorance."[48] The ISPP became a means to end Indigenous "primitive" living using religious conversion and educational programs to uplift a people. The ISPP was difficult to initially implement due to Mormon settler attitudes toward Indian people. Eventually the program would need institutional support from the LDS Church to facilitate the placement and welfare of the ISPP Indian children.

Mormon settlers' perception of Indigenous children and communities as deficient, void of educational, social, and cultural opportunities, became the justification for child removal. The home became a vital site of the Mormon settler colonial process; American Indian foster children would be inculcated with Mormon religious, economic, and educational beliefs. The removal of Indigenous children "constituted another crucial way to eliminate Indigenous people, but in a cultural and biological sense."[49] The physical removal of Indian children would "save" them from their lives of "backwardness and poverty" on the reservation, and the socialization within Mormon settler homes would civilize and assimilate Indigenous children into American and Mormon settler societies.

Mormon settler foster homes, like US Indian boarding schools, became exemplars of industry and civilization to Indigenous children and families. Mormon foster families became critical to the operationalization of Mormon settler colonial ideologies rooted in the notion of Mormon settlers as *the* standard.[50] The LDS Church gave Mormon settler families a handbook, the "Foster Parent Guide." The handbook highlights the key role of Mormon foster families, as models of "exemplary living," to motivate Indian foster children "to use their experiences [educational, spiritual, social, and cultural opportunities] for the benefit of themselves and their people."[51] Those Mormon settler foster families who participated did so because the ISPP was for their benefit, a means to advance their spiritual status within the LDS Church. One proclamation stated, "The sons and daughters of Zion will soon be required to donate a portion of their time in instructing the children of the forest [the Indians] for they must be educated and instructed in all arts of civil life, as well as in the Gospel." Indian foster children were expected to be treated like a member of the family: to do chores, participate in family activities, eat different foods, and attend church with their foster families. The family household routine exposed Indian foster children to activities centered around LDS Church religious beliefs within the home and family structure. The LDS Church made assumptions about Indigenous families and operated under the belief that Mormon settler foster families could model ideal home life and routines. This "model home" project was "designed to link the domestic transformations achieved" in the ISPP "to Indian family life back home [on] reservations."[52] Mormon leadership believed that the education Indian children were receiving on the reservation was inadequate and limited their religious, education, and economic potential. Despite removal from their deficient families, ISPP children were expected to return home and transform their families and communities.

The Mormon settler foster family as an ideal standard is evident on how social worker's and LDS Church members placed ISPP students. Based on the "professional judgment of the Placement Program's staff members following a review of all the factors presented by the natural family, the foster family, and the student," students were then matched with the best possible Mormon settler foster family.[53] Mormon settler foster families who wanted to participate had to have the economic resources to provide for their Mormon Indian foster child. Mormon families wishing to foster Mormon Indian children were selected based on "their [foster parents'] marital relationships, high moral standards, activity in the Church, age and sex of children [natural children], financial stability and desire to help a Lamanite child gain an education." The LDS Church wanted to find the best match for Indian children and Mormon foster families while also making sure that these families met basic standards for "their local licensed agency; those standards var[ied] from state to state." If Mormon settler applicants fulfilled these basic qualifications, they could participate in the ISPP and foster an Indigenous child. Indian foster children had to maintain good standing in the LDS Church, attending all church meetings and activities as they abstained from alcohol, tobacco, and premarital sex.

Indian children were expected to conform and adhere to Mormon religious standards. In essence, Mormon settler foster family homes became structures to impose Mormon civilizing ideologies designed to "eradicate Native thought, language, culture, and education."[54] The Mormon settler foster home itself was intended to be a welcoming space, but many Mormon Indian foster children found their homes to be a foreign space. Indian foster children adjusted to their new environment living with Mormon white foster families. Tonia Halona, ISPP student, found her foster family activities, such as prayers and activities every weekend, to be disconcerting because her family simply did not do these things.[55] Perhaps even more problematic for Tonia was that her foster parents wanted her to call them "Mom" and "Dad." Eventually Tonia acquiesced to the request after she became comfortable with the foster family.[56] While calling her foster parents "Mom" and "Dad" was a personal choice made by Tonia, the attempt to replace natural parents was indicative of systemic issues surrounding Indigenous child removal policies. Many Indigenous children had been removed from their homes and communities and placed into temporary foster care with the hope that Indigenous children would not be reunited with their families. For example, one ISPP social worker wrote to Diné parents in December 1969 and stated, "Many of you may be thinking of visiting your child and his foster family sometime during the Holidays. . . . I hope you will not do this. Most of the time [it] is not good for you or your child. It makes both of you homesick and your child must adjust again after you leave."[57] Even though many Indigenous parents voluntarily signed consent for their children to be placed into temporary foster homes as part of the ISPP, the impact on the family was great.[58] The LDS Church discouraged natural parents from maintaining strong ties to their children by not visiting them while on placement, thus weakening the bond between Indigenous children, families, and communities.

LDS Church officials and members assumed that their way of living, a largely middle-class patriarchal home organized by and reinforced around LDS Church

values, would considerably improve the lives of Indigenous peoples. Mormon foster home rituals became important in reinforcing gendered norms. For example,
Lamanite females were taught various domestic skills and learned to remain virtuous
women. Both female and male LDS Lamanite children were expected to maintain
their sexual purity until marriage and participated in various activities in the home
and at church that further entrenched gendered roles and religious ideology. These
ideologies were also reinforced in church lessons and in the homes.[59] The gendered
division of labor within Mormon settler foster homes was similar to US boarding
schools' gendered education and labor. Indian girls were taught domestic skills,
while the boys learned either vocational or technical skills that reinforced gender
expectations and roles.

Mormon foster families undermined Indigenous belief systems by asserting Mormon settler colonial ideologies as the only correct belief system. All
others, especially Indigenous ways of knowing, were considered wrong, unholy,
or uncivilized. Virginia Tulley remembers how her Mormon settler foster family
viewed Indigenous ceremonies as being from "Satan."[60] She never believed her
Mormon settler foster family's assertions. Tulley's Mormon settler foster family
was not the only family that condemned Indigenous ceremonies. Another ISPP
child, Ray Mitchell, vividly recalls one incident when his Mormon settler foster
mother condemned his religious beliefs. Mitchell's foster mother was giving a
lesson during Family Home Evening, a weekly religious activity conducted in
the home designed to inculcate Mormon children with Mormon religious values
and beliefs. For example, Mitchell's foster family had a Family Home Evening
lesson on the priesthood, held by only LDS males, further entrenching gendered
religious roles within the LDS Church. His Mormon settler foster mother stated
that "the power of the priesthood will heal man when he has the faith." Mitchell
responded to his foster mother's statement and shared that medicine men could
also heal. His foster mother responded quickly and bluntly: "That medicine man is
of the devil."[61] Many Mormon settler families did not understand or respect their
placement child's spiritual beliefs. Instead, the foster families often dismissed or
disrespected Indigenous traditional beliefs altogether. In the intimacy of the home,
Mormon settlers privileged their LDS Church doctrinal beliefs and categorized
Indigenous spiritual beliefs as unholy and, in doing so, dismissed Indigenous beliefs
as spiritually inferior. Mitchell's foster mother was not alone. Many others, including
non-Mormons, believed that Indigenous people's spiritual beliefs were indicative
of their savagery, or uncivilized nature. Mormon ISPP foster parents' rejection of
Indigenous spirituality aligned with US and other settler views that attempted to

destroy Indigenous spirituality through assimilationist policies, including access to sacred sites and the ability to simply practice all aspects of their spirituality. Living in Mormon foster homes made it nearly impossible to participate in ceremonial practices during the school year, a function of the ISPP as a technology of US and Mormon settler colonialism. Yet there were Indigenous children who refused to acquiesce to these pressures and instead never spoke of those things. "My responsibility, my duty there[,]" said Julius Ray Chavez, "was for schooling and for nothing else."[62] Julius Ray Chavez's grandparents did not want him to share his traditional beliefs with his Mormon settler foster family, preventing criticisms and pressure to let them go. Instead, his responsibility was to go and get an education but to remain Diné, which would include maintaining language, cultural, and spiritual practices. Indigenous families resisted overt and subversive attempts to become Mormon and instead learned to exist within these Mormon settler colonial structures. While some Mormon settler foster families pushed for complete civilization into Mormon settler society, others encouraged ISPP children to maintain ties to their culture through the preservation of their language and traditions. Emery Bowman, Diné, vividly remembers how his foster parents taught him about the LDS Church and doctrinal teachings. His foster mother stated:

> being a Lamanite is important, so you have to learn it. Don't leave it because that's what you are and that's what your kids will be. Your kids won't be Anglo. They'll have our language, but that's about it. To be Navajo is to be greatly religious. To understand the Navajo tradition and the Navajo religion is very complex. So learn it. I don't think Heavenly Father has anything against you learning who you are because you'll have to identify yourself when you get back there. How are you going to identify yourself if you don't know how to speak Navajo? She always used to get after me for that.[63]

Bowman's memory regarding his Mormon settler foster family stands in contrast to others because they reaffirmed Diné (Indigenous) identity and the importance of his language. Mormon settlers asserted themselves as proponents of Indian culture yet expected Indian children to learn about the dominant culture, especially Mormonism, while also keeping their culture intact. Indigenous youths were able to accept these differing worldviews, including spiritual beliefs. Tracy Neal Lavelle explains in *The Catholic Calumet* how "native models of spiritual transformation remained flexible enough to accommodate multiple perspectives at the same time," and the "thoughtful and varied responses" by Mormon Indian foster children highlight how different truths can exist alongside one another.[64] Indigenous peoples were flexible only because these infrastructures imposed these subject positions onto them. The literature and narrative surrounding the ISPP and Indigenous children emphasize this negotiation and in doing so renders Mormon settler colonialism invisible. Mormon settler foster families, while complicated, remain a technology of Mormon settler colonialism because the ISPP functions on Mormon settler terms.

The LDS Church and Mormon settler foster families had participated in the ISPP because they benefited from the ISPP. Clarence R. Bishop, first director of the ISPP, believed that Mormon settler foster families could benefit from having Indian children in their home. He believed that attitudes, such as those displayed by Thelma Buchanan, would change if they could learn to love Indian children and then eventually love a people.[65] One Mormon settler foster mother remembers how "stunned" she was when her husband had suggested they apply to foster a "placement student."[66] She recalls, "I hadn't thought about it much, but I don't think I even liked Indians very much. I'm not sure how I felt. But I resolved those feelings, and we did get our foster son; and I can hardly express how I feel now about our experiences. This young man took us outside ourselves. We have experienced love we never would have been able to experience otherwise. We have seen into his culture and sensed something of the great promise there. Our family will never be the same."

This Mormon settler foster parent's perspective highlights how Indigenous children remain the Other, despite claims of acceptance. Her experience reveals how this foster family's colonial gaze viewed this Indigenous child as an educational opportunity for their family in the comfort of their home. The relationship between Mormon settler foster family and Indigenous foster children was transactional as Mormon settlers consumed indigeneity on their terms. The ISPP was not about the education of an Indian foster child, but how Indian children could provide their Mormon settler foster families with experiences and education about Indians to change their attitudes about Indigenous peoples. Mormon settler foster families did not go to Indian reservations, communities, or families to learn about the culture or beliefs of the children they fostered. Instead, they accepted Indigenous cultures when presented in a neat, consumable package via Indian children living in their homes. The removal of Indigenous children into the ISPP and Mormon settler foster homes needs to be placed in the literature about Indigenous child removal in the twentieth century. From 1947 to 1980, 44,371 Indian foster students had participated in the ISPP.[67] While these numbers are an estimate, the number of participants demonstrates the enormity and reach of the LDS Church into tribal communities.

NEGOTIATING INDIGENEITY IN MORMON
SETTLER INFRASTRUCTURES

The literature on the ISPP and Indigenous participants focuses on those who largely remain embedded in the LDS Church or those who have chosen to have their stories documented. There is a diverse spectrum of Indigenous people's experiences within the ISPP, many of which are complicated at best. However, the stories that continue to dominate the narrative are those of people who stake a claim on what it means to be Indigenous and Mormon. There is also no space for those who are not in the archival record. Those critical voices have been silenced, ignored, or simply excluded because they challenge the fantasies of Mormon settlers around the ISPP, particularly its purpose and lasting impact. There are so many ISPP voices. I have selected a few to demonstrate how Indigenous children made sense of their identity within the Lamanite subject position. The Mormon settler colonial project defined and gave meaning to indigeneity using Lamanite discourse, yet this discourse about what it means to be Lamanite reflects US settler colonial policies about indigeneity. In both the US and Mormon settler colonial contexts, definitions of indigeneity, specifically the subject position of Indigenous peoples, is meant to serve the center of settler colonial power. Indigeneity is a settler colonial structure because the US government and the LDS Church define these subject positions and, in turn, because policies enforce these narrow definitions of indigeneity. These external definitions of indigeneity are an act of US and Mormon settler colonial power. Mormon settler colonial ideologies around indigeneity rely on US ideologies and policies designed to assimilate Indigenous peoples. In fact, Mormon settler colonialism complicates our understanding of indigeneity as a subject position in the United States because citizenship is not the requirement; rather, indigeneity is much more fluid, and one must simply be deemed Lamanite by Mormon settlers. Indigenous children not only had to wrestle with contestations over indigeneity within their tribal communities but also had to try to make sense of their place within Mormon settler foster families and American society simultaneously. The voices I utilize reveal how students negotiated their Lamanite subject position as they learned to exist in Mormon settler foster families and larger settler communities. Indigenous children existed on settler terms, whether simply as Indigenous, as Lamanite, or as Indian. The ISPP Indigenous children struggled to exist within Mormon settler structures even when they accepted US and Mormon settler subject positions of indigeneity. Indigenous children's accounts of their ISPP experiences expose how they made sense of self and identity within Mormon settler foster families, the LDS Church, and their tribal communities. While I use individual voices and experiences of ISPP students, they existed within the structures of Mormon settler colonialism, which impacted individuals, communities, and infrastructures. Indigenous parents may have voluntarily signed up their children as willing participants, but this does not negate Mormon settler colonial infrastructures in which these children existed. Mormon Indian children negotiated and made sense of their Indigenous identity and struggled to maintain their identity because of internal and external pressures to lay claim to their Lamanite subject position despite inherent contradictions with their tribal subject position. Finally, Mormon Indian children accepted, rejected, or negotiated a Lamanite subject position and their place in the LDS Church and within the context of Mormon settler colonialism.

One structure where ISPP Indigenous children confronted their subject position as Lamanite was in school. Many of the ISPP students were often in the minority at their respective schools sites, while the average Indian student experience on placement varied, with some students experiencing microaggressions and bullying because they were Indian. Racial microaggressions can be defined as "brief and commonplace daily verbal, behavioral and environmental indignities, whether intentional or unintentional, that communicate hostile, derogatory, or negative racial slights and insults to the target person or group."[68] The majority non-Indian classmates who attended school with Indigenous children were largely settlers and had very limited or no experiences with Indigenous children. Rhonda Lee knew that her classmates looked at her differently. "Sometimes they would remark and make comments like, 'You're just in here because you are a minority and they felt sorry for you.'"[69] Lee recalled how angry these comments made her, but rather than become discouraged, she felt compelled to work harder. These microaggressions that Lee experienced reflect how non-Indian children "communicate [using] denigrating, hidden messages." Her classmates attributed her presence in school to the fact that she was Indigenous, not because she was simply attending public schools just like them. Instead, she was only in school because she was "minority."[70] While this is just one specific example, this occurred with other students and reflects the daily racism students endured.

Julius Ray Chavez also remembered that he was the only "Indian kid" in his class, and on the first day of school he was beaten by three white classmates because he was Indian.[71] The harassment continued over time. He was taunted and called names by classmates. Classmates would call him an "Indian giver" and believed him to be a "good one," or a good Indian. Oftentimes, Chavez fought his tormentors and would get in trouble for protecting himself. Due to his experiences in school, Chavez became bitter and questioned his identity as Diné. Non-Indian children bullied Chavez because they viewed him as an outsider even though he was Mormon. He knew that because he was Indian, he had to prove to his classmates that he belonged in school. Unfortunately, Chavez was not alone. Mormon and non-Mormon settler children picked on Indian children simply for being Indian and used racial epithets to dehumanize them. These experiences highlight the tensions between settler and Indian children but, more importantly, emphasize how Indian children wrestled with their indigeneity because of settler anti-Indianism.

Despite being members of the LDS Church and assuming a Lamanite subject position, ISPP children were constantly reminded of their status as Indian. Some Mormon Indian children recalled various incidents of blatant racism expressed by Mormon settlers simply for being Indian. Mormon settlers constructed and assigned the Lamanite subject position to Indigenous peoples yet perpetuated racist notions about Indigenous peoples because of the very religious ideologies used to construct a Lamanite subject identity that perpetuated racist beliefs about Indigenous peoples as a savage, uncivilized people living in a degraded state. For example, Myrtle Hatch remembers that during a meeting of the Relief Society, the LDS Church women's auxiliary organization, a group of Mormon settler women were talking about her. Hatch recalls their comments: "Don't let your daughters hang around with Claude Hatch's girls. Their mother is an Indian, and you know how those Indian kids are. They get pregnant. . . . They'll lead them astray. They're not whole people; they're only half."[72] Hatch and her sisters were not seen as fully human, as evidenced by the racist attitudes of these Mormon settler women. Mormon settler women viewed Indigenous women as hypersexualized beings, a danger to Mormon female standards of beauty and purity.[73] This was exacerbated by the Indigenous women's biracial status. Being "half" Lamanite did nothing to save or civilize them; their Lamanite status would always mark them as the uncivilized Other. Mormon settler women's racist views of Indigenous women would negatively impact Indigenous children. Ken Sekaquaptewa's comments also attribute these racist attitudes toward Indians to white Mormon Utahans. Ken believed that there was underlying racism in many members of the LDS Church. He believed the culture of "Utah Mormons" to be "different."[74] Sekaquaptewa's comments dismiss "Utah Mormon" racism as unintentional. Nonetheless, Mormon settlers' prejudicial and racist attitudes toward Mormon Indian foster children undermine religious mandates to love and embrace Lamanite foster children as one's own. Whether intentional or not, racism and racist attitudes toward Lamanites persisted because the Lamanite subject position was predicated on anti-Indianism.

Mormon Indigenous members confronted aspects of their identity because there was an expectation that they would privilege their religious subject position. One ISPP student, Stephanie Chiquito, believed that Mormon Indigenous members had a problem giving up aspects of their indigeneity when they did not fit or mesh with LDS Church beliefs.[75] Lemuel Pedro also believed that "there's a difference between being an Indian, a Lamanite, and being an LDS. I think they should be LDS first, and Lamanites second."[76] Pedro's comments point to the differences between being Lamanite and being Mormon. Despite the Lamanite subject position being a production of Mormon settler colonialism, Pedro saw these two subject positions as being at odds with one another. Indigenous peoples could not be Indigenous and Mormon. Read another way, Indigenous peoples cannot be Indigenous; instead, they must assume the Mormon settler subject position. In essence, the Mormon settler subject position did not include Lamanites even when Lamanites were central and gave meaning to Mormon settler identity. In these interpretations, Lamanites remain on the periphery of Mormon settler society. There are other Mormon Indigenous peoples who claim both Mormon and Indigenous identities but struggle with balancing the Lamanite subject position. P. Jane Hafen, Taos Pueblo, came to her own conclusion:

> It is impossible to consider Native American issues and Mormonism without considering the Book of Mormon. I do not have a clue whether my people are literal descendants of Book of Mormon peoples, nor do I think it matters. For me, the Book of Mormon offers precepts for living rather than historical accounts. . . . The community of Mormonism is one of the most appealing aspects of my faith. . . . The diversity of our spiritual gifts and individual callings contribute to our communal wholeness. . . . This idealistic hope consoles doubts and soothes pains of history and racism. Being a Native American Mormon is not without trials and absurdities. . . . I am Mormon, and I will always be Taos Pueblo.[77]

These accounts make up the spectrum of Mormon Indigenous experiences and how individuals negotiate and make sense of what it meant to be Lamanite. Mormon Native students who had participated in the program and became LDS members felt torn between two cultures, "the Church and their own."[78] Members found it difficult to negotiate their identity and place in the LDS Church. Ken Sekaquaptewa served a mission for the LDS Church and realized that he could be both Indian and Mormon. He discovered that learning more about his Hopi culture gave him a deeper understanding of his identity and place both in and outside the LDS Church.[79]

Sekaquaptewa negotiated his identity; he could remain both Mormon and Hopi simultaneously. Other students felt as though their Indigenous and Mormon beliefs worked well together; they could be both Indigenous and Mormon.[80] Ernesteen Lynch articulated how her sense of self was founded in her "Navajoness."[81] Indian children made sense of their identity on their own terms but within these settler colonial structures, such as the ISPP. These individuals found that they could be Indian and Mormon and viewed the world through their Indigenous lens. Students learned to stay grounded in their Indigenous identity because they were able to make sense of the world around them through an Indigenous lens.

The very nature of these subject positions is incongruous, compelling some individuals to choose one at the expense of the other. Some Indigenous members chose to completely let go of their Indigenous identity and became immersed in Mormonism. Aneta Whaley did not consider herself to be Lamanite; she was a "latter-day Saint . . . before anything else."[82] While this is a small sampling of Indigenous voices, it highlights the diversity of experiences as these children struggled to make sense of their Indigenous identity within Mormon settler colonial structures, with many choosing to be only Mormon. While many chose to let go of their Indigenous identity, others chose to remain in the LDS Church and reject the Lamanite subject position because of its negative connotations. Emery Bowman remembers that "there was a time where I just hated being called a Navajo. I think every Indian Placement student has gone through that. They hate to be called Indian; they hate to be called Lamanite. What I hated was always having somebody come up to me in the ward and say, 'you're special. You're a special Lamanite.' After nine years that got to me."[83] Bowman recalls how this special Lamanite status bothered him because non-Indigenous Mormon members emphasized this subject position. Mormon settlers conflated his Navajo identity with being Lamanite, and ultimately Bowman rejected that subject position. Another student, Carl S. Moore, did not like being called a "Lamanite" because it meant that he was a "minority," and as a "second class citizen you don't know where you really stand."[84] Moore believed that being Indian or Lamanite automatically marginalized Mormon Indians within the LDS Church. Lewis J. Singer reacted like other Mormon Indian members. He recalled, "our Indian people resent the fact when they [Mormon whites] call them Lamanites. They don't like to be called Lamanites. Lamanite . . . denotes or infers that we are from Laman. . . . They [Lamanites] were always doing bad things and messing up. Because of some of that I think they kind of resent being called Lamanites."[85] Being Lamanite had a negative connotation because of racializing ideologies that marginalized and marked Lamanites as the Other. Mormon settlers treated Mormon

Indigenous members as if they were Lamanites from the Book of Mormon, a people marked with a skin of blackness for their wickedness.

Carl R. Moore's recollections about his ISPP experiences highlight how he negotiated and made sense of his identity as the Other. Moore remembers feeling like a "second class citizen" but reclaimed this Lamanite subject identity. "The term Lamanite has made me really feel proud of the changes that we made as a whole[;] . . . [we] are no longer the blood thirsty killers that were always equated with the wrong-doers."[86] Moore's account highlights tensions to exist as a second class citizen but reclaiming "Lamanite" because Indigenous peoples were no longer "blood thirsty killers." Missing from Moore's recollection and others is the right to exist outside the US and Mormon settler colonial constructs of indigeneity. US and Mormon settler colonial ideologies rely on the depiction of Indigenous peoples as perpetrators of violence to justify settler presence. Even though Moore articulates that we, Indigenous peoples, were no longer killers or wrongdoers, his perspective makes visible the insidious nature of US and Mormon settler colonialism to change the structures in which ISPP children could exist in the world. Julius Ray Chavez's experiences echoed Bowman's. "[Mormon] settlers always look[ed] at you as an Indian and not as a latter-day Saint or just a Saint like one of them without the barrier there of being an Indian."[87] Mormon settlers saw Indigenous peoples not as Mormon but instead as Lamanites even when ISPP children rejected this Lamanite subject position and wanted to be *just* Mormon. Mormon settler identity in the United States was equated with being white and occupied the center of these Mormon settler colonial infrastructures, and Indigenous children would never have access to the center or be white. Mormon Indian members still did not have complete control over their identity or even being seen as Mormons by non-Indian Mormons and therefore remained marginalized within these infrastructures.

In contrast, other ISPP students welcomed the term "Lamanite." Verlinda Adams said,

[I am] proud of who I am and proud of my heritage. It doesn't offend me at all. I know I come from the brother Laman and from that lineage. At least I know where I come from. It doesn't offend me at all, no. . . . To me it means that my people, the Lamanites, once they gain knowledge, once they gain a testimony, once they really see how much the Church can offer them, that they will grow, not only spiritually, but every other way. . . . I think that the blossoming as a rose is just gaining that knowledge, receiving the priesthood, receiving a testimony, and then going from there to grow spiritually.[88]

Adams internalized racialized ideologies about Indigenous peoples and accepted her status as Lamanite. Her recollections show her acceptance of this racialized identity and her assumption that her people could only grow through their acceptance of the LDS Church and being Lamanite. Her comments clearly link this notion of civilization to her people. Their "blossoming" could only occur when they converted, accepting religious ideologies that required Indigenous peoples to give up their indigeneity for a form of spirituality in which they could no longer exist from within their communities. There was power in being a Mormon settler, so much so that ISPP children existed because of Mormon settler colonial structures that preserved their whiteness.

One student, Audrey Boone, raised by her Mormon settler foster family, was instilled with "good habits and social manners. It's like I've become like them."[89] Boone's Mormon settler foster family taught her "good habits and social manners" based on white Mormon standards, and this young Indigenous girl internalized those teachings. Even though she does not explicitly state her desire to become white, she associates these good, civilized teachings with being Mormon. This was echoed by other ISSP children who viewed their people through a Mormon settler lens and perpetuated racialized views based on religious ideologies. Joseph R. Harlan embraced the LDS Church's perspective toward Indian culture and history. "I believe the Native Americans are the way they are and it's totally not their fault. They're following the traditions of their forefathers which are incorrect and this makes them blind. . . . They have rich promises made to them. You can read them in the Book of Mormon. I see them in that way. That's how I see Native Americans or other Lamanites."[90] Harlan sees the culture, spirituality, and history of his people as incorrect, yet this only holds true based on a Mormon settler framework. Harlan's perspective legitimizes Mormon settlers' claims about Indigenous peoples as inferior.

One ISPP participant perpetuated these beliefs about being first and foremost Mormon. Jimmy N. Benally, Mormon Indian member, raised his children to be members of the Church. "We teach them about their culture, but we don't dwell into the tradition. They know their dances and know about their culture. We don't push them to learn Navajo because that's not going to help them. Since we're members of the Church, we just raise them to be LDS."[91] Benally actively chose to curate a Mormon settler subject position for his children because he does not believe that their culture will do much to help them. He did not find their language or culture to be beneficial and instead wanted his children to be raised only as Mormon, or white. Benally does not believe that individuals can remain in two traditions and that LDS Indian members must give up their traditions and those who "dwell into" the traditions. They have left the Church because you can't do that. You can't afford to do that. You can live your culture and you can learn about your heritage[;] . . . that's what's holding back a lot of people. They can't get away from the tradition and at the same time live the gospel."[92] ISPP children moved away from claiming their language, history, and culture. Instead, they chose to curate a very specific Mormon subject position that meant that Indigenous peoples could never fully exist as Indigenous within the structures of Mormon settler colonialism despite the LDS Church's claims about Lamanites as a promised people. Lamanites would exist only when their status and presence served the Mormon settler colonial project.

Mormon Indian children not only faced challenges living in Mormon settler colonial spaces but also experienced opposition from their families and communities. When Mormon Indian children returned to the reservation, their transition was not easy. Tonia Halona recalled how she had both family support and criticism because of her participation in the ISPP. Halona viewed the ISPP as beneficial, but her family criticized her participation. They felt that her attitude changed. "They thought I came back white instead of Indian. They really put down the Church because they think the Church has a lot to do with it. They didn't like the white families taking the Indian students[;] . . . it was kind of hard."[93] Many families were critical of the LDS Church for removing Indian children from their homes yet became critical of their children when they returned home. Gabriel Cinniginnie criticized the LDS Church because "back on the reservation it seems the Indians are being assimilated spiritually that way also. It seems like the LDS Church is following the government's seven era Indian policy periods of assimilating the Indian."[94] Indian people also resisted the LDS Church's characterization of their cultural beliefs as "incorrect traditions." "That really gets my family going," Julius Ray Chavez said. "I think that kind of offends them."[95]

Claudine Arthur, one Navajo mother and Tribal government official, argued that the LDS Church only wanted Indian children who were "emotionally stable," from decent, good homes. Those are the children they want to take off to their homes in Utah and brainwash for their own purposes. If they really believe that home and family is good, then they must believe that it's best for children like these to be in their own homes with their own people."[96] Yet the LDS Church's removal of Indian children and motives behind the ISPP mimicked US boarding schools and foster care, where Indigenous homes and families had been cast as deficient and US and Mormon interventions were for the good of the Indian child. As Arthur poignantly argues, if the LDS Church and the US government wanted the best for Indian children, they should have been left with their families or communities. Yet

Indigenous children bore the brunt of their family and community outrage as they tried to make sense of their place within their community.

The individual choice to be baptized and leave for the ISPP became a personal indictment rather than a wholesale outrage against the LDS Church. Another student, James Dandy, said some of his people "think you are too Anglo. They think, 'You're too good for us. You're not like us anymore.' . . . I know my brothers and sisters struggled with that because they were littler than I was. . . . I had some relatives that had the same problem. They think I'm just too Mormon. They see you that you don't respect your culture anymore."[97] ISPP Indian children faced internal struggles to be Mormon *and* Indigenous, but Mormon Indian children could never be both, even in their communities. Their choice to be Mormon meant that they could not be fully Indigenous. The ISPP children returning to the reservation had to readjust to living at home as they endured family criticism regarding their Mormon status. The children had been disconnected from their families and community, often at great detriment to self. For example, Antoinette Dee remembers how people had called her "an 'apple,' red on the outside and white on the inside."[98] Dee did not believe that her community understood why she chose to leave the reservation. She did not choose to leave because she believed herself to be better than her people but because she wanted to have other opportunities not available in her community. These individual ISPP experiences demonstrate the complexity and ongoing negotiations of identity within Indigenous communities and by Mormon Indian children when forced to exist within these strict settler colonial constructs of indigeneity. Both Mormon and non-Mormon Indian people resisted the efforts made by the LDS Church to assimilate Indigenous people. Because the LDS Church condemned the cultural traditions of Indian people, Indian people resisted missionary efforts as a result of racist Mormon settler missionaries to convert Indian peoples to Mormonism.

EXTERNAL CRITICISM OF THE MORMON SETTLER COLONIAL PROJECT

The American Indian Movement (AIM) criticized the LDS Church's ISPP because of the detrimental impact on Indigenous children, people, and communities. AIM skillfully used mainstream media to draw attention to its campaign and in a letter to tribal councils in Utah called for a gathering at the biannual General Conference, held in April and October for members of the LDS Church, to listen to modern revelations and speeches from LDS Church authorities. AIM gathered at Temple Square on April 4–7, 1974. Utah AIM was strategic in its call for action. Its very presence confronted and was juxtaposed against Mormon settler colonial structures, in particular the center of LDS Church spiritual and political power: Temple Square. Utah AIM focused on issues around the ISPP and considered the program to be a "Cultural Genecidal [sic]" program.[99] American Indian children were removed at an early age to be educated; however, "the maine [sic] scope is to indoctrinate the Indian children in the teachings of their religion. As a result, we find that in many cases, the young child, upon completion of the program, the child [can] function in neither the Indian nor White societies."[100] American Indian children who had participated in the ISPP lost their language, culture, and traditions. AIM recognized the impact of the ISPP on the individual and, as noted in chapter 3, recognized how the ISPP and other tactics used by the LDS Church pitted "Indian against Indian." ISPP was a divisive program and negatively impacted Indigenous children and communities.

AIM acknowledged the larger number of Indigenous members of the LDS Church and said that these individuals and others have "turned to alcoholism because of the cultural genocide." AIM used the average lifespan of American Indians, including those living in Salt Lake City, to validate its argument regarding individuals living in settler spaces versus living on reservations. Ignoring gender, American Indians residing off-reservation, said by AIM then to live only 38.7 to 44 years on average compared to those living on-reservation.[101] All American Indians, on- or off-reservation, lived almost thirty years less than the average American in 1974. Life expectancy is representative of systemic issues contributing to the loss of American Indian life. AIM utilized the LDS Church's religious ideologies of Lamanites and racial uplift to "better help the Indian people" by reallocating funds and changing current programs. First and foremost, all "Indian Programs" should go through a process so that Indigenous people could give input on how these programs could better serve the people. Second, even though AIM wanted missionaries to be taken off reservations, it proposed that non-Indigenous missionaries should have a "working knowledge of the culture, traditions, religions, and languages of the people they would be working in." Third, AIM wanted to establish an advisory board for the LDS Church leadership, which would include changing hiring practices for Indigenous members in leadership positions. AIM also requested that the LDS Church allocate "$1,000,000 for the use of Indian non-denominational Indian self-help programs" and establish a nondenominational board to be chaired by an American Indian. Finally, AIM wanted the LDS Church to fund investigations of treaties made between the LDS Church and American Indians and "honor all treaties that has been negotiated with the church by Indian people." The LDS Church did not immediately respond and instead took AIM's request to church leadership.

Several months later, AIM accompanied a medicine man on July 7, 1974, to request the return of "two skulls of our ancestors" displayed in "the L.D.S. museum and information center." When the LDS Church did not respond, AIM encouraged tribal councils to adopt a resolution to reevaluate the relationship between tribal communities and the LDS Church due to ongoing cultural genocide and lack of support for Indigenous sovereignty. For more than two years AIM sought to work with the LDS Church, which did little to address issues facing tribal communities like "poverty, alcoholism, school dropout, unemployment, land and water losses to realize these programs are not effective" because "these policies of the church tend only to perpetuate Mormon superiority and keep the Indian peoples divided and dependent on Mormon colonialism."[102] In addition to addressing issues facing tribal communities, AIM also "wanted to discuss with the church the foolishness of expecting Indian peoples to blindly follow the Mormon way when it means we must deny our Indian souls while waiting for Mormon rewards after we are dead." AIM believed that American Indian people have "spent over a hundred years listening to their reason and yet they tell us to be reasonable while they dictate the terms that Indian peoples must exist in when they live on the lands now controlled by the Mormons. We feel that Indian people have been more than reasonable and in return we have been repaid with the white exploitive philosophy of the church. We want it known that we will no longer wait for their revalations [sic]."[103] In this letter, AIM confronted the LDS Church and was pointed in its criticisms despite over a hundred years of Mormon settler colonial efforts to save Indigenous peoples from themselves. AIM pushed back and (re)centered Indigenous spirituality and sovereignty as it appealed to the LDS Church to stop its destructive practices.

The ISPP and the homes of Mormon settler foster families were Mormon settler colonial structures designed to operationalize and embed Mormon settler ideologies about Indigenous peoples. The ISPP as a foster and educational program for Indigenous children has been largely excluded from US, Mormon, and Indigenous histories in the twentieth century. Mormon Indigenous children who had participated in the ISPP did so at great cost. Even as some individuals thrived in their Mormon settler foster families or embraced the Lamanite subject position, they did so within these Mormon settler colonial structures based on religious ideologies that marked Indigenous peoples as the Other. The LDS Church sought to remake Indigenous peoples into Lamanites, yet they would never become part of the Mormon settler colonial center or the Mormon subject position. Golden Buchanan, director of the ISPP, recognized the inherent contradictions in Mormon-Indian policies, including the ISPP. Buchanan acknowledged that it would be nearly impossible for Indigenous children to completely let go of their cultural traditions and beliefs. "We couldn't expect these people to completely drop all their customs and all of their sense of values and take over the white man's ways. I think any time we expect the Indians to do that we're being unfair to them, because again I say that they have much good in their culture."[104] Yet there was not much good in Indigenous culture when Mormon Indian children were being removed from their families and communities. Even in the language Buchanan used to talk about the good of Indigenous peoples he used the phrase "these people," highlighting how Indigenous peoples remained the racialized Other not only in his rhetoric but also in the design and purpose of the ISPP. The ISPP targeted Indigenous children as a means to civilize and racially uplift an entire people. Yet the civilization of Indigenous children would not happen, because Indigenous peoples would be relegated to their Lamanite status. Indigenous children could never become fully Mormon because they could never become white enough.

Mormon Indian children were taken from their homes and transported to various communities primarily throughout Utah to be fostered by predominantly Mormon settler foster families. The ISPP required that all participants be members of the LDS Church, increasing the number of Indigenous members. These Mormon settler foster homes became intimate sites of assimilation couched as religious benevolence. Many Mormon settler foster families had been invested in the ISPP not for the greater good of Indigenous children but instead because their good works would lead to the salvation of Lamanite children and ultimately their own eternal salvation. The push to fulfill these religious ideologies regarding Indigenous peoples as Lamanites would lead to the subjugation of Indigenous children. Many Indigenous children existed in between their Mormon and Indigenous identities, never being seen as fully Mormon or Indigenous. In order to fully understand the impact of Mormon settler colonialism on Indigenous identity, the narrative around ISPP children must be included to demonstrate that their contestations over identity occurred within a very racialized space as they sought to navigate the complicated constructions and expectations of indigeneity in their families and communities and in Mormon settler colonial structures. Some students were able to negotiate and exist within these structures, while others could not and never really felt as though they belonged in either space. The ISPP foster children reveal the complexity of indigeneity and the multiple ways Indigenous children chose to construct and make sense of their identity as Mormon and Indigenous. Finally, the ISPP was not just about the extension and application of Mormon settler colonialism but was also about how these structures advanced US settler colonialism that continued to push for the assimilation of Indigenous peoples and nations into mainstream American society. The structure of the ISPP forced Indigenous children to negotiate and exist within Mormon settler colonial constructs of indigeneity. The literature on the ISPP focuses on the Mormon Indian children who could exist within these Mormon settler colonial structures, further perpetuating the invisibility of the Mormon settler colonial project. These subject positions had been imposed onto Indigenous children, which is why it is disingenuous at best to argue that Mormon Indian children could exist as Lamanites. The production of the Lamanite subject position and the operationalization of the ISPP as a structure of Mormon settler colonialism had a detrimental impact on Indigenous children and communities as children were removed from their communities. Although the ISPP ended in 2000, when the last student graduated, the Mormon settler colonial project will never end. The LDS Church continues to cast Indigenous peoples as the Other, Lamanites, to secure their status and belonging as Mormon settlers.

CONCLUSION

MORMON SETTLER COLONIALISM'S ENDPOINT: ENDURING MORMON SETTLER AND LAMANITE DISCOURSE IN MORMON INFRASTRUCTURES

On March 12, 2021, the Church of Jesus Christ of Latter-day Saints (LDS Church) announced plans to renovate the historic "pioneer era" Salt Lake City Temple and the Manti Utah Temple. Desiring to increase accessibility, standardize ritual practices, and modernize temple structures, the LDS Church removed many of the historical and architectural elements, an ode to the pioneer subject position and narratives, considered significant to the cultural fabric of the church and its members. The Manti Utah Temple murals painted by Minerva Teichert, a renowned Mormon painter, were removed during the renovation and would not be reinstalled, causing public outcry. Much like the dissent following the Brigham Young statue's deface-ment at Brigham Young University, the removal of Teichert's murals was also met with opposing perspectives. Many advocated preserving Teichert's work for its historical and cultural value to the LDS Church and its members. Teichert was, after all, the first woman commissioned by the LDS Church to produce murals for an LDS temple. Historian Patrick Q. Mason states, "These are priceless cultural artifacts that can never be replaced if destroyed. The murals in the Manti Utah Temple by Minerva Teichert, one of the few prominent female LDS artists of the 20th century, are particularly stunning, even if some of the artistic elements no longer conform to current cultural sensibilities."[1]

Teichert's Manti Utah Temple murals filter history related to the American continent through a Mormon settler lens. Teichert's *The Pageantry of History,* which adorned the Manti Utah Temple's World Room, is especially significant, as the four-wall mural, measuring four thousand square feet, concludes on the front wall with Mormon settlers arriving in the Salt Lake Valley to establish a Mormon empire. Teichert's murals became an essential part of the Manti Utah Temple history, the Mormon settler subject position, and the history of the LDS Church. The murals depict widely held views of Mormon settlers' place in the region and the world. Teichert captures a Mormon settler perspective of the American continent, where Indigenous peoples exist on the periphery even when they are the literal center of the mural, dominating space in the front of the room, because Indigenous peoples exist to sanction Mormon settler presence. Ultimately Mormon settler desires prevailed, despite knowing that racist depictions of Indigenous peoples do not align with modern "cultural sensibilities," because the quest to preserve Teichert's artistic contributions as a Mormon female painter sustained Mormon settler narratives regarding a Mormon settler subject position. The refusal to remove Mormon settler art legitimizes the harmful representation of Indigenous peoples, an act of Indigenous dispossession as Indigenous peoples disappear from the narrative and the land. Mormon settler presence became naturalized at the expense of Indigenous peoples and others who pushed back against Mormon settler representation of Indigenous peoples. The LDS Church acquiesced to the demands made by those who wanted to preserve Teichert's murals. The church then began "seeking the advice of international experts in the field of art preservation during this process" to assuage those demanding for the preservation of these murals.[2] The LDS Church hoped to preserve, restore, and publicly display the murals in the future.

The public commotion over the removal of Teichert's murals in the Manti Utah Temple has further shown how many Mormon settlers, including direct descendants, are invested in Mormon settler structures that enforce and reify Mormon settler colonial structures and systems. Ultimately, Mormon settler desires became the dominating voice, and the LDS Church made efforts to preserve this mythical settler past that forces Mormon settler narratives and processes onto Indigenous peoples and the general public. The Mormon settler desire was to preserve these necessary murals to mark spaces and histories as distinctly Mormon and settler. Teichert's murals depict and reinforce a mythical Mormon settler past, or pioneer past, in which Indigenous peoples existed only in relation to Mormon settlers. Mormon settlers, including Teichert, used their religious ideologies about Mormon Zion, or empire, to shape how Mormon and non-Mormon settlers viewed the world.

Another portion of the mural, *The Pageantry of History,* begins with the Tower of Babel in Babylon and concludes with the Mormon Zion on the American continent. Teichert includes a depiction of Christopher Columbus, a fulfillment of Nephi's prophecy as found in the Book of Mormon in which Nephi has a vision regarding the discovery and colonization of the American continent. Nephi writes, "I beheld the Spirit of God, that it came down and wrought upon the man; and he went forth upon the many waters, even unto the seed of my [Nephi's] brethren, who were in the promised land."[3] He does not name Christopher Columbus specifically, yet Columbus's arrival into the New World fulfilled Nephi's prophecy and signals the possibility of a Mormon Zion. Within the larger mural, Teichert's "Indian Brave as the symbol of the American Continent" compares Columbus with other settlers, including Pilgrims who appear on the various walls within the room.[4] The "Indian Brave" appears at the front of the room, centered between two curtained entrances, a focal point for visitors. Teichert's "Indian Brave" is depicted barefoot and wearing an eagle feather headdress and two braids, and his arms are outstretched as if welcoming settlers to this space, or land. The depiction of a Mormon Zion is the mural's pinnacle, as it "stands as a bright beacon of hope and a symbol of eternal life. There the king of kings will reign in righteousness. There love will abound. There the repentant may rest from their labors."[5] In the artistic and physical form, Mormon Zion is the realization of the Mormon settler empire through dispossession and the disappearance of Indigenous peoples. Indigenous peoples exist as figments of settler imagination. Teichert's "Indian Brave" embodied and engendered stereotypes of Indigenous men and, by extension, Indigenous peoples as stoic, uncivilized, and innocent. Teichert's art, including the inclusion of Indigenous peoples, demonstrates a move toward settler innocence. The mural became part of the (re)making of a Mormon settler narrative in which Indigenous peoples exist only to usher in Mormon Zion. In the process, Mormon settler belonging is secured. This Mormon move to settler innocence demonstrates how Mormon settler colonialism functions in art and within Mormon settler infrastructures as Lamanites remain the Other.

The Manti Utah Temple and other temples such as the Nauvoo and Kirtland Temples became Mormon settler structures that claim and mark land as Mormon settler land. The "pioneer temples" in Utah also contributed to the making of a Mormon empire in the American West. The structures themselves became Mormon settler markers, claiming land for exclusive Mormon use. Only worthy members of the LDS Church can enter into these spaces. The temple became the source of Mormon settler colonial power, a physical representation of the power held by the LDS Church and its members to (re)make the land to serve their purposes. The religious power of temples further sanctions and sustains Mormon settler presence, and Indigenous peoples can be present only when they are in service to and sustain the center of Mormon empire. The Manti Utah Temple and the Salt Lake City Temple and murals are symbolic of Mormon settler power, and in the modern era, Mormon settlers and those who buy into this subject position entrench themselves in Mormon settler infrastructures, especially when their presence is challenged. Modern Mormon settlers, like other settlers, fear their dispossession, and the push to have Teichert's murals removed represents their symbolic demise and access to land and challenges their narrative about their belonging and presence.

THE LAMANITE IN MORMON SETTLER RELIGIOUS DISCOURSE

These stereotypes and images of Indigenous peoples as Lamanites persist because the LDS Church continues to produce Mormon settler religious discourse that reinforces and perpetuates the racialization of Indigenous peoples. Given the narratives about the Lamanite subject position and history and Lamanites as the racial and spiritual Other, the LDS Church continues to define and give meaning to Lamanite histories in religious discourse. In 2020, the LDS Church published and globally distributed the Sunday school manual *Come Follow Me.* The manual is the text for a yearlong curriculum introduced by the LDS Church using the Book of Mormon and is meant to instruct individuals and members on how to teach doctrine in the home. The print manual has a brief note to explain the Lamanite "curse": "The dark skin was placed upon the Lamanites so that they could be distinguished from the Nephites and to keep the two peoples from mixing. . . . The dark skin was the sign of the curse. The curse was the withdrawal of the Spirit of the Lord. . . . Dark skin . . . is no longer to be considered a sign of the curse."[6] Despite revisions made in 1984 to the Book of Mormon that changed the racialized language describing Lamanites as "white and delightsome" to "pure and delightsome," the 2020 *Come, Follow Me* manual for individuals and families includes the problematic trope about Indigenous peoples as a cursed people even though "dark skin" no longer signals their cursed status. The manual's reference to these historical teachings continues to shape and sustain racialized Lamanite discourse in the LDS Church. While the LDS Church may not have active Lamanite programs, as long as the term "Lamanite" exists in religious texts, Mormon settler colonialism will persist.

The continual reference and inclusion of these racist religious ideologies about Lamanites in LDS Church curriculum will endure for another generation, since the LDS Church distributed the 2020 manual to over sixteen million LDS members.[7]

An LDS Church spokesperson, Irene Caso, acknowledged that "there was an error that resulted in printing material that doesn't reflect the church's current views on the topic. To correct this, the LDS church modified the online manual." The modified online content begins with a brief reference that the "curse of the Lamanites was that they were 'cut off from [the Lord's] presence . . . because of their iniquity,'" meaning that Lamanites did not have the "Spirit of the Lord" until they "embraced the gospel of Jesus Christ."[8] There was an acknowledgment that Lamanites had been marked with dark skin to distinguish them from Nephites, but the mark became "irrelevant as an indicator of the Lamanites' standing before God," and "in our day that dark skin is not a sign of divine disfavor or cursing." Yet both versions reference the Lamanite curse and connect the mark or curse with racialized status and indigeneity even if that is not the current metric used to categorize Lamanites. The change to the online version does little to change the narrative about Lamanites as a cursed people because in 2020 physical copies of the manual had been provided to and were utilized by millions of members of the faith. Caso declined to comment on any action by the LDS Church to change the circulated printed manual that was most accessible and available to its members. By keeping this physical text, the LDS Church demonstrates that disrupting racist ideologies about Lamanites does not serve its best interests. These ideologies about Lamanites serve the structures of Mormon settler colonialism and maintain a racialized hierarchy within the church. According to Jerri Harwell, an associate professor in English at Salt Lake Community College, maintains that refusal to reprint the revised *Come, Follow Me* manual "will essentially reset the clock and allow another generation to perpetuate such racist beliefs."[9] The LDS Church has disavowed theories that equate unrighteousness with one's race, yet the globally published religious manual contains racialized discourse that is specifically harmful to Indigenous peoples who are *still* categorized as Lamanites by Mormons.

Refusal to (re)write and (re)right racist rhetoric sustains Mormon settler colonialism in the modern era. Simultaneously, the LDS Church erases racial differences by citing the 2018 speech by current LDS Church president Russell M. Nelson at the Worldwide Priesthood Celebration. In the speech, Nelson stated that Jesus's doctrine, or LDS Church gospel, is the "doctrine of equal opportunity for His children. . . . Differences in culture, language, gender, race, and nationality face into insignificance as the faithful enter the covenant path and come unto our beloved Redeemer."[10] Flattening and dismissing diversities of race, culture, and gender as "differences" also erases the lived experiences of those whose subject positions are rooted in these categories. The color-blind rhetoric utilized by Nelson is "new racism," defined by Eduardo Bonilla-Silva as "practices [that] have emerged that are more sophisticated and subtle than those typical of the Jim Crow Era[;] . . . these practices are as effective as the old ones in maintaining the racial status quo."[11] The LDS Church's Official Declaration 2 stated that "all worthy male members of the Church may be ordained to the priesthood without regard for race or color," which appeared in a letter to church member on June 8, 1978, a response to the expansion of global missionary work. Yet not much has changed structurally within the LDS Church. The highest positions of leadership remains primarily white despite most of the LDS Church's membership living outside the United States. Only 6 percent of the LDS Church's global membership is Black.[12] One group of Mormon Black college students at Brigham Young University, the Black Menaces, have turned to the social media platform TikTok to hold their peers and institution responsible for creating a more inclusive environment and raising awareness of the burdens that Mormon Black students carry in educating their peers.

Despite the 2021 "Report and Recommendations of the BYU Committee on Race, Equity, and Belonging," no structural changes have been made to make the campus more inclusive and welcoming to Black students, who make up less than 1 percent of the student population. In the meantime, the Black Menaces continue to ask their peers about "race, identity, and politics."[13] Deseret Book, a for-profit business owned by the LDS Church, published in 2023 W. Paul Reeve's *Let's Talk About Race and the Priesthood*, which discusses the origins of the priesthood ban and "race relations both within and outside of the Church, the effects of implementing and eventually removing the policy, and other questions surrounding this sensitive topic."[14] The desire to better understand the priesthood ban and the subsequent impact on the experiences of Mormon Blacks is contrary to Nelson's claims that racial differences do not matter. Race matters, especially when structures maintain the oppression of marginalized peoples.

Racism persists in the structure that perpetuates racial inequality, especially since those decision-making positions do not reflect the diversity and experiences of their membership. The center of Mormon settler colonial power emanates from Salt Lake City, Utah, outwardly to the world. As a very American religious institution, the LDS Church must remake settler colonial structures that maintain the othering of marginalized peoples, including Indigenous peoples. Nelson's move toward a color-blind religious rhetoric, or Jesus-centered doctrine, further erases those whose very existence is at odds with Mormon, or white, settler subject position and discourse. In the United States, people of color simply cannot check their identity even if they choose to do so because racism exists "as a structure, that is, as a network of social relations at social, political, economic, and ideological levels that shapes the life chances of the various races."[15] This subtle change in rhetoric about race and racism as a structure is important in understanding if these racial structures have undergone transformative change. Unfortunately, racial structures is driven by "new racism" that continues to maintain racial inequalities, including racialized discourse and practices. The LDS Church continues to maintain a religious, historical narrative that deliberately marks people of color, including Indigenous peoples, as the Other despite attempts to flatten race within the LDS Church.

The Mormon settler colonial presence persists as Mormon settlers continue to live on stolen lands and reify Mormon settler structures that erase Indigenous peoples from their lands, history, and identity. My intention is to name and make visible Mormon settler colonialism and demonstrate its effectiveness in defining and naming Indigenous peoples as Lamanites using religious settler texts such as the Book of Mormon and the Doctrine and Covenants. In this book I make visible Mormon settler colonialism in various manifestations and the intimate ways Mormon settler structures have invaded and erased the lives of Indigenous peoples. Despite Mormon settler policies that sought Indigenous possession, whether physical, cultural, or spiritual via LDS conversion and acceptance of the Lamanite subject position, Indigenous peoples have remained. Indigenous peoples must define their identity and history on their own terms without settler colonial interference. Indigenous peoples have the power to define the future of our nations, and this does not require a subject position and a history that mark them as the Other on their lands. Indigenous origin stories give meaning to who we are as a people and our connection to land, one another, and the world around us. The Lamanite subject position and history does not exist in this context. Indigenous peoples will always be Indigenous, even outside of the Mormon settler colonial context.

Mormon settler colonialism, in all its expressions, has been rendered invisible, naturalized, and marked as *the* normative. Yet the impacts on the material lives of Indigenous peoples are real. Indigenous children have been negatively impacted by the Mormon settler belief that Lamanites must be saved via conversion and acceptance of the Book of Mormon as Indigenous history and identity. Indigenous children have been harmed by being labeled and treated as Lamanite. In 2016, four Navajo citizens filed a lawsuit against the LDS Church in the Window Rock District Court regarding abuse they experienced as children when they participated in the Indian Student Placement Program (ISPP). Since then several others have also filed their own lawsuits, including a Crow woman in Washington state.[16] The abuse happened in the homes of Mormon settler foster families, and the LDS Church did not protect Indigenous children. While the LDS Church has refused to comment on these lawsuits, apologetics have articulated that the abuse was done in the homes of LDS settler members outside the purview of the LDS Church. However, the LDS Church was responsible for the ISPP and removed children from their homes in hopes of saving them. Instead, Indigenous children had been exposed to abuse. The ISPP was part of national policies of Indian child removal and foster care used to assimilate Indigenous children. Yet the LDS Church has largely escaped critique because the ISPP was a private religious foster care system.

The only difference between the ISPP and state foster care systems is that the LDS Church relied on its members to fund the program. Portrayed as the fulfillment of religious doctrine, many Mormon settler families fostered Indigenous children. Those Indigenous children have been irreparably harmed and continue to be harmed by the silence of Mormon settler foster families and the LDS Church. One Navajo man recalls how he has spent his adulthood avoiding the abuse he experienced as a seventh grader. "It's horrible. You relive it. You see the person who did this. You see their silhouette. . . . It broke me. When a Native American is broken, he has to fix himself."[17] This individual only came forward after reading about the abuse and lawsuits of two Navajo siblings who had participated in the ISPP. Their lawyer, Craig Vernon, filed the lawsuits in Navajo Nation tribal court as an exercise of tribal sovereignty over its citizens. These Navajo children are tribal citizens, and Vernon has argued that the LDS Church failed to protect them and others. In the lawsuit, the victims are seeking an apology and compensation from the LDS Church.

The LDS Church has denied that the Navajo Nation tribal court has jurisdiction because the abuse occurred off-reservation. A US district court judge, Robert J. Shelby, ruled against the LDS Church's petition to move the lawsuit to Utah federal courts because the church failed to meet the "substantial burden of showing that tribal court jurisdiction is clearly foreclosed."[18] Shelby's decision reaffirmed and secured the sovereign tie between child and Tribal Nations. While several victims and the LDS Church chose to settle out of tribal court in 2018, their cases highlight the ongoing trauma and harm caused by the LDS Church against Indigenous children. The ISPP harmed Indigenous children, especially those who have experienced spiritual, cultural, and physical violence under the guise of religious redemption and for simply being Lamanite. Young Indigenous children have been forever changed by their experience in the ISPP and as members of the LDS Church. The backbone and purpose of the ISPP was to assimilate Indigenous peoples under the guise of educational opportunities. Indigenous children in the ISPP represent the spectrum of Indigenous identity and experiences of Mormon Indigenous members today. The Manti Utah Temple murals, the LDS Church 2020 handbook, and current lawsuits demonstrate contestations over being Lamanite. There is no endpoint to Mormon settler colonialism as long as Mormon settler infrastructures continue to demarcate space, narrative, and land as Mormon. The persistence of Lamanite in Mormon discourse, even on the margins, and the technologies of Mormon settler colonialism will continue to exist, and Indigenous peoples will always remain Lamanite. Only when these Mormon settler infrastructures have been dismantled can Indigenous peoples exist on their own terms, a contradiction to the Mormon settler colonial project.

I acknowledge the diverse range of indigeneity, particularly as it intersects with Mormons' religious subject position, Lamanite, especially those who remain active and practicing members of the LDS Church. This book is not meant to diminish or erase their experiences as faithful members who have made Mormon settler space their own, but there must also be room for the voices and experiences of those who do not readily accept, reject, or have a complicated relationship with their Mormon and Lamanite subject positions. There must also be space for those who make visible and reject Mormon settler colonial structures. Indigenous peoples in the margins challenge the history and presence of Mormon settler colonialism. It is for those individuals who continue to occupy and still live in the periphery of Mormon settler society and narrative that I write this book.

NOTES

INTRODUCTION

1. "Brigham Young Statue Vandalized at BYU Campus," *Deseret News*, June 19, https://www
.deseret.com/utah/2020/6/19/21297184/brigham-young-statue-vandalized-byu-campus.

2. Peggy Fletcher Stack, "Descendants of Slaveholder Smoot Argue Renaming BYU
Building 'Accomplishes Nothing' in Addressing Racism," *Salt Lake Tribune*, September 2,
2020, https://www.sltrib.com/religion/2020/09/02/descendants-slaveholder/.

3. "Committee Formed to Examine Race and Inequality at BYU," Brigham Young University, June 17, 2020, https://news.byu.edu/announcements/committee-formed-to-examine
-race-and-inequality-at-byu.

4. Aubrey Eyre, "Native American Professor Joins BYU Committee Examining Race,
Inequality," *Deseret News*, https://www.deseret.com/utah/2020/7/11/21321231/byu-native
-american-professor-joins-byu-committee-examining-race-and-inequality; and Farina King,
"BYU's Committee on Race and Inequality Needs a Native American Representative," petition to Brigham Young University, BYU president Keven J. Worthen, and Academic Vice
President C. Shane Reese, https://www.change.org/p/c-shane-reese-byu-s-committee-on
-race-and-inequality-needs-a-native-american-representative.

5. "Report and Recommendations of the BYU Committee on Race, Equity, and Belonging, Report," Brigham Young University, February 2021, https://brightspotcdn.byu.edu/12
/58/d61b3164487da5946d13471e7567/byu-race-equity-belonging-report-feb21.pdf.

6. Aileen Moreton-Robinson, *The White Possessive: Property, Power, and Indigenous Sovereignty* (Minneapolis: University of Minnesota Press, 2015), xiii.

7. 2 Nephi 5:20–23.

8. Linda Tuhiwai Smith, *Decolonizing Methodologies: Research and Indigenous Peoples*,
2nd ed. (London: Zed Books, 2012), 22.

9. Patrick Wolfe, "Settler Colonialism and the Elimination of the Native," *Journal of
Genocide Research* 8, no 4. (2006), 388.

10. Smith, *Decolonizing Methodologies*, 24.

11. Maile Arvin, *Possessing Polynesians: The Science of Settler Colonial Whiteness in Hawai'i
and Oceania* (Durham, NC: Duke University Press, 2019), 15.

12. Arvin, *Possessing Polynesians*, 16.

13. Arvin, 3.

14. Arvin, 3.

15. K. Mohrman, *Exceptionally Queer: Mormon Peculiarity and U.S. Nationalism* (Minneapolis: University of Minnesota, 2022), 15.

16. Aileen Moreton-Robinson, *The White Possessive: Property, Power, and Indigenous Sovereignty* (Minneapolis: University of Minnesota Press, 2015), xi.

17. Moreton-Robinson, *The White Possessive*, xi–xii.

18. Moreton-Robinson, xii.

19. Moreton-Robinson, xx.

20. Erika Marie Bsumek, *The Foundations of Glen Canyon Dam: Infrastructures of Dispossession on the Colorado Plateau* (Austin: University of Texas Tech, 2023), 5.

21. Cynthia Prescott, *Pioneer Mother Monuments: Constructing Cultural Memory* (Norman: University of Oklahoma Press, 2019), 14.

22. Tracey Banivanua Mar, "Settler-Colonial Landscapes and Narratives of Possession," *Arena Journal* no. 37–38 (January 2012): 176.

23. Lorenzo Veracini, *Settler Colonialism: A Theoretical Overview* (New York: Palgrave Macmillan, 2010), 75.

24. Mar, "Settler-Colonial Landscapes," 180.

25. "Joanna Brooks on Past LDS Leaders' Racist Views and How White Supremacy Took Root," Episode 134, *Mormon Land*, June 17, 2020, https://soundcloud.com/mormonland /joanna-brooks-on-past-lds-leaders-racist-views-and-how-white-supremacy-took-root -episode-134.

26. "Joanna Brooks on Past LDS Leaders' Racist Views."

27. "Joanna Brooks on Past LDS Leaders' Racist Views."

28. "Priesthood," The Church of Jesus Christ of Latter-day Saints, https://www .churchofjesuschrist.org/study/manual/gospel-topics/priesthood?lang=eng.

29. "Official Declaration 2," The Church of Jesus Christ of Latter-day Saints, https://www .churchofjesuschrist.org/study/scriptures/dc-testament/od/2?lang=eng.

30. 2 Nephi 26:33.

31. See W. Paul Reeve, *Let's Talk about Race and Priesthood* (Salt Lake City: Deseret Book, 2023); Quincy D. Newell, *Your Sister in the Gospel: The Life of Jane Manning James, a Nineteenth Century Black* Mormon (Oxford: Oxford University Press, 2019); Matthew L. Harris and Newell G. Bringhurst, eds., *The Mormon Church and Blacks: A Documentary History* (Champaign: University of Illinois Press, 2015); and Newell G. Bringhurst, *Saints, Slaves, & Blacks: A Changing Place of Black People within Mormonism* (Sandy, UT: Greg Kofford Books, 2018).

32. See Elise Boxer, "The Book of Mormon as Mormon Settler Colonialism," in *Essays on American Indian and Mormon History*, ed. P. Jane Hafen and Brenden W. Rensink, 3–22 (Salt Lake City: University of Utah Press, 2019); and Elise Boxer, "'This Is the Place!': Disrupting Mormon Settler Colonialism," in *Decolonizing Mormonism: Approaching a Postcolonial Zion*, ed. Gina Colvin and Joanna Brooks, 77–99 (Salt Lake City: University of Utah Press, 2018).

33. Veracini, *Settler Colonialism*, 18.

34. Veracini, 19.

35. Elizabeth Strakosch and Alissa Macoun, "The Vanishing Endpoint of Settler Colonialism," *Arena Journal*, nos. 37–28 (January 2012): 41.

36. Veracini, *Settler Colonialism*, 20.

37. W. Paul Reeve, *Religion of a Different Color: Race and the Mormon Struggle for Whiteness* (New York: Oxford University Press, 2015), 54.

38. William W. Phelps, "Free People of Color," *Evening and Morning Star*, vol. 2, no. 14 (July 1833): 218–19, https://contentdm.lib.byu.edu/digital/collection/NCMP1820-1846/id/5850/.

39. Veracini, *Settler Colonialism*, 3.

40. Matthew Garrett, *Making Lamanites: Mormons, Native Americans, and the Indian Student Placement Program, 1947–2000* (Salt Lake City: University of Utah Press, 2016), 8.

41. Garrett, *Making Lamanites* 8.

42. Veracini, *Settler Colonialism*, 16.

43. Veracini, 4.

44. Andrew Denson, *Monuments to Absence: Cherokee Removal and the Contests over Southern Memory* (Chapel Hill: University of North Carolina Press, 2017), 12.

45. Veracini, *Settler Colonialism*, 15.

46. For a more in-depth description of this interaction, see Boxer, "This Is the Place!"

47. Lisa Ford, *Settler Sovereignty: Jurisdiction and Indigenous People in America and Australia, 1788–1836* (Cambridge, MA: Harvard University Press, 2010), 3.

48. Ford, *Settler Sovereignty*, 13.

CHAPTER 1

1. Tom Lynch, *Outback and Out West: The Settler-Colonial Environmental Imaginary* (Lincoln: University of Nebraska Press, 2022), 25.

2. Doctrine and Covenants, 20:1.

3. Book of Mormon, "Introduction."

4. Book of Mormon, "Brief Explanation about the Book of Mormon."

5. Richard Lyman Bushman and Dean C. Jessee, "Joseph Smith and His Papers: An Introduction," The Joseph Smith Papers, https://www.josephsmithpapers.org/articles/joseph-smith-and-his-papers-an-introduction.

6. Richard Lyman Bushman, *Joseph Smith: Rough Stone Rolling; A Cultural Biography of Mormonism's Founder* (New York: Knopf, 2005), 23.

7. Bushman and Jessee, "Joseph Smith and His Papers."

8. Bushman, *Joseph Smith*, 26.

9. Bushman, 25.

10. *The Pearl of Great Price: A Selection from the Revelations, Translations, and Narrations of Joseph Smith, First Prophet, Seer, and Revelator to the Church of Jesus Christ of Latter-day Saints* (Salt Lake City: Church of Jesus Christ of Latter-day Saints, 1979), 49.

11. The Church of Jesus Christ of Latter-day Saints, *The Truth Restored: A Short History of the Church of Jesus Christ of Latter-day Saints* (Salt Lake City: Church of Jesus Christ of Latter-day Saints, 2001), 8.

12. The Hill Cumorah where Joseph Smith located the Book of Mormon was so named after his communications with the Angel Moroni. Hill Cumorah is a specific reference in the Book of Mormon where the last battle between the two great civilizations, Lamanites and Nephites, took place. Lamanites killed all the Nephites, but the prophet Moroni (later

known as the Angel Moroni) who appeared and talked to Joseph Smith finished writing about the destruction of the Nephite people, and the most sacred portion of these "plates" were hidden by Moroni's father, Mormon, in the Hill Cumorah. Hence, this reference to "Hill Cumorah" comes specifically from the Book of Mormon. See The Church of Jesus Christ of Latter-day Saints, "Moroni Hides the Plates in the Hill Cumorah," http://www .lds.org/ldsorg/v/index.jsp?vgnextoid=637e1b08f338c010VgnVCM1000004d82620aRC RD&locale=0&sourceId=c61df48fa2d20110VgnVCM100000176f620a____&hideNav=1.

13. Book of Mormon, 1 Nephi 1:1–3.

14. Book of Mormon, 1 Nephi 1:9–11.

15. Book of Mormon, 1 Nephi 1: 13.

16. Doctrine and Covenants, 57:1–2.

17. Book of Mormon, 1 Nephi 2:2.

18. Book of Mormon, 1 Nephi 2:20.

19. Book of Mormon, 1 Nephi 9:4.

20. Book of Mormon, 2 Nephi 5:6.

21. Book of Mormon, 2 Nephi 5:20–23 (emphasis added).

22. Book of Mormon, Enos 11:20.

23. Vern Swanson, "The Book of Mormon Art of Arnold Friberg, Painter of Scripture," *Journal of Book of Mormon Studies* 10, no. 1 (2001): 29; and Trent Toone, "Insight into Arnold Friberg's Book of Mormon Paintings," *Deseret News*, March 21, 2012, https://www.deseret .com/2012/5/21/20502627/insight-into-arnold-friberg-s-book-of-mormon-paintings.

24. Book of Mormon, 2 Nephi 30:6 (pre-1981 editions).

25. Book of Mormon, "Three Witnesses."

26. Andrew H. Hedges, Andrew, Alex D. Smith, and Richard Lloyd Anderson, eds., *Joseph Smith Papers: Journals*, Vol. 2, *December 1841–April 1843*, (Salt Lake City: Church Historian's Press, 2011), 349.

27. Hedges et al., *Joseph Smith Papers: Journals*, 2:354.

28. Doctrine and Covenants, 28:8.

29. "Covenant of Oliver Cowdery and Others," October 17, 1830, The Joseph Smith Papers, https://www.josephsmithpapers.org/paper-summary/covenant-of-oliver-cowdery -and-others-17-october-1830/1.

30. Joseph Smith, *History of the Church of Jesus Christ of Latter-day Saints: Period I, History of Joseph Smith, the Prophet, by Himself*, Vol. I, introduction and notes by B. H. Roberts (Salt Lake City: Deseret Book, 1948), 118.

31. Joseph Smith, *History of the Church of Jesus Christ of Latter-day Saints: Period I, History of Joseph Smith, the Prophet, by Himself*, Vol. 2, introduction and notes by B. H. Roberts (Salt Lake City: Deseret Book, 1948), 358.

32. Leland Gentry, "Light on the 'Mission to the Lamanites,'" *BYU Studies Quarterly* 36, no. 2, article 13 (1996): 228.

33. Smith, *History of the Church of Jesus Christ of Latter-day Saints*, 1:183–84.

34. Smith, 1:185.

35. Warren A. Jennings, "The First Mormon Mission to the Lamanites," *Kansas Historical Quarterly* 37 (Autumn 1971): 295.

36. Smith, *History of the Church of Jesus Christ of Latter-day Saints*, 1:185.

37. Doctrine and Covenants, 21:1.

38. Doctrine and Covenants, 38:31–32.

39. Doctrine and Covenants, title page and introduction.

40. Doctrine and Covenants, title page and introduction.

41. "Lectures on Theology (Lectures on Faith)," The Church of Jesus Christ of Latter-day Saints," https://www.churchofjesuschrist.org/study/history/topics/lectures-on-faith?lang=eng.

42. Doctrine and Covenants, 3:20.

43. Doctrine and Covenants, 3:18–20.

44. Book of Mormon, Mosiah 9:12, Mormon 5:15, and 1 Nephi 12:23.

45. Book of Mormon, Alma 24:18.

46. *Conference Reports of the Church of Jesus Christ of Latter-day Saints; 1920–1929,* October 1926), Church History Library, https://catalog.churchofjesuschrist.org/assets/90127c74–5f98–44cc-b15b-0c7444de4ac8/0/39, 40.

47. Book of Mormon, Introduction.

48. Book of Mormon, Introduction (emphasis added).

49. Carrie A. Moore, "Debate Renewed with Change in Book of Mormon Introduction," *Deseret News*, November 8, 2007.

CHAPTER 2

The epigraph is from Matthew J. Grow et al., *The Joseph Smith Papers: Administrative Records, Council of Fifty, Minutes*, Vol. 1, *March 1844–January 1846* (Salt Lake City: Church Historian's Press, 2016), 68.

1. Eve Tuck and Wayne Yang, "Decolonization Is Not a Metaphor," *Decolonization: Indigeneity, Education & Society* 1, no. 1 (2012): 9–10.

2. Doctrine and Covenants, 105:9–10.

3. *Our Heritage: A Brief History of the Church of Jesus Christ of Latter-day Saints* (Salt Lake City: Church of Jesus Christ of Latter-day Saints, 1996), 51.

4. Richard Lyman Bushman, *Joseph Smith: Rough Stone Rolling; A Cultural Biography of Mormonism's Founder* (New York: Knopf, 2005), 382.

5. Bushman, *Joseph Smith*, 382.

6. Bushman, 383.

7. Bushman, 384.

8. For additional information about the Wisconsin Territory pineries, see Dennis Rowley, "The Mormon Experience in the Wisconsin Pineries, 1841–1845," *BYU Studies Quarterly* 32, no. 1 (1992): 121.

9. Grow et al., *The Joseph Smith Papers: Administrative Records, Council of Fifty, Minutes,* 1:128.

10. For additional information about the Missouri Mormon War and the extermination order, see "The Missouri Mormon War," Missouri State Archives, https://www.sos.mo.gov/archives/resources/mormon.asp.

11. Grow et al., *The Joseph Smith Papers: Administrative Records, Council of Fifty, Minutes*, 1:xxv.

12. Grow et al., 1:xxvi.

13. Grow et al., 1:xxiii.

14. Grow et al., 1:96.

15. Grow et al., 1:44.

16. Grow et al., 1:xxxii.

17. Grow et al., 1:xxi.

18. Grow et al., 1:xxv.

19. Grow et al., 1:116.

20. Council Minutes, March 21, 1844, in Grow et al., *The Joseph Smith Papers: Administrative Records, Council of Fifty, Minutes,* 1:57.

21. Grow et al., *The Joseph Smith Papers: Administrative Records, Council of Fifty, Minutes,* 1:xlv.

22. Bushman, *Joseph Smith,* 514.

23. Bushman, *Joseph Smith,* 514–15.

24. Grow et al., *The Joseph Smith Papers: Administrative Records, Council of Fifty, Minutes,* 1:xxi.

25. "Treaty with the Sioux, etc. 1825," Amazon Web Services, https://govtrackus.s3 .amazonaws.com/legislink/pdf/stat/7/STATUTE-7-Pg272.pdf.

26. Rowley, "The Mormon Experience in the Wisconsin Pineries," 121.

27. Francis Paul Prucha, *The Great Father: The United States Government and the American Indians,* Vol. 1 (Lincoln: University of Nebraska Press, 1984), 245.

28. Prucha, *The Great Father,* 1:252.

29. Prucha, *The Great Father,* 1:254.

30. Prucha, *The Great Father,* 1:257.

31. Grow et al., *The Joseph Smith Papers: Administrative Records, Council of Fifty, Minutes,* 1:32.

32. Grow et al., 1:25.

33. Grow et al., 1:18.

34. Grow et al., 1:21.

35. Grow et al., 1:25.

36. For comprehensive discussion on Indigenous sovereignty and the US settler state, see Walter R. Echo-Hawk, *In the Courts of the Conqueror: The 10 Worst Indian Law Cases Ever Decided* (Golden, CO: Fulcrum, 2010); Vine Deloria Jr. and Clifford M. Lytle, *American Indians, American Justice* (Austin: University of Texas Press, 1983); and Prucha, *The Great Father: The United States Government and the American Indians,* 2 vols. (Lincoln: University of Nebraska Press), 1984.

37. "To Repeal Section 2141 of the Revised Statutes to Remove the Prohibition on Certain Alcohol Manufacturing on Indian Lands," Report 115-703, 15th Congress, 2nd session, May 24, 2018, https://www.congress.gov/115/crpt/hrpt703/CRPT-115hrpt703.pdf.

38. Grow et al., *The Joseph Smith Papers: Administrative Records, Council of Fifty, Minutes,* 1:25.

39. Grow et al., 1:25.

40. Grow et al., 1:27.

41. Grow et al., 1:25.

42. Grow et al., 1:27.

43. Grow et al., 1:32.

44. Grow et al., 1:34.

45. Grow et al., 1:27–28.

46. Grow et al., 1:29.

47. Grow et al., 1:73–74.

48. Grow et al., 1:75.

49. Grow et al., 1:73.

50. Grow et al., 1:76.

51. Andrew H. Hedges, Alex D. Smith, and Brent M. Rogers, eds., *The Joseph Smith Papers: Journals*, Vol. 3, *May 1843–June 1844* (Salt Lake City: Church Historian's Press, 2015), 198.

52. Grow et al., *The Joseph Smith Papers: Administrative Records, Council of Fifty, Minutes*, 1:40.

53. Grow et al., 1:29.

54. Grow et al., 1:30–31.

55. Grow et al., 1:34.

56. Grow et al., 1:29.

57. Hedges, *Journals* 3:204.

58. Grow et al., *The Joseph Smith Papers: Administrative Records, Council of Fifty, Minutes*, 1:69.

59. Grow et al., 1:55.

60. Grow et al., 1:67 (brackets appear in the author's quote).

61. Grow et al., 1:137.

62. Grow et al., 1:143.

63. Grow et al., 1:151.

64. Grow et al., 1:156.

65. Grow et al., 1:178.

66. Grow et al., 1:181.

67. Grow et al., 1:326.

68. Grow et al., 1:328.

69. Grow et al., 1:329.

70. Grow et al., 1:328.

71. Grow et al., 1:350.

72. Grow et al., 1:323.

73. Lorenzo Veracini, *Settler Colonialism: A Theoretical Overview* (New York: Palgrave Macmillan, 2010), 8.

74. Veracini, *Settler Colonialism*, 14.

75. Grow et al., *The Joseph Smith Papers: Administrative Records, Council of Fifty, Minutes*, 1:110.

76. Grow et al., 1:395.

CHAPTER 3

1. Sean P. Means, "How Is Utah Celebrating Pioneer Day? With Parades, Fireworks and Music—and, For Some, Pie and Beer," *Salt Lake Tribune*, July 18, 2019. https://www.sltrib .com/artsliving/2019/07/18/how-is-utah-celebrating/.

2. "Fewer Mormons Live in Utah's Biggest County, New Figures Show," *The Spectrum*, December 15, 2018, https://www.thespectrum.com/story/news/2018/12/15/mormons-utah -fewer-lds-church-members-live-salt-lake-county/2323877002/.

3. Joanne Barker, *Native Acts: Law, Recognition, and Cultural Authenticity* (Durham, NC: Duke University Press, 2011), 5.

4. Tom Lynch, *Outback and Out West: The Settler-Colonial Environmental Imaginary* (Lincoln: University of Nebraska Press, 2022), 25.

5. Eve Tuck and Wayne Yang, "Decolonization Is Not a Metaphor," *Decolonization: Indigeneity, Education & Society* 1, no. 1 (2012): 5.

6. Tuck and Yang, "Decolonization Is Not a Metaphor," 6.

7. Lisa Blee and Jean M. O'Brien, *Monumental Mobility: The Memory Work of Massasoit* (Durham, NC: University of North Carolina Press), 202.

8. Lynch, *Outback and Out West*, 24.

9. Adria L. Imada, "Aloha 'O': Settler-Colonial Nostalgia and the Genealogy of a Love Song," *American Indian Culture and Research Journal* 37, no. 2 (2013): 36.

10. Jared Farmer, *On Zion's Mount: Mormons, Indians, and the American Landscape* (Cambridge, MA: Harvard University Press, 2008).

11. Doctrine and Covenants, 136:1.

12. Pioneer Monument State Park, Utah State Park and Recreation Commission, This Is the Place Monument, West Side Inscription, page 2, Series 23449, box 1, folder 15, This Is the Place Heritage Park Records, Division of Parks and Recreation, Department of Natural Resources, Utah Division of Archives and Record Service, Salt Lake City, Utah.

13. Pioneer Monument State Park, Utah State Park and Recreation Commission, "This Is the Place" Monument, West Side Inscription, Series 23449, box 7, folder 18, item 10.

14. "Wilford Woodruff Journal 1847 January–December 1853," MS1352, Church History Library, Salt Lake City, Utah, https://catalog.churchofjesuschrist.org/assets/a5c827b5-938d -4a08-b80e-71570704e323/0/83?lang=eng, July 24, 1847.

15. "Wilford Woodruff Journal 1847 January–December 1853."

16. Pioneer Monument State Park, Utah State Park and Recreation Commission, "This Is the Place" Monument, West Side Inscription, page 2, Series 23449, box 1, folder 15.

17. Mark Rifkin, *Settler Common Sense* (Minneapolis: University of Minnesota Press, 2014), xvi.

18. "Foundations of Faith: Treasures from the Historical Collections of The Church of Jesus Christ of Latter-day Saints," The Church of Jesus Christ of Latter-day Saints," https://history.churchofjesuschrist.org/landing/library/foundations-of-faith?lang=eng.

19. *Laws of the State of Utah, Passed at the Special and First Regular Sessions of the Legislature of the State of Utah, Passed by Congress and the State Constitution, Adopted by Convention May 8, 1895, Salt Lake City, the State Capital, in January, February, March, and April 1896;*

Also the Enabling Act, Passed by Congress and the State Constitution, Adopted by Convention May 8, 1895, and Ratified by the People at the General Election, November 5, 1895, Published by Authority (Salt Lake City: Deseret News Publishing, 1896).

20. Harold H. Jenson, "Utah's First 24th Celebration," *The Improvement Era* 45, no. 7 (July 1942): 435, https://archive.org/details/improvementera4507unse/mode/2up.

21. Laurel Thatcher Ulrich, *A House Full of Females: Plural Marriage and Women's Rights in Early Mormonism, 1835–1870* (New York: Knopf, 2017), 206.

22. Jenson, "Utah's First 24th Celebration," 435.

23. D. W. Meinig, "The Mormon Nation," *Journal of Mormon History* 22, no. 1 (1996): 41.

24. W. Paul Reeve, *Religion of a Different Color: Race and the Mormon Struggle for Whiteness* (New York: Oxford University Press, 2017), 80.

25. Joseph Fielding Smith, *Essentials in Church History* (Salt Lake City: Desert News Press, 1922), 411.

26. "The Historic Trek," The Church of Jesus Christ of Latter-day Saints, http://www.lds.org/newsroom/page/0,15606,3899–1—-2–314,00htm#.

27. Henry A. Smith, "Achievements of Mormon Pioneers Now Recorded in Enduring Granite and Bronze" *Deseret News* July 19, 1947.

28. Thomas P. Brown, "'This Is the Place' Monument," *The Headlight*, November 1945, 5.

29. Welcome to Pioneer Monument State Park, Series 23449, box 2, folder 8, This Is the Place Heritage Park Records, Division of Parks and Recreation, Department of Natural Resources, Utah Division of Archives and Record Service, Salt Lake City, Utah.

30. Wayne K. Hinton, "Mahroni Young and the Church: A View of Mormonism and Art," *Dialogue* 7, no. 4 (Winter 1972): 40.

31. Cynthia Prescott, *Pioneer Mother Monuments: Constructing Cultural Memory* (Norman: University of Oklahoma Press, 2019), 155.

32. Welcome to Pioneer Monument State Park, Series 23449, box 2, folder 8.

33. Welcome to Pioneer Monument State Park, Series 23449, box 7, folder 6, item 4.

34. Cynthia Prescott, *Pioneer Monument Mothers*, 156.

35. Prescott, 157.

36. Chief Washakie, This Is the Place Monument, inscription on Chief Washakie statue.

37. Patrick Wolfe, "Settler Colonialism and the Elimination of the Native," *Journal of Genocide Research* 8, no 4. (2006), 388.

38. Welcome to Pioneer Monument State Park, Series 23449, box 2, folder 8.

39. Tuck and Yang, "Decolonization Is Not a Metaphor," 6.

40. "Native American Village", This Is the Place Heritage Park https://www.thisistheplace.org/todays-fun/native-american-village, accessed August 5, 2008.

41. Ned Blackhawk, *Violence over the Land: Indians and Empires in the American West* (Cambridge, MA: Harvard University Press, 2008); and Brigham D. Madsen, *The Shoshoni Frontier and the Bear River Massacre* (Salt Lake City: University of Utah Press, 1985).

42. "Preliminary Master Development Plan," February 1971, Series 23449, box 7, folder 2, item 9, This Is the Place Heritage Park Records, Division of Parks and Recreation, Department of Natural Resources, Utah Division of Archives and Record Service, Salt Lake City, Utah.

43. "Preliminary Master Development Plan," item 7.

44. "Pres. Smith Realizes Dream at Dedication," *Deseret News,* July 24, 1947, 1.

45. "Pres. Smith Realizes Dream at Dedication," 1.

46. "Scenes, Sidelights as Utah's Centennial Reaches Climax." *Salt Lake Tribune,* July 25, 1947.

47. John H. Harrington, "Heap Big Injun Cometh," *Salt Lake Tribune,* March 9, 1947.

48. Eric A. Eliason, "The Cultural Dynamics of Historical Self-Fashioning: Mormon Pioneer Nostalgia, American Culture, and the International Church," *Journal of Mormon History* 28, no. 2 (Fall 2002): 152.

49. "Miscellaneous Items Deposited in Copper Box of 'This Is The Place' Monument," June 6, 1947, Series 23449, box 7, folder 6, item 2, This Is the Place Heritage Park Records, Division of Parks and Recreation, Department of Natural Resources, Utah Division of Archives and Record Service, Salt Lake City, Utah.

50. "Preliminary Master Development Plan."

51. "Mormon Pioneer: National Historical Trail, Illinois, Iowa, Nebraska, Wyoming, Utah; Draft Comprehensive Plan and Environmental Assessment, June 1981," Series 23449, box 7, folder 18, item 3, This Is the Place Heritage Park Records, Division of Parks and Recreation, Department of Natural Resources, Utah Division of Archives and Record Service, Salt Lake City, Utah.

52. "Mormon Pioneer," item 10.

53. "Preliminary Master Development Plan," item 6.

54. "Pioneer Trail State Park," Letter by Vincent P. Foley to Advisory Council member on May 19, 1976, Series 23449, box 11, folder 6, This Is the Place Heritage Park Records, Division of Parks and Recreation, Department of Natural Resources, Utah Division of Archives and Record Service, Salt Lake City, Utah.

55. "Interim Report," Pioneer Trail Advisory Council, Vincent P. Foley, superintendent, Pioneer Trail Development Project, March 21, 1975, Series 23449, box 10, folder 1, item 6, This Is the Place Heritage Park Records, Division of Parks and Recreation, Department of Natural Resources, Utah Division of Archives and Record Service, Salt Lake City, Utah.

56. "Project Proposal," Pioneer Trail State Park, Division of Parks and Recreation, Utah Department of Natural Resources, April 15, 1969, Series 23449, box 8, folder 3, item 1, This Is the Place Heritage Park Records, Division of Parks and Recreation, Department of Natural Resources, Utah Division of Archives and Record Service, Salt Lake City, Utah.

57. "Project Proposal," items 2 and 3.

58. "Interim Report," item 10.

59. "Interim Report," item 11.

60. "Interim Report," item 12.

61. "Interim Report," item 11.

62. "Interim Report," item 12.

63. "Interim Report," item 10.

64. "Interim Report," item 11.

65. Letter to Elizabeth Griffith, Utah American Revolution Bicentennial Commission, from Vincent P. Foley, December 11, 1975, Series 23449, box 8, folder 1, item 2, This

Is the Place Heritage Park Records, Division of Parks and Recreation, Department of Natural Resources, Utah Division of Archives and Record Service, Salt Lake City, Utah.

66. Letter from James D. Moyle to Mr. LaCee Harris, March 31, 1976, Series 23449, box 11, folder 6, This Is the Place Heritage Park Records, Division of Parks and Recreation, Department of Natural Resources, Utah Division of Archives and Record Service, Salt Lake City, Utah.

67. "Interim Report," item 11.

68. "At Dedication: Dignitaries Laud Indian Activity Amphitheater," *Salt Lake Tribune* July 30, 1976, 24.

69. "This Is the Place Heritage Park," Utah Agenda, https://utahagenda.com/this-is -the-place-heritage-park/.

70. "Native American Village," This Is the Place Heritage Park, https://www.thisistheplace .org/todays-fun/native-american-village.

71. "A Declaration to the Mormon Church, Spencer W. Kimball," Series 23449, box 11, folder 6, item 1, Division of Parks and Recreation, Department of Natural Resources. Utah Division of Archives and Record Service, Salt Lake City, Utah

72. "An Open Letter to the Tribal Councils and the Mormon Church," From the Office of the National Chairman American Indian Movement, Series 23449, box 11, folder 6, p. 3, Division of Parks and Recreation, Department of Natural Resources, Utah Division of Archives and Record Service, Salt Lake City, Utah.

CHAPTER 4

1. For information regarding the history of the ISPP, see Robert S. McPherson, *Navajo Tradition, Mormon Life: The Autobiography and Teachings of Jim Dandy* (Salt Lake City: University of Utah, 2012); Matthew R. Garrett, "Mormons, Indians and Lamanites: The Indian Student Placement Program, 1947–2000 (PhD diss., Arizona State University, 2010); Lynette Riggs, "The Church of Jesus Christ of Latter-day Saints' Indian Student Placement Service: A History" (PhD diss., Utah State University, 2008); Clarence R. Bishop, "Indian Placement: A History of the Indian Student Placement Program of the Church of Jesus Christ of Latter-day Saints" (Master's thesis, University of Utah, 1967); Kay H. Cox, *Without Reservation* (Salt Lake City: Bookcraft, 1964); George P. Lee, *Silent Courage: An Indian Story* (Salt Lake City: Deseret Book, 1987); Dale L. Shumway and Margene Shumway, eds., *The Blossoming: Dramatic Accounts of the Lives of Native Americans in the Foster Care Program of the Church of Jesus Christ of Latter-day Saints* (Orem, UT: Granite, 2002); Dale L. Shumway and Margene Shumway, eds., *The Blossoming II: Dramatic Accounts of the Lives of Native Americans in the Foster Care Program of the Church of Jesus Christ of Latter-day Saints* (Orem, UT: Granite, 2007); James B. Allen, "The Rise and Decline of the LDS Indian Student Placement Program, 1947–1996," in *Mormons, Scripture, and the Ancient World: Studies in Honor of John L. Sorenson,* ed. Davis Bitton, 85–119 (Provo, UT: Foundation for Ancient Mormon Research, 1998); Tona J. Hangen, "A Place Called Home: Studying the Indian Placement Program," *Dialogue: A Journal of Mormon Though* 16, no. 1 (1983): 62–88; Brandon Morgan, "Educating the Lamanites: A Brief History of the LDS Indian Student Placement Program," *Journal of Mormon History* vol. 35, no. 4 (Fall 2009): 191–217; Martin D. Topper,

"Mormon Placement: The Effects of Missionary Foster Families on Navajo Adolescents," *Ethos* 7, no. 2 (Summer 1979): 142–60; John Birch, "Helen John: The Beginnings of Indian Placement," *Dialogue: A Journal of Mormon Thought* 18, no. 4 (1977): 119–19; and Bruce A. Chadwick, Stan L. Albrecht, and Howard M. Bahr, "Evaluation of an Indian Student Placement Program," *Social Casework* 17, no. 9 (November 1986): 515–24.

2. David Wallace Adams, *Education for Extinction: American Indians and the Boarding School Experience, 1875–1928* (Lawrence: University of Kansas Press, 1995); John Bloom, *To Show What an Indian Can Do: Sports at Native American Boarding Schools* (Minneapolis: University of Minnesota Press, 2000); Clifford Trafzer and Jean A. Keller, eds., *Boarding School Blues: Revisiting American Indian Educational Experiences* (Lincoln: University of Nebraska Press, 2006); K. Tsianina Lomawaima and Teresa L. McCarty, *"To Remain an Indian": Lessons in Democracy from a Century of Native American Education* (New York: Teachers College Press, 2006); Amelia V. Katanski, *Learning to Write "Indian": The Boarding-School Experience and American Indian Literature* (Norman: University of Oklahoma Press, 2005); Jon Allen Reyhner and Jeanne Eder, *American Indian Education: A History* (Norman: University of Oklahoma Press, 2004); Brenda J. Child, *Boarding School Seasons: American Indian Families, 1900–1940* (Lincoln: University of Nebraska Press, 1998); and K. Tsianina Lomawaima, *They Called It Prairie Light: The Story of Chilocco Indian School* (Lincoln: University of Nebraska Press, 1994).

3. Book of Mormon, 1980. For a brief explanation regarding the change in language from "white and delightsome" to "pure and delightsome," see "Changes to the Book of Mormon," The Church of Jesus Christ of Latter-day Saints, https://www.churchofjesuschrist.org/study /history/topics/changes-to-the-book-of-mormon?lang=eng.

4. Patrick Wolfe, "Settler Colonialism and the Elimination of the Native," *Journal of Genocide Research* 8, no. 4 (December 2006), 388.

5. "'Kill the Indian in Him, and Save the Man': R. H. Pratt on the Education of Native Americans," Carlisle Indian School Digital Resource Center, https://carlisleindian.dickinson .edu/teach/kill-indian-him-and-save-man-r-h-pratt-education-native-americans.

6. Adams, *Education for Extinction*, 12–13.

7. Boarding schools as institutions of assimilation rooted in Christianity have a long history and can be dated back to as early as the 1600s when John Eliot, a Puritan missionary, created "praying towns" in Massachusetts. "Praying towns" separated Indian people from their communities so they could be fully Christianized while also segregating them from settler communities. Indian converts lived in "praying towns," physically separated from their tribal communities, so they could be moved away from any negative influences that could potentially prevent their successful and complete conversion to Christianity.

8. Lomawaima and McCarty, *"To Remain an Indian,"* 4.

9. For the purpose of this chapter, I employ either Indian or American Indian to reflect the LDS Church's terminology used to describe the ISPP and its participants. I utilize the term "Indigenous" in my own analysis to acknowledge the diversity of tribal nations. James Riding In and Susan A. Miller state in *Native Historians Write Back: Decolonizing American Indian History* (Lubbock: Texas Tech University Press, 2011) that the term "Indigenous does not refer to *original* occupation of an area (although that is

a popular sense of the word), but to a set of principles that . . . Indigenous peoples live [by] in [their] communities" (1).

10. Helen Rose John Hall, October 10, 1978, MS 51201, transcript, 2, Archives, The Church of Jesus Christ of Latter-day Saints Library, Salt Lake City, Utah.

11. Bishop, "Indian Placement," 31.

12. Hall transcript, 2.

13. Thomas Quentin Cannon, interview by Loretta L. Hefner, 28 March 1979, OH 498, Typescript, 11, The James Moyle Oral History Program. Archives, Historical Department of the Church of Jesus Christ Latter-day Saints, Salt Lake City, Utah, 5.

14. Jon Stewart and Peter Wiley, "Cultural Genocide," *Penthouse*, June 1981, 84.

15. Golden R. Buchanan, Dictation, Vol. 2, 5, The James Moyle Oral History Program, Archives, Historical Department of the Church of Jesus Christ of Latter-day Saints, Salt Lake City, Utah; and Thelma S. Buchanan, interview by William Hartley, October 12, 1976, OH 670, Typescript, Interview Vol. 2, 5, The James Moyle Oral History Program, Archives, Historical Department of the Church of Jesus Christ of Latter-day Saints Library, Salt Lake City, Utah.

16. Buchanan interview, 5.

17. Ned Blackhawk, *Violence Over the Land: Indians and Empires in the Early American West* (Cambridge: Harvard University Press, 2008), 5.

18. For the most recent monograph that illustrates this point, see Todd M. Compton, *A Frontier Life: Jacob Hamblin, Explorer and Indian Missionary* (Salt Lake City: University of Utah Press, 2013). Discussion of this subject can also be found in Jared Farmer, *On Zion's Mount, On Zion's Mount: Mormons, Indians and the American Landscape* (Cambridge, MA: Harvard University Press, 2008); Armand L. Mauss, *All Abraham's Children: Changing Mormon Conceptions of Race and Lineage* (Urbana: University of Illinois Press, 2003); and John Barnes, "Memory, Commemoration, and the Bear River Massacre of 1863" (Master's thesis, Utah State University, 2004).

19. Book of Mormon, Enos 1:20.

20. For information regarding Mormon settlers who had displaced local Indians, Utes, from their traditional homeland, Utah Lake, see Jared Farmer, *On Zion's Mount: Mormons, Indians and the American Landscape* (Cambridge, MA: Harvard University Press, 2008) Blackhawk, *Violence Over the Land*, is also useful for examining the complex relationships between Indians in the American West and the shifting relationships between the various groups that ultimately had an impact on Indigenous peoples and lands.

21. Bishop, "Indian Placement," 33.

22. Buchanan dictation, Vol. 2, 4.

23. Buchanan, 13.

24. Buchanan, 12.

25. Buchanan, 4.

26. Miles Jensen, May 18, 1983, OH 665, interview by Gordon Irving, Historical Department, Church of Jesus Christ of Latter-day Saints, Salt Lake City, Utah.

27. Bishop, "Indian Placement," 42.

28. Bishop, 44.

29. Bishop, 46.

30. Bishop, 47.

31. Bishop, 48. See also Cannon oral history.

32. Indian Student Placement Service Reunion Program 2000, MS 16468, Archives, The Church of Jesus Christ of Latter-day Saints. Salt Lake City, Utah.

33. Church of Jesus Christ of Latter-day Saints, "Miscellaneous Missionary Lessons for Teaching the Navaho," Americana Collection, L. Tom Perry Special Collections, Harold B. Lee Library, Brigham Young University, Provo, Utah.

34. "Foster Parent Guide," L.D.S. Indian Student Placement Program, The Church of Jesus Christ of Latter-day Saints, 1965, Americana Collection–Quarto, L. Tom Perry Special Collections, Harold B. Lee Library, Brigham Young University, Provo, Utah.

35. Riggs, "The Church of Jesus Christ of Latter-day Saints' Indian Student Placement Service," 85.

36. Church of Jesus Christ of Latter-day Saints, "Miscellaneous Missionary Lessons for Teaching the Navaho," Americana Collection, L. Tom Perry Special Collections, Harold B. Lee Library, Brigham Young University, Provo, Utah.

37. Jensen oral history, 2.

38. "Treaty with the Navaho, 1868," in *Indian Affairs: Laws and Treaties*, Vol. 2, compiled and edited by Charles J. Kappler, (Washington, DC: US Government Printing Office, 1904), https://dc.library.okstate.edu/digital/collection/kapplers/id/29605.

39. Donald Mose Jr., interview by Jim M. Dandy, November 6, 1990, in Monument Valley, Utah, transcript, 2, MSS OH 1165, LDS Native American Oral History Project, Charles Redd Center for Western Studies, L. Tom Perry Special Collections, Harold B. Lee Library, Brigham Young University, Provo, Utah.

40. Julius Ray Chavez, interview by Odessa Neaman, June 27, 1990, in Provo, Utah, transcript, 7, MSS OH 1180, LDS Native American Oral History Project, Charles Redd Center for Western Studies, L. Tom Perry Special Collections, Harold B. Lee Library, Brigham Young University, Provo, Utah.

41. Chavez, oral history, 9.

42. Jensen oral history, 2.

43. Jackie Webster Hainsworth, interview by Rebecca Vorimo, June 14, 1994, transcript, 7, MSS OH 1667, LDS Missionary Oral History Project, Charles Redd Center for Western Studies, L. Tom Perry Special Collections, Harold B. Lee Library, Brigham Young University, Provo, Utah.

44. "The Placement Program: How Interested Families Can Help," *Ensign* (August 1972): 78.

45. Matthew West, interview by Jeff Anderson, October 20, 1998, Archives, LDS Church's Historical Department, Salt Lake City, Utah.

46. Ray R. Mitchell, interview by Matthew K. Heiss, April 28, 1992, 2, OH 1536, The James Moyle Oral History Program, Archives, Historical Department of the Church of Jesus Christ of Latter-day Saints Archives, Salt Lake City, Utah.

47. Cannon oral history.

48. Buchanan dictation, Vol. 2, 14.

49. Margaret D. Jacobs, *White Mother to a Dark Race: Settler Colonialism, Maternalism, and the Removal of Indigenous Children in the American West and Australia, 1880–1940* (Lincoln: University of Nebraska, 2009), 4.

50. Jacobs, *White Mother to a Dark Race*, 4.

51. "Foster Parent Guide."

52. K. Tsianina Lomawaima, "The Unnatural History of American Indian Education," in *Next Steps: Research and Practice to Advance Indian Education* (Charleston, WV: Eric Clearinghouse on Rural), 17.

53. "Indian Placement: The Three Most Common Questions," *Ensign* 6, no.7 (July 1976): 35.

54. Lomawaima and McCarty, *"To Remain an Indian,"* xxii.

55. Tonia Halona, 2, interview by Jim M. Dandy, April 10, 1991, MS OH 1446, 2, The LDS Native American Oral History Project, Charles Redd Center for Western Studies, L. Tom Perry Special Collections, Harold B. Lee Library. Brigham Young University, Provo, Utah.

56. Halona oral history, 3.

57. Margaret D. Jacobs, *A Generation Removed: The Fostering & Adoption of Indigenous Children in the Postwar World* (Lincoln: University of Nebraska Press, 2014), 87.

58. For additional information on the impact on children and communities, see Jacob, *A Generation Removed*; and Lisa M. Poupart, "The Familiar Face of Genocide: Internalized Oppression among American Indians," *Indigenous Women in the Americas* 18, no. 2 (Spring 2003): 86–100.

59. Wallace, *Education for Extinction*, 175.

60. Virginia Morris Tso Tulley, interview by Matthew K. Heiss, April 25, 1997, in Window Rock, AZ, typescript, The James Moyle Oral History Program, Archives, Historical Department of the Church of Jesus Christ of Latter-day Saints Library, Salt Lake City, Utah.

61. Mitchell oral history, 2.

62. Chavez oral history, 10.

63. Emery Bowman, interview by Deborah Lewis, January 27, 1990, Provo, Utah, transcript, 14, MSS OH 1152, LDS Native American Oral History Project, Charles Redd Center for Western Studies, L. Tom Perry Special Collections, Harold B. Lee Library, Brigham Young University, Provo, Utah.

64. Tracy Neal Leavelle, *The Catholic Calumet: Colonial Conversions in French and Indian North America* (Baltimore: University of Pennsylvania Press, 2014), 115.

65. Bishop, "Indian Placement," 11.

66. "Foster Parent Guide."

67. Riggs, "The Church of Jesus Christ of Latter-day Saints' Indian Student Placement Service," 107, 113.

68. Derald Wing Sue et al., "Racial Microaggressions and Difficult Dialogues on Race in the Classroom," *Cultural Diversity and Ethnic Minority Psychology* 15, no. 2 (2009): 183.

69. Rhonda J. Lee, interview by Jim M. Dandy, April 10, 1991, in Provo, Utah, typescript, 8, MSS OH 1197, LDS Native American Oral History Project, Charles Redd Center for Western Studies, L. Tom Perry Special Collections, Harold B. Lee Library, Brigham Young University, Provo, Utah.

70. Sue et al., "Racial Microaggressions and Difficult Dialogues on Race in the Classroom," 183.

71. Chavez oral history, 11.

72. Myrtle Hatch, interview by Ernesteen B. Lynch, August 23, 1989. in Kirkland, New Mexico, transcript, 9, MSS OH 1143, LDS Native American Oral History Project, Charles Redd Center for Western Studies, L. Tom Perry Special Collections, Harold B. Lee Library, Brigham Young University, Provo, Utah.

73. For information on Indigenous women and stereotypes, see Rayna Green, "The Pocahontas Perpex: The Image of Indian Women in American Culture," in *Native American Voices: A Reader*, ed. Susan Lobo, Steve Talbot, and Traci L. Morris, 159–65 (Boston: Prentice Hall, 2010).

74. Ken Sekaquatewa, interview by Odessa Neaman, June 11, 1990, Provo, Utah, transcript, 9, MSS OH 1184, LDS Native American Oral History Project, Charles Redd Center for Western Studies, L. Tom Perry Special Collections, Harold B. Lee Library, Brigham Young University, Provo, Utah.

75. Stephanie Chiquito, interview by Jim M. Dandy, April 11, 1991, in Provo, Utah, transcript, 8, MSS OH 1994, LDS Native American Oral History Project, Charles Redd Center for Western Studies, L. Tom Perry Special Collections, Harold B. Lee Library, Brigham Young University, Provo, Utah. Chiquito also discussions problems on reservations, such as alcoholism.

76. Lemuel Pedro, interview by Malcolm T. Pappan, April 1, 1990, MS OH 1146, 7, The LDS Native American Oral History Project, Charles Redd Center for Western Studies. L. Tom Perry Special Collections, Harold B. Lee Library, Brigham Young University, Provo, Utah.

77. P. Jane Hafen, "The Being and Place of a Native American Mormon," in *New Genesis: A Mormon Reader on Land and Community*, ed. Terry Tempest Williams, William B. Smart, and Gibbs M. Smith, (Salt Lake City: Gibbs Smith, 1998), 39–40.

78. Walter D. Atene, interview by Jim M. Dandy, November 3, 1990. MS OH 1186, 5, The LDS Native American Oral History Project, Charles Redd Center for Western Studies, L. Tom Perry Special Collections, Harold B. Lee Library. Brigham Young University, Provo, Utah.

79. Ken Sekaquaptewa, interview by Odessa Neaman, June 11, 1990, MS OH 1184, 12–13, The LDS Native American Oral History Project, Charles Redd Center for Western Studies, L. Tom Perry Special Collections, Harold B. Lee Library, Brigham Young University, Provo, Utah.

80. Robert S. McPherson, *Navajo Tradition, Mormon Life: The Autobiography and Teachings of Jim Dandy* (Salt Lake City: University of Utah, 2012); and George P. Lee, *Silent Courage: An Indian Story* (Salt Lake City: Deseret Book, 1987.

81. Ernesteen B. Lynch, interview by Jessie Embry, May 17, 1990, MS OH 1488, 29, The LDS Native American Oral History Project, Charles Redd Center for Western Studies, L. Tom Perry Special Collections, Harold B. Lee Library, Brigham Young University, Provo, Utah.

82. Aneta Whaley, interview by Jim M. Dandy, November 15, 1990. in Monument Valley, Utah, transcript, 2, MSS OH 1164, LDS Native American Oral History Project, Charles

Redd Center for Western Studies, L. Tom Perry Special Collections, Harold B. Lee Library, Brigham Young University, Provo, Utah.

83. Bowman interview, 14.

84. Carl R. Moore Sr., interview by Angela Moore Fields, April 24, 1990, in Provo, Utah, transcript, 32, MSS OH 1157, LDS Native American Oral History Project, Charles Redd Center for Western Studies, L. Tom Perry Special Collections, Harold B. Lee Library, Brigham Young University, Provo, Utah.

85. Lewis J. Singer, interview by Jim M. Dandy, October 23, 1990, in Blanding, Utah, transcript, 4, MSS OH 1185, LDS Native American Oral History Project, Charles Redd Center for Western Studies, L. Tom Perry Special Collections, Harold B. Lee Library, Brigham Young University, Provo, Utah.

86. Carl R. Moore, interview by Jim A. Dandy, MS OH 1164, The LDS Native American Oral History Project, Charles Redd Center for Western Studies, L. Tom Perry Special Collections, Harold B. Lee Library, Brigham Young University, Provo, Utah.

87. Chavez oral history, 19.

88. Adams, *Education for Extinction*, 8, 12.

89. Audrey Boone, interview by Malcolm T. Pappan, April 6, 1990, MS OH 1164, 15, The LDS Native American Oral History Project, Charles Redd Center for Western Studies, L. Tom Perry Special Collections, Harold B. Lee Library. Brigham Young University, Provo, Utah.

90. Joseph R. Harlan, interview by Malcolm T. Pappan, August 12, 1990, in Macy, Nebraska, transcript, 12, MSS OH 1181, LDS Native American Oral History Project, Charles Redd Center for Western Studies, L. Tom Perry Special Collections, Harold B. Lee Library, Brigham Young University, Provo, Utah.

91. Jimmy N. Benally, interview by Odessa Neaman, July 18, 1990 in Provo, Utah, transcript, 9, MSS OH 1176, LDS Native American Oral History Project, Charles Redd Center for Western Studies, L. Tom Perry Special Collections, Harold B. Lee Library, Brigham Young University, Provo, Utah.

92. Benally interview, 18.

93. Halona oral history, 4.

94. Gabriel Holyan Cinniginnie, interview by Malcolm T. Pappan, April 9, 1990, in Provo, Utah, transcript, 13, MSS OH 1171, LDS Native American Oral History Project, Charles Redd Center for Western Studies, L. Tom Perry Special Collections, Harold B. Lee Library, Brigham Young University, Provo, Utah.

95. Chavez oral history, 22.

96. Stewart and Wiley, "Cultural Genocide," 84.

97. James Lee Dandy, interview by Jesse Embry, October 2, 1990, MS OH 985, 9, The LDS Native American Oral History Project, Charles Redd Center for Western Studies, L. Tom Perry Special Collections, Harold B. Lee Library. Brigham Young University, Provo, Utah.

98. Antoinette Dee, interview by Jim M. Dandy, November 15, 1990, in Monument Valley, Utah, transcript, 4, MSS OH 985, LDS Native American Oral History Project, Charles Redd Center for Western Studies, L. Tom Perry Special Collections, Harold B. Lee Library, Brigham Young University, Provo, Utah.

99. Utah AIM, Letter to Tribal Council, Series 23449, box 11, folder 6, page 1, Division of Parks and Recreation, Department of Natural Resources. Utah Division of Archives and Record Service, Salt Lake City, Utah.

100. Utah AIM, Letter to Tribal Council, 2.

101. Utah AIM, 2.

102. John Trudell, "An Open Letter to the Tribal Councils and the Mormon Church. From the Office of the National Chairman American Indian Movement," Series 23449, box 11, folder 6, page 1, Division of Parks and Recreation, Department of Natural Resources, Utah Division of Archives and Record Service, Salt Lake City, Utah.

103. Trudell, "An Open Letter to the Tribal Councils and the Mormon Church," page 2.

104. Buchanan dictation, Vol. 2, 14.

CONCLUSION

1. Peggy Fletcher Stack, "In a Loss for Preservation, LDS Church Removes Historic Murals from Salt Lake Temple," *Salt Lake Tribune*, March 12, 2021, https://www.sltrib.com/religion/2021/03/12/lds-church-removes/?fbclid=IwAR1sN4elrcKj9UdDCPBIrCafzCMGfzGo_ouNvBK-YmUx7Y92DnhfKooyPAg.

2. "A First Presidency Update on Historic Temple Renovations: New Details Released about the Salt Lake and Manti Temples," Church of Jesus Christ of Latter-day Saints, March 25, 2022, https://newsroom.churchofjesuschrist.org/article/salt-lake-manti-temples-update-march-2021.

3. Book of Mormon 1 Nephi 13:12.

4. Doris R. Dant, "Minerva Teichart's Manti Temple Murals," *BYU Studies Quarterly* 38, no. 3 (1999): 23, 25.

5. Dant, "Minerva Teichart's Manti Temple Murals," 26.

6. *Come, Follow Me—For Individuals and Families: Living, Learning, and Teaching the Gospel of Jesus Christ* (Salt Lake City: Church of Jesus Christ of Latter-day Saints, 2019), 24.

7. Peggy Fletcher Stack, "Error Printed in LDS Church Manual Could Revive Racial Criticisms," *Salt Lake Tribune*, January 18, 2020, https://www.sltrib.com/religion/2020/01/18/error-printed-lds-church/.

8. "2 Nephi 1–5," Church of Jesus Christ of Latter-day Saints, https://www.churchofjesuschrist.org/study/manual/come-follow-me-for-individuals-and-families-book-of-mormon-2020/06?lang=eng.

9. Stack, "Error Printed in LDS Church Manual Could Revive Racial Criticism."

10. Stack.

11. Eduardo Bonilla-Silva, *Racism without Racists: Color-Blind Racism and the Persistence of Racial Inequality in America*, 4th ed. (New York: Rowman & Littlefield, 2014), 25.

12. Angela Yang, "Black Mormons Turn to TikTok to Hold Majority-White School Accountable on Race," NBC News, April 21, 2022, https://www.nbcnews.com/news/nbcblk/black-mormons-turn-tiktok-hold-majority-white-school-accountable-race-rcna25366.

13. Yang, "Black Mormons Turn to TikTok."

14. Description, "Let's Talk about Race and the Priesthood," Deseret Book, https://www.deseretbook.com/product/P6012982.html?cgid=books_gospel-voices_let-s-talk-book-collection.

15. Bonilla-Silva, *Racism without Racists*, 26.

16. Brady McCombs, "Mormon Church Sued by Fourth Navajo Alleging Sexual Abuse," Associated Press, June 7, 2016; and Felicia Fonseca, "New Lawsuits Say Mormon Church Failed to Protect American Indian Children," *Salt Lake Tribune*, August 15, 2017, https://www.sltrib.com/religion/local/2017/08/16/new-lawsuits-say-mormon-church-failed-to-protect-american-indian-children/.

17. McCombs, "Mormon Church Sued by Fourth Navajo Alleging Sexual Abuse"; and Fonseca, "New Lawsuits Say Mormon Church Failed to Protect American Indian Children."

18. Dennis Romboy, "Judge Denies LDS Request to Move Sex Abuse Case to Federal Court," November 16, 2016, KSL.com, https://www.ksl.com/article/42235579.

BIBLIOGRAPHY

PRIMARY SOURCES

MANUSCRIPTS/SPECIAL COLLECTIONS

American Indian Service Records, 1949–1973. CR 245 6. Archives, Church History Library. The Church of Jesus Christ of Latter-day Saints, Salt Lake City, Utah.

Armand L. Mauss Papers, 1960–2004. MSS B 1015. Utah State Historical Society, Salt Lake City, Utah.

Church of Jesus Christ of Latter-day Saints. "Miscellaneous Missionary Lessons for Teaching the Navaho." Americana Collection. L. Tom Special Collections. Harold B. Lee Library, Brigham Young University, Provo, Utah.

Dee Winterton Collection, 1935–1984. L. Tom Special Collections, Harold B. Lee Library, Brigham Young University, Provo, Utah.

Ernest Mahan Papers. Special Collections and Archives, Utah State University, Logan, Utah.

"Foster Parent Guide." L.D.S. Indian Student Placement Program. The Church of Jesus Christ of Latter-day Saints, 1965. Americana Collection–Quarto, L. Tom Perry Special Collections. Harold B. Lee Library. Brigham Young University, Provo, Utah.

Indian Student Placement Program Files, 1950–1998. CR 245 2. Archives, Church History Library. The Church of Jesus Christ of Latter-day Saints, Salt Lake City, Utah.

Indian Student Placement Service Reunion Program 2000. MS 16468. Archives, Church History Library. The Church of Jesus Christ of Latter-day Saints, Salt Lake City, Utah.

LDS Native American Oral History Project. L. Tom Special Collections, Harold B. Lee Library. Brigham Young University, Provo, Utah.

Proofs and Negatives of BYU Folk Dancers, Lamanite Generation, Young Ambassadors, and Other Entertainers, 1975–1986. L. Tom Special Collections, Harold B. Lee Library. Brigham Young University, Provo, Utah.

This Is the Place Heritage Park Records. Series 23449. Division of Parks and Recreation, Department of Natural Resources. Utah Division of Archives and Record Service, Salt Lake City, Utah.

UA 518, Records of the University Program Bureau. University Archives, L. Tom Perry Special Collections, Harold B. Lee Library, Brigham Young University.

UA 1129, Entertainment Division Collection. University Archives; L. Tom Perry Special Collections, Harold B. Lee Library, Brigham Young University.

Wagenen, Glen Van, to Foster Parents, August 1972. CR 245 9. Archives, Church History Library. The Church of Jesus Christ of Latter-day Saints, Salt Lake City, Utah.

Will Bagley Papers, Manuscripts. J. Willard Marriott Digital Library, University of Utah, Salt Lake City, Utah.

ORAL HISTORIES

Adams, Verlinda Cochise. Interview by Matthew K. Heiss. April 29, 1992. OH 1174. The James Moyle Oral History Program. Archives, Historical Department of the Church of Jesus Christ of Latter-day Saints, Salt Lake City, Utah.

Ashdown, Rex R. Interview by Loretta L. Hefner. 1979. OH 424. Typescript. The James Moyle Oral History Program. Archives, Historical Department of the Church of Jesus Christ of Latter-day Saints, Salt Lake City, Utah.

Atene, Walter D. Interview by Jim M. Dandy, November 3, 1990. MS OH 1186. The LDS Native American Oral History Project. Charles Redd Center for Western Studies, L. Tom Perry Special Collections, Harold B. Lee Library. Brigham Young University, Provo, Utah.

Baptiso, Daisy. Interview by Deborah Lewis. January 1, 1990. MS OH 1162. The LDS Native American Oral History Project. Charles Redd Center for Western Studies, L. Tom Perry Special Collections, Harold B. Lee Library. Brigham Young University, Provo, Utah.

Benally, Jimmy N. Interview by Odessa Neaman. July 18, 1980. MS OH 1176. The LDS Native American Oral History Project. Charles Redd Center for Western Studies. L. Tom Perry Special Collections, Harold B. Lee Library. Brigham Young University, Provo, Utah.

Benally, Thomas. Interview by Matthew K. Heiss. April 26, 1997. The James Moyle Oral History Program. Archives, Historical Department of the Church of Jesus Christ of Latter-day Saints, Salt Lake City, Utah.

Boone, Audrey. Interview by Malcolm T. Pappan. April 6, 1990. MS OH 1164. The LDS Native American Oral History Project. Charles Redd Center for Western Studies. L. Tom Perry Special Collections, Harold B. Lee Library. Brigham Young University, Provo, Utah.

Bowman, Emery. Interview by Deborah Lewis. April 27, 1990. MS OH 1152. The LDS Native American Oral History Project. Charles Redd Center for Western Studies. L. Tom Perry Special Collections, Harold B. Lee Library. Brigham Young University, Provo, Utah.

Buchanan, Golden R. Dictation, Vol. 2. The James Moyle Oral History Program. Archives, Historical Department of the Church of Jesus Christ of Latter-day Saints, Salt Lake City, Utah.

Buchanan, Thelma S. Interview by William Hartley. October 12, 1976. OH 670. Typescript. Interview 2. The James Moyle Oral History Program. Archives, Historical Department of the Church of Jesus Christ of Latter-day Saints, Salt Lake City, Utah.

Cannon, Thomas Quentin. Interview by Loretta L. Hefner. March 20, 1979. OH 498. Typescript. The James Moyle Oral History Program. Archives, Historical Department of The Church of Jesus Christ of Latter-day Saints, Salt Lake City, Utah.

Chavez, Julius Ray. Interview by Odessa Neaman. June 27, 1990. MS OH 1180. The LDS Native American Oral History Project. Charles Redd Center for Western Studies. L. Tom Perry Special Collections, Harold B. Lee Library. Brigham Young University, Provo, Utah.

Chiquito, Stephani. Interview by Jim M. Dandy. April 10, 1991. MS OH 1194. The LDS Native American Oral History Project. Charles Redd Center for Western Studies. L. Tom Perry Special Collections, Harold B. Lee Library. Brigham Young University, Provo, Utah.

Cinniginnie, Gabriel Holyan. Interview by Malcolm T. Pappan. April 9, 1990. MS OH 1171. The LDS Native American Oral History Project. Charles Redd Center for Western Studies. L. Tom Perry Special Collections, Harold B. Lee Library. Brigham Young University, Provo, Utah.

Crouch, Amy Avery. December 21, 1978. MS 5120 2. Transcript. Archives, The Church of Jesus Christ of Latter-day Saints, Salt Lake City, Utah.

Dandy, James Lee. Interview by Jesse Embry. October 2, 1990. MS OH 985. The LDS Native American Oral History Project. Charles Redd Center for Western Studies. L. Tom Perry Special Collections, Harold B. Lee Library. Brigham Young University, Provo, Utah.

Dee, Antoinette. Interview by Jim M. Dandy. November 15, 1990. MS OH 985. The LDS Native American Oral History Project. Charles Redd Center for Western Studies. L. Tom Perry Special Collections, Harold B. Lee Library. Brigham Young University, Provo, Utah.

Deschine, Wilson Yazzie. Interview by Matthew K. Heiss. April 30, 1992. OH 1526. Typescript. The James Moyle Oral History Program. Archives, Historical Department of the Church of Jesus Christ of Latter-day Saints. Salt Lake City, Utah.

Fifita, Donna. Interview by Odessa Neaman. June 5, 1990. MS OH 1177. The LDS Native American Oral History Project. Charles Redd Center for Western Studies. L. Tom Perry Special Collections, Harold B. Lee Library. Brigham Young University, Provo, Utah.

Hainsworth, Jackie Webster. Interview by Rebecca Vorimo. June 14, 1994. MSS OH 1667. The LDS Missionary Oral History Project. Charles Redd Center for Western Studies. L. Tom Perry Special Collections, Harold B. Lee Library. Brigham Young University, Provo, Utah.

Hall, Helen Rose John. October 10, 1978. MS 51201. Transcript. James Moyle Oral History Program, Archives Historical Department of The Church of Jesus Christ of Latter-day Saints. Salt Lake City, Utah.

Halona, Tonia. Interview by Jim M. Dandy. April 10, 1991. MS OH 1446. The LDS Native American Oral History Project. Charles Redd Center for Western Studies. L. Tom Perry Special Collections, Harold B. Lee Library. Brigham Young University, Provo, Utah.

Hatch, Myrtle. Interview by Ernesteen B. Lynch. August 23, 1989. MS OH 1143. The LDS Native American Oral History Project. Charles Redd Center for Western Studies. L. Tom Perry Special Collections, Harold B. Lee Library. Brigham Young University, Provo, Utah.

Holiday, Kee H. Interview by Matthew K. Heiss. The James Moyle Oral History Program. Archives, Historical Department of the Church of Jesus Christ of Latter-day Saints. Salt Lake City, Utah.

Jensen, Miles Herbert. Dictation. December 13, 1973. OH 817. Typescript. The James Moyle Oral History Program. Archives, Historical Department of the Church of Jesus Christ of Latter-day Saints. Salt Lake City, Utah.

Klain, Victoria. Interview by Farina King. November 11, 1997. The LDS Native American Oral History Project. Charles Redd Center for Western Studies, L. Tom Perry Special Collections, Harold B. Lee Library. Brigham Young University, Provo, Utah.

Lee, Rhonda J. Interview by Jim M. Dandy. April 10, 1991. MS OH 1197. The LDS Native American Oral History Project. Charles Redd Center for Western Studies. L. Tom Perry Special Collections, Harold B. Lee Library. Brigham Young University, Provo, Utah.

Lopez, Alexia. Interview by Ernesteen B. Lynch. August 10, 1989. MS OH 985. The LDS Native American Oral History Project. Charles Redd Center for Western Studies. L. Tom Perry Special Collections, Harold B. Lee Library. Brigham Young University, Provo, Utah.

Lynch, Ernesteen B. Interview by Jessie Embry, May 17, 1990. MS OH 1488. The LDS Native American Oral History Project, Charles Redd Center for Western Studies, L. Tom Perry Special Collections, Harold B. Lee Library. Brigham Young University, Provo, Utah.

Mitchell, Ray R. Interview by Matthew K. Heiss. April 28, 1992. OH 1536. The James Moyle Oral History Program. Archives, Historical Department of the Church of Jesus Christ of Latter-day Saints, Salt Lake City, Utah.

Moore, Carl R. Interview by Jim M. Dandy. November 15, 1989. MS OH 1164. The LDS Native American Oral History Project. Charles Redd Center for Western Studies. L. Tom Perry Special Collections, Harold B. Lee Library. Brigham Young University, Provo, Utah.

Mose, Donald, Jr. Interview by Jim M. Dandy. November 6, 1990. MS OH 1165. The LDS Native American Oral History Project. Charles Redd Center for Western Studies. L. Tom Perry Special Collections, Harold B. Lee Library. Brigham Young University, Provo, Utah.

Pedro, Lemuel. Interview by Malcolm T. Pappan. April 1, 1990. MS OH 1146. The LDS Native American Oral History Project. Charles Redd Center for Western Studies. L. Tom Perry Special Collections, Harold B. Lee Library. Brigham Young University, Provo, Utah.

Sekaquaptewa, Ken. Interview by Odessa Neaman. June 11, 1990. MS OH 1184. The LDS Native American Oral History Project. Charles Redd Center for Western Studies. L. Tom Perry Special Collections, Harold B. Lee Library. Brigham Young University, Provo, Utah.

Singer, Lewis J. Interview by Jim M. Dandy. October 23, 1990. MS OH 1185. The LDS Native American Oral History Project. Charles Redd Center for Western Studies. L. Tom Perry Special Collections, Harold B. Lee Library. Brigham Young University, Provo, Utah.

Tulley, Virginia Morris Tso. Interview by Matthew K. Heiss. April 25, 1997. Typescript. The James Moyle Oral History Program. Archives, Historical Department of the Church of Jesus Christ of Latter-day Saints. Salt Lake City, Utah.

West, Matthew. Interview by Jeff Anderson. October 20, 1998. Archives, Church History Library. The Church of Jesus Christ of Latter-Day Saint Historical Department, Salt Lake City, Utah.

Whaley, Aneta. Interview by Jim M. Dandy. November 15, 1990. The LDS Native American Oral History Project. Charles Redd Center for Western Studies. L. Tom Perry Special Collections, Harold B. Lee Library. Brigham Young University, Provo, Utah.

PUBLISHED PRIMARY SOURCES

Ashurst-McGee, Mark, David W. Grua, Elizabeth Kuehn, Alexander L. Baugh, and Brenden W. Rensink, eds. *The Joseph Smith Papers: Documents*, Vol. 6, *February 1838–August 1839.* Salt Lake City: Church Historian's Press, 2017.

Bagley, Will, ed. *Kingdom in the West: The Mormons and the American Frontier*, Vol. 16, *The Whites Want Every Thing: Indian-Mormon Relations, 1847–1877.* Norman, OK: Arthur H. Clark, 2019.

Bashore, Melvin L. "'Where the Prophets of God Live': A Brief Overview of the Mormon Trail Experience." Brigham Young University Overland Diaries and Letters, 1846–1869. https://overlandtrails.lib.byu.edu/essay_mtrail.php.

Bible, King James Version. Reprint. Salt Lake City: Church of Jesus Christ of Latter-day Saints, 2002.

Book of Mormon. Reprint. Salt Lake City: Church of Jesus Christ of Latter-day Saints, 1944.

The Book of Mormon: Another Testament of Jesus Christ. Reprint. Salt Lake City: Church of Jesus Christ of Latter-day Saints, 1981.

Book of Mormon: Another Testament of Jesus Christ. Reprint. Salt Lake City: Church of Jesus Christ of Latter-day Saints, 2002.

Children's Songbook. Salt Lake City: Deseret Book, 1989.

Church Educational System. *Church History in the Fulness of Times: The History of the Church of Jesus Christ of Latter-day Saint,* 2nd ed. Salt Lake City: Church of Jesus Christ of Latter-day Saints, 2003.

The Church of Jesus Christ of Latter-day Saints. *The Truth Restored: A Short History of the Church of Jesus Christ of Latter-day Saints.* Salt Lake City: Church of Jesus Christ of Latter-day Saints, 2001.

Dirkmaat, Gerrit J., Brent M. Rogers, Grant Underwood, Robert J. Woodford, and William G. Hartley, eds. *The Joseph Smith Papers: Documents,* Vol. 3, *February 1833–March 1834.* Salt Lake City: Church Historian's Press, 2014.

Excommunication of a Mormon Church Leader: Containing the Letters of Dr. George P. Lee. Salt Lake City: Utah Lighthouse Ministry. Americana collection. Special Collections. Harold B. Lee Library, Brigham Young University, Provo, Utah.

Godfrey, Matthew C., Mark Ashurst-McGee, Grant Underwood, Robert J. Woodford, and William G. Hartley, eds. *The Joseph Smith Papers: Documents,* Vol. 2, *July 1831–January 1833.* Salt Lake City: Church Historian's Press, 2013.

Godfrey, Matthew C., Spencer W. McBride, Alex D. Smith, and Christopher James Blythe, eds. *The Joseph Smith Papers: Documents,* Vol. 7, *September 1839–January 1841.* Salt Lake City: Church Historian's Press, 2018.

Godfrey, Matthew C., Brenden W. Rensink, Alex D. Smith, Max H. Parkin, and Alexander L. Baugh, eds. *The Joseph Smith Papers: Documents,* Vol. 4, *April 1834–September 1835.* Salt Lake City: Church Historian's Press, 2016.

Grow, Matthew J., Ronald K. Esplin, Mark Ashurst-McGee, Gerrit J. Dirkmaat, and Jeffrey D. Mahas, eds. *The Joseph Smith Papers: Administrative Records, Council of Fifty, Minutes,* Vol. 1, *March 1844–January 1846.* Salt Lake City: Church Historian's Press, 2016.

Hedges, Andrew H., Alex D. Smith, and Brent M. Rogers, eds. *The Joseph Smith Papers: Journals,* Vol. 3, *May 1843 June 1844.* Salt Lake City: Church Historian's Press, 2015.

Hyde, William. *William Hyde's Journal, Part 2.* https://penelope.uchicago.edu/Thayer/E/Gazetteer/People/William_Hyde/Journal/2*.html.

Hymns of the Church of Jesus Christ of Latter-day Saints. Salt Lake City: Deseret Book, 1985.

Lyman, Albert R. "A Voice Calling." Salt Lake City: Church of Jesus Christ of Latter-day Saints.

MacKay, Michael Hubbard, Gerrit J. Dirkmaat, Grant Underwood, Robert J. Woodford, and William G. Hartley, eds. *The Joseph Smith Papers: Documents,* Vol. 1, *July 1828–June 1831.* Salt Lake City: Church Historian's Press, 2013.

"News Four Notebook." KSL-TV, April 1967. Videorecording. Archives. The Church of Jesus Christ of Latter-day Saints. Salt Lake City, Utah.

Our Heritage: A Brief History of the Church of Jesus Christ of Latter-day Saints. Salt Lake City: Church of Jesus Christ of Latter-day Saints, 1996.

The Pearl of Great Price: A Selection from the Revelations, Translations, and Narrations of Joseph Smith, First Prophet, Seer, and Revelator to the Church of Jesus Christ of Latter-day Saints. Salt Lake City: Church of Jesus Christ of Latter-day Saints, 1979.

Pearson, Don H., and T. Edgar Lyon. *This Is the Place Monument Story and History.* 2nd printing. Salt Lake City: n.p., 1958.

Pratt, Parley P., and Parker Pratt Robison. *Writings of Parley Parker Pratt: One of the First Missionaries and a Member of the First Quorum of the Twelve Apostles of the Church of Jesus Christ of Latter- day Saints.* Salt Lake City: Deseret News Press, 1952.

Rogers, Brent M., Mason K. Allred, Gerrit J. Dirkmaat, and Brett D. Dowdle, eds. *The Joseph Smith Papers: Documents,* Vol. 8, *February–November 1841.* Salt Lake City: Church Historian's Press, 2019.

Rogers, Brent M., Elizabeth A. Kuehn, Christian K. Heimburger, Max H. Parkin, Alexander L. Baugh, and Steven C. Harper, eds. *The Joseph Smith Papers: Documents,* Vol. 5, *October 1835–January 1838.* Salt Lake City: Church Historian's Press, 2017.

Smith, Joseph. *The Doctrine and Covenants of the Church of Jesus Christ of Latter-day Saints: Containing Revelations Given to Joseph Smith, the Prophet, with Some Additions by His Successors in the Presidency of the Church.* Salt Lake City: Church of Jesus Christ of Latter-day Saints, 1979.

Smith, Joseph Fielding. *Essentials in Church History.* Salt Lake City: Deseret News Press, 1922.

"Still the Place at 170." *Wild West,* August 2017, 50–57.

Turner, Frederick Jackson. "The Significance of the Frontier in American History." *Proceedings of the Forty-First Annual Meeting of the State Historical Society of Wisconsin* (Madison, WI, 1894), 79–112.

Woodruff, Wilford. *Wilford Woodruff Journal, January 1847–December 1953.* https://catalog .churchofjesuschrist.org/assets/a5c827b5-938d-4a08-b80e-71570704e323/0/83?lang =eng. MS1352, Church History Library, Salt Lake City, Utah.

Young, Brigham. "Proper Treatment of the Indians, etc." In *Journal of Discourse: Delivered by President Young, His Two Counselors, The Twelve Apostles, and Others,* Vol. 6. London: LDS Book Depot, 1859,

GOVERNMENT DOCUMENTS

Indian Child Welfare Act of 1977: Hearing before the United States Senate, Select Committee on Indian Affairs, Ninety-fifth Congress, First Session, on S. 1214; To Establish Standards

for the Placement of Indian Children in Foster or Adoptive Homes, to Prevent the Breakup of Indian Families, and for Other Purposes. Washington, DC: US Government Printing Office, 1977.

Kappler, Charles J., comp. and ed. "Treaty of the Navaho." In *Indian Affairs: Laws and Treaties*, Vol. 2. https://dc.library.okstate.edu/digital/collection/kapplers/id/29605.

Laws of the State of Utah Passed at the Special and First Regular Sessions of the Legislature of the State of Utah. Passed by Congress and the State Constitution, Adopted by Convention May 8, 1895. Salt Lake City, the State Capital in January, February, March, and April 1896. Also the Enabling Act, Passed by Congress and the State Constitution, Adopted by Convention May 8, 1895, and Ratified by the People at the General Election November 5, 1895. Published by Authority. Salt Lake City: Deseret News Publishing Company, 1896.

"The National Trails System Act." National Park Service. https://www.nps.gov/subjects/nationaltrailssystem/upload/National-Trails-System-Act-Amended-2019.pdf.

Nixon, Richard M. "Special Message on Indian Affairs." Congress, July 8, 1970. https://www.epa.gov/sites/default/files/2013-08/documents/president-nixon70.pdf.

"Treaty with the Navaho, 1868." In *Indian Affairs: Laws and Treaties*, Vol. 2. Compiled and edited by Charles J. Kappler. Washington, DC: US Government Printing Office, 1904). https://dc.library.okstate.edu/digital/collection/kapplers/id/29605

US Congress, Senate, Committee on Labor and Public Welfare. *Indian Education: A National Tragedy—A National Challenge 1969 Report.* 91st Congress, 1st session. Washington, DC: US Government Printing Office, 1969.

NEWSPAPERS AND PERIODICALS

The Christmas News
Church News
Daily Herald
Deseret News
Ensign
The Friend
The Headlight
Improvement Era
Indian Liahona
Intermountain News
The Lamanite
Millennial Star
New York Times
Penthouse
Provo Daily Herald
The Richfield Reaper
Salt Lake City Daily Herald
Salt Lake City Tribune
Seattle Post-Intelligencer

The Spectrum
Utah Statesmen
Uintah Basin Standard

SECONDARY SOURCES
BOOKS

Adams, David. *Education for Extinction: American Indians and the Boarding School Experience, 1875–1928.* Lawrence: University of Kansas Press, 1995.

Aikau, Hokulani K. *A Chosen People, a Promised Land: Mormonism and Race in Hawai'i.* Minneapolis: University of Minnesota Press, 2012.

Alexander, Thomas G. *Mormonism in Transition: A History of the Latter-day Saints, 1890–1930.* Edited by Illini Books. Urbana: University of Illinois, 1996.

Allen, Theodore. *The Invention of the White Race.* Haymarket series. London: Verso, 1994.

Almaguer, Tomás. *Racial Fault Lines: The Historical Origins of White Supremacy in California.* Berkeley: University of California Press, 1994.

Anderson, Benedict. *Imagined Communities: Reflections on the Origin and Spread of Nationalism.* Rev. ed. London: Verso, 1991.

Arrington, Leonard J., and Davis Bitton. *The Mormon Experience: A History of the Latter-day Saints.* 2nd ed. Urbana: University of Illinois Press, 1992.

Arrington, Leonard J., Davis Bitton, and Maureen Ursenbach Beecher. *New Views of Mormon History: A Collection of Essays in Honor of Leonard J. Arrington.* Salt Lake City: University of Utah Press, 1987.

Arvin, Maile. *Possessing Polynesians: The Science of Settler Colonial Whiteness in Hawai'i and Oceania.* Durham, NC: Duke University Press, 2019.

Azuma, Eiichiro. *Between Two Empires: Race, History, and Transnationalism in Japanese America.* New York: Oxford University Press, 2005.

Bagley, Will. *Blood of the Prophets: Brigham Young and the Massacre at Mountain Meadows.* Norman: University of Oklahoma Press, 2002.

Barker, Joanne. *Native Acts: Law, Recognition, and Cultural Authenticity.* Durham, NC: Duke University Press, 2011.

Barney, Garold. *Mormons, Indians and the Ghost Dance Religion of 1890.* 2nd ed. Boulder, CO: Bäuu, 2010.

Bederman, Gail. *Manliness & Civilization: A Cultural History of Gender and Race in the United States, 1880–1917.* Women in Culture and Society. Chicago: University of Chicago Press, 1995.

Bennett, John Cook. *The History of the Saints, or, an Exposé of Joe Smith and Mormonism.* 3rd ed. Urbana: University of Illinois Press, [1842] 2000.

Bennett, Richard Edmond. *Mormons at the Missouri, 1846–1852: "And should we die—."* Norman: University of Oklahoma Press, 1987.

———. *We'll Find The Place: The Mormon Exodus, 1846–1848.* Norman: University of Oklahoma Press, 2009.

Bensen, Taft Ezra. *This Nation Shall Endure.* Salt Lake City: Deseret Book, 1979.

Blackhawk, Ned. *Violence over the Land: Indians and Empires in the Early American West.* Cambridge, MA: Harvard University Press, 2006.

Blee, Lisa, and Jean M. O'Brien. *Monumental Mobility: The Memory Work of Massasoit* Durham, NC: University of North Carolina Press.

Bloom, John. *To Show What an Indian Can Do: Sports at Native American Boarding Schools.* Minneapolis: University of Minnesota Press, 2000.

Bodnar, John. *Remaking America: Public Memory, Commemoration, and Patriotism in the Twentieth Century.* Princeton, NJ: Princeton University Press, 1992.

Bonilla-Silva, Eduardo. *Racism without Racists: Color-blind Racism and the Persistence of Racial Inequality in the United States.* New York: Rowman and Littlefield, 2003.

Bringhurst, Newell G., and Darron T. Smith, eds. *Black and Mormon.* Urbana: University of Illinois Press, 2004.

Brodie, Fawn McKay. *No Man Knows My History: The Life of Joseph Smith, the Mormon Prophet.* New York: Knopf, 1966.

Brooks, Juanita. *Journal of the Southern Indian Mission: Diary of Thomas D. Brown.* Logan: Utah State University Press, 1972.

———, ed. *The Mountain Meadows Massacre.* 2nd ed. Norman: University of Oklahoma Press, 1970.

Brown, Michael K. *Whitewashing Race: The Myth of a Color-blind Society.* Berkeley: University of California Press, 2003.

Bsumek, Erika Marie. *The Foundations of Glen Canyon Dam: Infrastructures of Dispossession on the Colorado Plateau.* Austin: University of Texas Tech, 2023.

Bushman, Richard Lyman. *From Puritan to Yankee; Character and the Social Order in Connecticut, 1690–1765.* Cambridge, MA: Harvard University Press, 1967.

———. *Joseph Smith, Rough Stone Rolling: A Cultural Biography of Mormonism's Founder.* New York: Knopf, 2005.

———. *Joseph Smith and the Beginnings of Mormonism.* Urbana: University of Illinois Press, 1984.

Bushman, Richard Lyman, Reid Larkin Neilson, and Jed Woodworth. *Believing History: Latter-day Saint Essays.* New York: Columbia University Press, 2004.

Butler, Jon, Grant Wacker, and Randall Herbert Balmer. *Religion in American Life: A Short History.* Oxford: Oxford University Press, 2003.

Byrd, Jodi A. *The Transit of Empire: Indigenous Critiques of Colonialism.* Minneapolis: University of Minnesota Press, 2011.

Cannon, Hugh J. *David O. McKay: Around the World.* Provo, UT: Spring Creek Book Company, 2005.

Chan, Sucheng, Douglas Henry Daniels, Mario T. Garcia, and Terry P. Wilson., eds. *Peoples of Color in the American West.* Lexington, MA: D. C. Heath, 1994.

Chidester, David. *Patterns of Power: Religion and Politics in American Culture.* Englewood Cliffs, NJ: Prentice Hall, 1988.

———. *Savage Systems: Colonialism and Comparative Religion in Southern Africa,* Studies in Religion and Culture. Charlottesville: University Press of Virginia, 1996.

———. *Word and Light: Seeing, Hearing, and Religious Discourse.* Urbana: University of Illinois Press, 1992.

Child, Brenda J. *Boarding School Seasons: American Indian Families, 1900–1940.* Lincoln: University of Nebraska Press, 1998.

Chireau, Yvonne Patricia, and Nathaniel Deutsch. *Black Zion: African American Religious Encounters with Judaism.* Religion in America Series. New York; Oxford: Oxford University Press, 2000.

Colvin, Gina, and Joanna Brooks. *Decolonizing Mormonism: Approaching a Postcolonial Zion.* Salt Lake City: University of Utah Press, 2018.

Compton, Todd M. *A Frontier Life: Jacob Hamblin, Explorer and Indian Missionary.* Salt Lake City: University of Utah Press, 2013.

Cope, Adrianne. *The Coming of Elijah.* Woodsboro, MD: Parables, 2006.

Costo, Rupert, and Jeanette Henry Costo. "The Crime of Genocide: A United Nations Convention Aimed at Preventing Destruction of Groups and at Punishing Those Responsible." In *Native American Voices: A reader,* 2nd ed., ed. Susan Lobo an Steve Talbot, 163–65. Upper Saddle River, NJ: Prentice Hall, 2001.

Cox, Kay H. *Without Reservation.* Salt Lake City: Bookcraft, 1980.

Crosby, Caroline Barnes, Edward Leo Lyman, Susan Ward Payne, and S. George Ellsworth. *No Place to Call Home: The 1807–1857 Life Writings of Caroline Barnes Crosby, Chronicler of Outlying Mormon Communities,* Vol. 7, *Life Writings of Frontier Women.* Logan: Utah State University Press, 2005.

Daughters of Utah Pioneers. *Indian Tribes and the Utah Pioneers.* n.p.: International Society of Daughters of Utah Pioneers, n.d.

Delgado, Richard, and Jean Stefancic. *Critical Race Theory: An Introduction.* With a Forward by Angela Harris. New York: New York University Press, 2001.

Deloria, Vine, Jr., and Clifford M. Lytle. *American Indians, American Justice.* Austin: University of Texas Press, 1983.

Denson, Andrew. *Monuments to Absence: Cherokee Removal and the Contests over Southern Memory.* Chapel Hill: University of North Carolina Press, 2017.

Dormady, Jason H., and Jared M. Tamez, eds. *Just South of Zion: The Mormons in Mexico and Its Borderlands.* Albuquerque: University of New Mexico Press, 2015.

Echo-Hawk, Walter R. *In the Courts of the Conqueror: The 10 Worst Indian Law Cases Ever Decided.* Golden, CO: Fulcrum, 2010.

Esplin, Scott C., Richard E. Bennett, Susan Easton Black, and Craig K. Manskill, eds. *Far Away in the West: Reflections on the Mormon Pioneer Trail.* Provo, UT: Deseret Book, 2015.

Evans, Jessica, Stuart Hall, and Open University. *Visual Culture: The Reader.* London: Sage in association with the Open University, 1999.

Farmer, Jared. *On Zion's Mount: Mormons, Indians, and the American Landscape.* Cambridge, MA: Harvard University Press, 2008.

Flake, Kathleen. *The Politics of American Religious Identity: The Seating of Senator Reed Smoot, Mormon Apostle.* Chapel Hill: University of North Carolina Press, 2004.

Flamming, Douglas. *Bound for Freedom: Black Los Angeles in Jim Crow America.* Berkeley: University of California Press, 2005.

Fluhman, J. Spencer. *"A Peculiar People": Anti-Mormonism and the Making of Religion in Nineteenth-Century America*. Chapel Hill: University of North Carolina Press, 2012.

Foley, Neil. *The White Scourge: Mexicans, Blacks, and Poor Whites in Texas Cotton Culture*. American Crossroads, Vol. 2. Berkeley: University of California Press, 1997.

Frankenberg, Ruth. *Displacing Whiteness: Essays in Social and Cultural Criticism*. Durham, NC: Duke University Press, 1997.

———. *White Women, Race Matters: The Social Construction of Whiteness*. Minneapolis: University of Minnesota, 1993.

Fredrickson, George M. *Racism: A Short History*. Princeton, NJ: Princeton University Press, 2002.

———. *White Supremacy: A Comparative Study in American and South African History*. New York: Oxford University Press, 1981.

Garrett, Matthew. *Making Lamanite: Mormons, Native Americans and the Indian Student Placement Program, 1947–2000*. Salt Lake City: University of Utah, 2016.

Gaustad, Edwin S. *A Documentary History of Religion in America*. Grand Rapids, MI: Eerdmans, 1982.

———. *A Religious History of America*. New rev. ed. San Francisco: Harper & Row, 1990.

Givens, Terryl. *By the Hand of Mormon: The American Scripture That Launched a New World Religion*. Oxford: Oxford University Press, 2002.

———. *The Viper on the Hearth: Mormons, Myths, and the Construction of Heresy*. Religion in America Series. New York: Oxford University Press, 1997.

Goldschmidt, Henry, and Elizabeth A. McAlister. *Race, Nation, and Religion in the Americas*. Oxford: Oxford University Press, 2004.

Gottlieb, Robert, and Peter Booth Wiley. *America's Saints: The Rise of Mormon Power*. New York: Putnam, 1984.

Grow, Matthew J., and R. Eric Smith, eds. *The Council of Fifty: What the Records Reveal about Mormon History*. Provo, UT: Deseret Book, 2017.

Guglielmo, Thomas A. *White on Arrival: Italians, Race, Color, and Power in Chicago, 1890–1945*. New York: Oxford University Press, 2003.

Gunnison, Lieutenant J. W. *The Mormons, or Latter-day Saints in the Great Salt Lake: A History of Their Rise and Progress, Peculiar Doctrines, Present Condition, and Prospects, Derived from Personal Observation, during a Residence among Them*. Philadelphia: J. B. Lippincott, 1857.

Hafen, LeRoy R., and Ann W. Hafen. *Handcarts to Zion: The Story of a Unique Western Migration 1856–1860 with Contemporary Journals, Accounts, Reports; and Rosters of Members of the Ten Handcart Companies*. Pioneers edition. Glendale, CA: Arthur H. Clark, 1960.

Hafen, P. Jane. "The Being and Place of a Native American Mormon." In *New Genesis: A Mormon Reader on Land and Community*, ed. Terry Tempest Williams, William B. Smart and Gibbs M. Smith, 35–41. Salt Lake City: Gibbs Smith 1998.

Hafen, P. Jane, and Brenden W. Rensink, eds. *Essays on American Indian and Mormon History*. Salt Lake City: University of Utah Press, 2019.

Hall, Stuart, ed. *Representation: Cultural Representations and Signifying Practices*. Thousand Oaks, CA: Sage, 1997.

Hallwas, John E., and Roger D. Launius, eds. *Cultures in Conflict: A Documentary History of the Mormon War in Illinois.* Logan: Utah State University Press, 1995.

Hammond, John J. *Island Adventure: The Hawaiian Mission of Francis A. Hammond, 1851–1865.* Salt Lake City: Signature Books, 2016.

Hampshire, Annette P. *Mormonism in Conflict, the Nauvoo Years.* Studies in Religion and Society, Vol. 11. New York: E. Mellen, 1985.

Haney-Lopez, Ian. *Racism on Trial: The Chicano Fight for Justice.* Cambridge, MA: Belknap Press of Harvard University Press, 2003.

———. *White by Law: The Legal Construction of Race.* Critical America. New York: New York University Press, 1996.

Harris, Matthew L., and Newell G. Bringhurst, eds. *The Mormon Church & Blacks: A Documentary History.* Urbana: University of Illinois Press, 2015.

Hayashi, Brian Masaru. *For the Sake of Our Japanese Brethern: Assimilation, Nationalism, and Protestantism among the Japanese of Los Angeles, 1895–1942.* Stanford, CA: Stanford University Press, 1995.

Hill, William E. *The Mormon Trail: Yesterday and Today.* Logan: Utah State University Press, 1996.

Hine, Robert V., and John Mack Faragher. *The American West: A New Interpretive History.* New Haven, CT: Yale University Press, 2000.

Hirsh, James. S. *Riot and Remembrance: The Tulsa Race War and Its Legacy.* Boston: Houghton Mifflin, 2002.

Hooks, Bell. "Representing Whiteness in the Black Imagination." In *Displacing Whiteness: Essays in Social and Cultural Criticism*, ed. Ruth Frankenberg, 165–79. Durham, NC: Duke University Press, 1997.

Horsman, Reginald. *Race and Manifest Destiny: The Origins of American Racial Anglo-Saxonism.* Cambridge, MA: Harvard University Press, 1981.

Hudson, Angela Pulley. *Real Native Genius: How an Ex-Slave and a White Mormon Became Famous Indians.* Chapel Hill: University of North Carolina, 2015.

Hyde, Anne F. *Empires, Nations & Families: A History of the North American West, 1800–1860.* Lincoln: University of Nebraska Press, 2011.

Ignatiev, Noel. *How the Irish Became White.* New York: Routledge, 1995.

Jacobs, Margaret. *A Generation Removed: The Fostering and Adoption of Indigenous Children in the Postwar World.* Lincoln: University of Nebraska Press, 2014.

———. *White Mother to a Dark Race: Settler Colonialism, Maternalism, and the Removal of Indigenous Children in the American West and Australia, 1880–1940.* Lincoln: University of Nebraska Press, 2009.

Jacobs, Wilbur R. *Dispossessing the American Indian: Indians and Whites on the Colonial Frontier.* Norman: University of Oklahoma Press, 1985.

Jacobson, Cardell K., John P. Hoffmann, and Tim B. Heaton. *Revisiting Thomas F. O'dea's* The Mormons*: Contemporary Perspectives.* Salt Lake City: University of Utah Press, 2008.

Jacobson, Matthew Frye. *Whiteness of a Different Color: European Immigrants and the Alchemy of Race.* Cambridge, MA: Harvard University Press, 1998.

Johnson, Paul E. *A Shopkeeper's Millenium: Society and Revivals in Rochester, New York, 1815–1837.* American Century Series. New York: Hill and Wang, 1978.

Jordan, Winthrop D. *The White Man's Burden: Historical Origins of Racism in the United States.* New York: Oxford University Press, 1974.

———. *White Over Black: American Attitudes toward the Negro, 1550–1812.* Chapel Hill: University of North Carolina Press, 1968

Justice, Daniel Heath. *Why Indigenous Literatures Matter.* Waterloo, Ontario: Wilfrid Laurier University Press, 2018.

Kaplan, Amy. *The Anarchy of Empire in the Making of U.S. Culture.* Cambridge, MA: Harvard University Press, 2002.

Kaplan, Amy, and Donald E. Pease. *Cultures of United States Imperialism.* New Americanists. Durham, NC: Duke University Press, 1993.

Kimball, Edward L. *Lengthen Your Stride: The Presidency of Spencer W. Kimball.* Salt Lake City: Deseret Book, 2005.

Kimball, Edward L., and Andrew E. Kimball Jr. *Spencer W. Kimball: The Early and Apostolic Years.* Salt Lake City: Deseret Book, 2006.

———. *Spencer W. Kimball: Twelfth President of the Church of Jesus Christ of Latter-day Saints.* Salt Lake City: Bookcraft, 1977.

King, Farina. *Diné dóó Gáamalii: Navajo Latter-day Saint Experiences in the Twentieth Century.* Lawrence: University of Kansas, 2023.

Knack, Martha. *Boundaries Between: The Southern Paiutes, 1775–1995.* Lincoln: University of Nebraska Press, 2001.

Leavelle, Tracy Neal. *The Catholic Calumet: Colonial Conversions in French and Indian North America.* Philadelphia: University of Pennsylvania Press, 2014.

Lee, George P. *Silent Courage: An Indian Story.* Salt Lake City: Bookcraft, 1974.

Leong, Karen J. *The China Mystique: Pearl S. Buck, Anna May Wong, Mayling Soong, and the Transformation of American Orientalism.* Berkeley: University of California Press, 2005.

LeSueur, Stephen C. *The 1838 Mormon War in Missouri.* Columbia: University of Missouri Press, 1987.

Lewis, David Rich. *Neither Wolf nor Dog: American Indians, Environment, and Agrarian Change.* New York: Oxford University Press, 1994.

Livingston, John P. *Same Drum, Different Beat: The Story of Dale T. Tingey and American Indian Services.* Provo, UT: Religious Studies Center, Brigham Young University, 2003.

Limerick, Patricia Nelson. *The Legacy of Conquest: The Unbroken Past of the American West.* New York: Norton, 1987.

Lindsey, Donal F. *Indians at Hampton Institute, 1877–1923.* Urbana: University of Illinois, 1995.

Lipsitz, George. *The Possessive Investment in Whiteness: How White People Profit from Identity Politics.* Philadelphia: Temple University Press, 2006.

Lomawaima, K. Tsianina. *They Called It Prairie Light: The Story of Chilocco Indian School.* Lincoln: University of Nebraska Press, 1994.

Lomawaima, K. Tsianina, and Teresa L. McCarty. *"To Remain an Indian": Lessons in Democracy from a Century of Native American Education.* New York: Teachers College Press, 2006.

Loomba, Ania. *Colonialism/Postcolonialism.* New York: Routledge, 2005.

Love, Eric Tyrone Lowery. *Race over Empire: Racism and U.S. Imperialism, 1865–1900.* Chapel Hill: University of North Carolina Press, 2004.

Luce, Willard. *Jerry Lindsey: Explorer to the San Juan.* Salt Lake City: Deseret Book, 1958.

Lund, John Lewis. *The Church and the Negro: A Discussion of Mormons, Negroes and the Priesthood.* Salt Lake City: Paramount Publishers, 1967.

Madsen, Brigham D. *The Shoshoni Frontier and the Bear River Massacre.* Salt Lake City: University of Utah Press, 1985.

Maffly-Kipp, Laurie F. "Looking West: Mormonism and the Pacific World." In *The Mormon History Association's Tanner Lectures: The First Twenty Years,* ed. Dean L. May and Reid L. Neilson with Richard Lyman Bushman, Jan Shipps, and Thomas G. Alexander, 123–41. Urbana: University of Illinois Press, 2006.

Marsden, George M. *Religion and American Culture.* San Diego: Harcourt Brace Jovanovich, 1990.

Martin, Joel W., and Mark A. Nicolas, eds. *Native Americans, Christianity, and the Reshaping of the American Religious Landscape.* Chapel Hill: University of North California Press, 2010.

Martins, Marcus H. *Blacks and the Mormon Priesthood: Setting the Record Straight.* Orem, UT: Millennial Press, 2007.

Marty, Martin E. *Pilgrims in Their Own Land: 500 Years of Religion in America.* Boston: Little, Brown, 1984.

Marty, Martin E., and R. Scott Appleby. *Religion, Ethnicity, and Self-identity: Nations in Turmoil.* Hanover, NH: University Press of New England, 1997.

Mauss, Armand L. *All Abraham's Children: Changing Mormon Conceptions of Race and Lineage.* Urbana: University of Illinois Press, 2003.

———. *The Angel and the Beehive: The Mormon Struggle with Assimilation.* Urbana: University of Illinois Press, 1994.

Mauss, Armand L., and Julie Camille Wolfe, eds. *This Land of Promises: The Rise and Fall of Social Problems in America.* Philadelphia: J. B. Lippincott, 1977.

McConkie, Bruce R. *Mormon Doctrine.* Salt Lake City: Deseret Book, 1966.

McKiernan, F. Mark, Alma R. Blair, and Paul M. Edwards, eds. *The Restoration Movement: Essays in Mormon History.* Lawrence, KS: Coronado, 1973.

McPherson, Robert S. *Navajo Traditions, Mormon Life: The Autobiography and Teachings of Jim Dandy.* Salt Lake City: University of Utah Press, 2012.

Memmi, Albert. *The Colonizer and the Colonized.* Boston: Beacon, 1991.

Mills, Charles W. *The Racial Contract.* Ithaca, NY: Cornell University Press, 1997.

Milner, Clyde A., and Allan G. Bogue. *A New Significance: Re-envisioning the History of the American West.* New York: Oxford University Press, 1996.

Milner, Clyde A., Carol A. O'Connor, and Martha A. Sandweiss. *The Oxford History of the American West.* New York: Oxford University Press, 1994.

Mohrman, K. *Exceptionally Queer: Mormon Peculiarity and U.S. Nationalism.* Minneapolis: University of Minnesota, 2022.

Moore, Beth S. *Bones in the Well: The Haun's Mill Massacre, 1838: A Documentary History.* Norman, OK: Arthur H. Clark, 2006.

Moreton-Robinson, Aileen. *The White Possessive: Property, Power, and Indigenous Sovereignty.* Minneapolis: University of Minnesota Press, 2015.

Mueller, Max Perry. *Race and the Making of the Mormon People.* Chapel Hill: University of North Carolina Press, 2017.

Murdoch, David Hamilton. *The American West: The Invention of a Myth.* Cardiff: Welsh Academic Press, 2001.

Murray, Alice Yang. *Historical Memories of the Japanese Internment and the Struggle for Redress.* Redwood City, CA: Stanford University Press, 2007.

Murray, Iain Hamish, and Banner of Truth Trust. *Revival and Revivalism: The Making and Marring of American Evangelicalism, 1750–1858.* Edinburgh, UK: Banner of Truth Trust, 1994.

Neilson, Reid Larkin, and Terryl Givens. *Joseph Smith, Jr.: Reappraisals after Two Centuries.* Oxford: Oxford University Press, 2009.

Newton, Marjorie. *Mormon and Maori.* Salt Lake City: Greg Kofford Books, 2014.

Nibley, Hugh. *Brother Brigham Challenges the Saints.* The Collected Works of Hugh Nibley, Vol. 13. Salt Lake City: Deseret Book, 1994.

———. *The Prophetic Book of Mormon.* The Collected Works of Hugh Nibley, Vol. 8. Salt Lake City: Deseret Book, 1989.

Nieto-Phillips, John M. *The Language of Blood: The Making of Spanish-American Identity in New Mexico, 1880s–1930s.* Albuquerque: University of New Mexico, 2004.

Niezen, Ronald. *Spirit Wars: Native North American Religious in the Age of Nation-building.* Berkeley: University of California Press, 2000.

O'Dea, Thomas. *The Mormons.* Chicago: University of Chicago Press, 1957.

Omi, Michael, and Howard Winant. *Racial Formation in the United States: From the 1960s to the 1990s.* 2nd ed. New York: Routledge, 1994.

Pagan, Eduardo Obregon. *Murder at the Sleepy Lagoon: Zoot Suits, Race, and Riot in Wartime L.A.* Chapel Hill: University of North Carolina Press, 2003.

Parker, Dorothy R. *Phoenix Indian School: The Second Half-Century.* Tucson: University of Arizona Press, 1996.

Pascoe, Peggy. *What Comes Naturally: Miscegenation Law and the Making of Race in America.* Oxford: Oxford University Press, 2009.

Peterson, Charles S. *Take Up Your Mission: Mormon Colonizing along the Little Colorado River, 1870–1900.* Tucson: University of Arizona Press, 1973.

Peterson, John Alton. *Utah's Black War.* Salt Lake City: University of Utah Press, 1998.

Prescott, Cynthia. *Pioneer Monument Mothers: Constructing Cultural Memory.* Norman: University of Oklahoma Press, 2019.

Prentiss, Craig R. *Religion and the Creation of Race and Ethnicity: An Introduction.* Race, Religion, and Ethnicity. New York; London: New York University Press, 2003.

Proctor, Maurine Jensen, and Scot Facer Proctor. *The Gathering: Mormon Pioneers on the Trail to Zion.* Salt Lake City: Deseret Book, 1996.

Prucha, Paul Francis. *The Great Father: The United States Government and the American Indians.* 2 vols. Lincoln: University of Nebraska Press, 1984.

Quinn, D. Michael. *The Mormon Hierarchy: Origins of Power.* Salt Lake City: Signature Books in association with Smith Research Associations, 1984.

Raboteau, Albert J. *A Fire in the Bones: Reflections on African-American Religious History.* Boston: Beacon, 1995.

Reeve, Paul. *Making Space on the Western Frontier: Mormons, Miners, and Southern Paiutes.* Urbana: University of Illinois Press, 2006.

———. *Religion of a Different Color: Race and the Mormon Struggle for Whiteness.* New York: Oxford University Press, 2017.

Reyner, Jon Allen, and Jeanne Eder. *American Indian Education: A History.* Norman: University of Oklahoma Press, 2004.

Richards, Legrand. *A Marvelous Work and a Wonder.* Salt Lake City: Deseret Book, 1976.

Riding In, James, and Susan Miller. *Native Historians Write Back: Decolonizing American Indian History.* Lubbock: Texas Tech University Press, 2011.

Roediger, David R. *Towards the Abolition of Whiteness: Essays on Race, Politics, and Working Class History.* The Haymarket Series. London: Verso, 1994.

———. *The Wages of Whiteness: Race and the Making of the American Working Class.* The Haymarket Series. London: Verso, 2007.

Rogers, Brent M. *Unpopular Sovereignty: Mormons and the Federal Management of Early Utah Territory.* Lincoln: University of Nebraska Press, 2017.

Rust, Val Dean. *Radical Origins: Early Mormon Converts and Their Colonial Ancestors.* Urbana: University of Illinois Press, 2004.

Ryan, Mary P. *Cradle of the Middle Class: The Family in Oneida County, New York, 1790–1865.* Interdisciplinary Perspectives on Modern History. Cambridge: Cambridge University Press, 1981.

Said, Edward W. *Orientalism.* New York: Vintage Books, 1978.

———. *Culture and Imperialism.* New York: Vintage Books, 1994.

Seed, Patricia. *Ceremonies of Possession in Europe's Conquest of the New World, 1492–1640.* Cambridge: Cambridge University Press, 1995.

Sekaquaptewa, Helen, and Louise Udall. *Me and Mine: The Life Story of Helen Sekaquaptewa.* Tucson: University of Arizona Press, 1969.

Shumway, Dale L., and Margene Shumway, eds. *The Blossoming: Dramatic Accounts of the Lives of Native Americans in the Foster Care Program of the Church of Jesus Christ of Latter-day Saints.* Orem, UT: Granite, 2002.

———. *The Blossoming II: Dramatic Accounts of the Lives of Native Americans in the Foster Care Program of the Church of Jesus Christ of Latter-day Saints.* Orem, UT: Granite, 2007.

Silva, NoeNoe. *Aloha Betrayed: Native Hawaiian Resistance to American Colonialism.* Durham, NC: Duke University Press, 2004.

Simpson, Caroline Chung. *An Absent Presence: Japanese Americans in Postwar American Culture, 1945–1960.* Durham, NC: Duke University Press, 2001.

Slotkin, Richard. *Regeneration through Violence: The Mythology of the American Frontier, 1600–1860.* Middletown, CT: Wesleyan University Press, 1973.

Smith, Andrea. *Conquest: Sexual Violence and American Indian Genocide.* Boston: South End Press, 2005.

Smith, George D. *Faithful History: Essays on Writing Mormon History*. Salt Lake City: Signature Books, 1992.

Smith, Gibb, William Smart, and Terry Tempest Williams, eds. *New Genesis: A Mormon Reader on Land and Community*. Salt Lake City: Gibbs Smith, 1998.

Smith, Linda Tuhiwai. *Decolonizing Methodologies: Research and Indigenous Peoples*. 2nd ed. London: Zed Books, 2012.

Smoak, Gregory E. *Ghost Dance and Identity: Prophetic Religion and American Indian Ethnogenesis in the Nineteenth Century*. Berkeley: University of California Press, 2008.

Southerton, Simon G. *Losing a Lost Tribe: Native Americans, DNA, and the Mormon Church*. Salt Lake City: Signature Books, 2004.

Stegner, Wallace Earle. *The Gathering of Zion: The Story of the Mormon Trail*. Salt Lake City: Westwater, 1981.

Szasz, Margaret Connell. *Education and the American Indian: The Road to Self-Determination since 1928*. Albuquerque: University of New Mexico, 1999.

———. *Indian Education in the American Colonies, 1607–1783*. Indigenous Education. Lincoln: University of Nebraska Press, 2007.

Tate, Michael L. *Indians and Emigrants: Encounters on the Overland Trails*. Norman: University of Oklahoma Press, 2006.

Taylor, Quintard. *In Search of the Racial Frontier: African Americans in the American West, 1528–1990*. New York: Norton, 1998.

Taylor, Quintard, and Shirley Ann Wilson Moore. *African American Women Confront the West, 1600–2000*. Norman: University of Oklahoma Press, 2003.

Thomas, David Hurst. *Skull Wars: Kennewick Man, Archaeology, and the Battle for Native American Identity*. New York: Basic Books, 2000.

Trafzer, Clifford, and Jean A. Keller, eds. *Boarding School Blues: Revisiting American Indian Educational Experiences*. Lincoln: University of Nebraska Press, 2000.

Trask, Huanani Kay. *From a Native Daughter: Colonialism and Sovereignty in Hawai'i*. Monroe: Common Courage Press, 1993. Reprint, Honolulu: University of Hawaii Press, 1999.

Trennert, Robert A. *The Phoenix Indian School: Forced Assimilation in Arizona, 1891–1935*. Norman: University of Oklahoma Press, 1988.

Tullis, F. LaMond. *Martyrs in Mexico: A Mormon Story of Revolution and Redemption*. Provo, UT: Religious Studies Center, 2018.

———. *Mormons in Mexico: The Dynamics of Faith and Culture*. Logan: Utah State University Press, 1987.

Turner, John G. *Brigham Young: Pioneer Prophet*. Cambridge, MA: Belknap Press of Harvard University Press, 2012.

Ulrich, Laurel Thatcher. *A House Full of Females: Plural Marriage and Women's Rights in Early Mormonism*. New York: Knopf, 2018.

Underwood, Grant, ed. *Voyages of Faith: Explorations in Mormon Pacific History*. Provo, UT: Brigham University Press, 2000.

Venebles, Robert W. *American Indian History: Five Centuries of Conflict & Coexistence*, Vol. 1, *Conquest of a Continent, 1492-1783*. Santa Fe: Clear Light Publishers, 2004.

————. *American Indian History: Five Centuries of Conflict and Coexistence*, Vol. 2, *Confrontation, Adaptation & Assimilation 1793–Present*. Santa Fe: Clear Light Publishers, 2004.

Veracini, Lorenzo. *Settler Colonialism: A Theoretical Overview*. New York: Palgrave Macmillan, 2010.

Walker, Ronald W., Richard E. Turley Jr., and Glen M. Leonard. *Massacre at Mountain Meadows*. Oxford: Oxford University Press, 2008.

Wallace Earle Stegner. *The Gathering of Zion: The Story of the Mormon Trail*. Salt Lake City: Westwater, 1981.

Walters, Ronald W. *The Price of Racial Reconciliation: The Politics of Race and Ethnicity*. Ann Arbor: University of Michigan Press, 2008.

Williams, Robert A., Jr. *Like a Loaded Weapon: The Rehnquist Court, Indian Rights, and the Legal History of Racism in America*. Minneapolis: University of Minnesota Press, 2005.

Wilson, John Frederick. *Religion and the American Nation: Historiography and History*. George H. Shriver Lecture Series in Religion in American History, Vol. 1. Athens: University of Georgia Press, 2003.

Wilson, Waziyatawin Angela, and Michael Yellow Bird, eds. *For Indigenous Eyes Only: A Decolonization Handbook*. Santa Fe: School of American Research, 2005.

Wolfe, Patrick. "Settler Colonialism and the Elimination of the Native." *Journal of Genocide Research* 8, no 4. (2006), 387–409.

————. *Settler Colonialism and the Transformation of Anthropology: The Politics and Poetics of an Ethnograph Event*. Writing Past Imperialism. London: Cassell, 1999.

Worster, Donald. *Under Western Skies: Nature and History in the American West*. New York: Oxford University Press, 1992.

CHAPTERS IN BOOKS

Allen, James B., "The Rise and Decline of the LDS Indian Student Placement Program, 1947 1996." In *Mormons, Scripture, and the Ancient World: Studies in Honor of John L. Sorenson*, ed. Davis Bitton, 85–119. Provo, UT: Foundation for Ancient Mormon Research, 1998.

Green, Reyna. "The Pocahontas Perplex: The Image of Indian Women in American Culture." In *Native American Voices: A Reader*, ed. Susan Lobo, Steve Talbot, and Traci L. Morris, 204–11. Boston: Prentice Hall, 2010.

Lomawaima, K. Tsianina. "The Unnatural History of American Indian Education." In *Next Steps: Research and Practice to Advance Indian Education*, ed. Karen Gayton Swisher and John Tippeconnic III, 3–31. Charleston, WV: Eric Clearinghouse on Rural, 1999. https://files.eric.ed.gov/fulltext/ED427903.pdf.

Patterson, Sara M. "Everyone Can Be a Pioneer: The Sesquicentennial Celebrations of Mormon Arrival in the Salt Lake Valley." In *Out of Obscurity: Mormonism since 1945*, ed. Patrick Q. Mason and John G. Turner, 302–17. New York: Oxford University Press, 2016.

JOURNAL ARTICLES

Birch, John. "Helen John: The Beginnings of Indian Placement." *Dialogue: A Journal of Mormon Thought* 18, no. 4 (Winter 1985):119–29.

Chadwick, Bruce A., Stan L. Albrecht, and Howard M. Bahr. "Evaluation of an Indian Student Placement Program." *Social Casework* 17, no. 9 (November 1986): 515–24.

Coates, Lawrence G. "Brigham Young and Mormon Indian Policies: The Formative Period, 1836–1851." *Brigham Young University Studies* 18, no. 3 (Spring 1978): 428–52.

———. "The Mormons and the Ghost Dance." *Dialogue: A Journal of Mormon Thought* 18, no. 4 (Winter 1985): 89–111.

Douglas, Norman. "The Sons of Lehi and the Seed of Cain: Racial Myths in Mormon Scripture and Their Reliance to the Pacific Islands." *Journal of Religious History* 8, no. 1 (June 1974): 90–104.

Duffy, John-Charles. "The Use of 'Lamanite' in Official LDS Discourse." *Journal of Mormon History* 34, no. 1 (Winter 2008): 118–67.

Dyer, Richard. "White." *Screen* 29, no. 4 (Autumn 1988): 44–65.

Eliason, Eric A. "The Cultural Dynamics of Historical Self-Fashioning: Mormon Pioneer Nostalgia, American Culture, and the International Church." *Journal of Mormon History* 28, no. 2 (Fall 2002): 139–73.

Embry, Jessie. "Indian Placement Program Families: A Mission to the Lamanites." *Journal of Mormon History* 40, no. 2 (Spring 2014): 235–76.

England, Eugene. "'Lamanites' and the Spirit of the Lord." *Dialogue: A Journal of Mormon Thought* 18, no. 4 (Winter 1985): 25–32.

Flake, Kathleen. "Re-placing Memory: Latter-day Saint Use of Historical Monuments and Narrative in the Early Twentieth Century." *Religion and American Culture: A Journal of Interpretation* 13, no. 1 (Winter 2003): 69–109.

Franks, Travis. "Make Settler Fantasy Strange Again: Unsettling Normative White Masculinity in Robert E. Howard's Weird West." *Western American Literatures* 54, no. 3 (Fall 2019): 295–322.

Garroutte, Eva Marie. "The Racial Formation of American Indians: Negotiating Legitimate Identities within Tribal and Federal Law." *American Indian Quarterly* 25, no. 2 (Spring 2001): 224–39.

Gentry, Leland. "Light on the 'Mission to the Lamanites.'" *BYU Studies Quarterly* 36, no. 2, article 13 (1996):227–34.

Hangen, Tona J. "A Place to Call Home: Studying the Indian Student Placement Program." *Dialogue: A Journal of Mormon Thought* 16, no. 1 (1983): 62–88.

Harper, Steven C. "Missionaries in the American Religious Marketplace: Mormon Proselyting in the 1830s." *Journal of Mormon History* 24, no. 2 (Fall 1998): 1–29.

Harris, Cheryl I. "Whiteness as Property." *Harvard Law Review* 106, no. 8 (June 1993): 1707–91.

Hinton, Wayne K. "Mahroni Young and the Church: A View of Mormonism and Art." *Dialogue: A Journal of Mormon Thought* 7, no. 4 (1972): 35–43.

Hunter, J. Michael. "The Monument to Brigham Young and the Pioneers: One Hundred Years of Controversy." *Utah Historical Quarterly* 68, no. 4 (Fall 2000): 332–50.

Imada, Adria L. "'Aloha 'Oe'": Settler-Colonial Nostalgia and the Geneaology of a Love Song." *American Indian Culture and Research Journal* 37, no. 2 (2013): 35–52.

Jennings, Warren A. "The First Mormon Mission to the Lamanites." *Kansas Historical Quarterly* 37 (Autumn 1971): 288–99.

Keane, Colleen. "Where Have All the Children Gone? Controversy over Native Child Placement by Mormon Church." *Wassaja/The Indian Historian* 15 (September–October 1982): 12–13.

Laga, Barry. "In Lieu of History: Mormon Monuments and the Shaping of Memory." *Dialogue: A Journal of Mormon Thought* 43, no. 4 (Winter 2010): 131–52.

Mar, Tracey Banivanua. "Settler-Colonial Landscapes and Narratives of Possession." *Arena Journal*, nos. 37–38 (January 2012): 176–98.

Meinig, D. W. "The Mormon Nation and the American Empire." *Journal of Mormon History* 22, no. 1 (1996): 33–51.

Morgan, Brandon. "Educating the Lamanites: A Brief History of the LDS Indian Student Placement Program." *Journal of Mormon History* 35, no. 4 (Fall 2009): 191–217.

Murphy, Thomas. "Laban's Ghost: On Writing and Transgression." *Dialogue: A Journal of Mormon Thought* 30, no. 2 (1997): 105–28.

———. "Other Mormon Histories: Lamanite Subjectivity in Mexico." *Journal of Mormon History* 26, no. 2 (2000): 179–214.

Pack, Elbert Eugene. "Ambivalent and Ambiguous." *Sunstone Magazine* 72 (August 1989): 6–7.

Peterson, Charles S. "Jacob Hamblin, Apostle to the Lamanites." *Journal of Mormon History* 2 (1975): 21–34.

Poupart, Lisa M. "The Familiar Face of Genocide: Internalized Oppression among American Indians." *Indigenous Women in the Americas* 18, no. 2 (Spring 2003): 86–100.

Ramos-Zayas, Ana Y. "Racializing the 'Invisible' Race: Latino Constructions of 'White Culture' and Whiteness in Chicago." *Urban Anthropology & Studies of Cultural Systems & World Economic Development* 30, no. 4 (Winter 2001): 341–80.

Rosaldo, Renato. "Imperialist Nostalgia." *Representations* 26 (Spring 1989): 107–22.

Rowley, Dennis. "The Mormon Experience in the Wisconsin Pineries, 1841–1845." *BYU Studies Quarterly* 32, no. 1 (1992), 119–48.

Smith, Darron. "The Persistence of Racialized Discourse in Mormonism." *Sunstone: Mormon Experience, Scholarship, Issues & Art* 126 (March 2003): 31–33.

Strakosch, Elizabeth, and Alissa Macoun. "The Vanishing Endpoint of Settler Colonialism." *Arena Journal*, nos. 37–28 (January 2012): 40–62.

Sue, Derald Wing, et al. "Racial Microaggressions and Difficult Dialogues on Race in the Classroom." *Cultural Diversity and Ethnic Minority Psychology* 35, no. 2 (2009): 183–90.

Swanson, Vern. "The Book of Mormon Art of Arnold Friberg, Painter of Scripture." *Journal of Book of Mormon Studies* 10, no. 1 (2001): 26–35, 79.

Thelan, David. "Memory and American History." *Journal of American History* 75, no. 4 (March 1989): 1117–29.

Topper, Martin D. "Mormon Placement: The Effects of Missionary Foster Families on Navajo Adolescents." *Ethos* 7, no. 2 (Summer 1979): 142–60.

Tvedtnes, John A. "The Charge of 'Racism' in the Book of Mormon." *FARMS Review* 15, no. 2 (2003): 183–97.

Vicenti Carpio, Myla. "(Un)disturbing Exhibitions: Indigenous Historical Memory at the NMAI." *American Indian Quarterly* 30, nos. 3–4 (Summer–Fall 2006): 619–31.

Walker, Ronald. "Toward a Reconstruction of Mormon and Indian Relations, 1847–1877." *Brigham Young University Studies* 2, no. 4 (1989): 23–42.

Whittaker, David J. "Mormons and Native Americans: A Historical and Bibliographical Introduction." *Dialogue: A Journal of Mormon Thought* 18, no. 4 (Winter 1985): 33–64.

Wolfe, Patrick. "Settler Colonialism and the Elimination of the Native." *Journal of Genocide Research.* 8, no. 4 (2006): 93–152.

———. "The Settler Complex: An Introduction." *American Indian Culture and Research Journal.* 37, no. 2 (2013): 1–22.

PAPER PRESENTATION

Coles, Sasha. "The Pioneer Spirit: Nation Building, Heritage Tourism and the LDS Church." Paper presented at the Western History Association, San Diego, CA, 2018.

DISSERTATIONS AND THESES

Aikau, Hokulani. "Polynesian Pioneers: Twentieth Century Religious Racial Formations and Migration in Hawai'i." PhD diss., University of Minnesota, 2005.

Barnes, John. "Memory, Commemoration, and the Bear River Massacre of 1863." MSc thesis, Utah State University, 2004.

Bishop, Clarence R. "Indian Placement: A History of the Indian Student Placement Program of the Church of Jesus Christ of Latter-day Saints." Master's thesis, University of Utah, 1967.

Kitchen, Richard Darrell. *Mormon-Indian Relations in Deseret: Intermarraige and Indenture, 1847–1877.* PhD diss, Arizona State University, 2002.

Poupart, Lisa M. "Silenced Voices: Patriarchy, Cultural Imperialism and Marginalized Others." PhD diss., Arizona State University, 1996.

Riggs, Lynette. "The Church of Jesus Christ of Latter-day Saints' Indian Student Placement Program: A History." PhD diss., Utah State University, 2008.

INTERNET SOURCES

Bashore, Melvin L. "'Where the Prophets of God Live': A Brief Overview of the Mormon Trail Experience." Brigham Young University Overland Diaries and Letters, 1846–1869. https://overlandtrails.lib.byu.edu/essay_mtrail.php.

"Black History Timeline." Blacklds.org. http://www.blacklds.org/history.

"The Historic Trek." The Church of Jesus Christ of Latter-day Saints. http://www.lds.org/newsroom/page/0,15606,3899-1—-2–314,00htm#, accessed March 6, 2006.

Madsen, Brigham D. "Bear River Massacre." Utah History Encyclopedia. https://www.uen.org/utah_history_encyclopedia/b/BEAR_RIVER_MASSACRE.shtml.

"Mormon Battalion Fact Sheet." The Church of Jesus Christ of Latter-day Saints. https://newsroom.churchofjesuschrist.org/additional-resource/mormon-battalion-fact-sheet#:~:text=Roughly%20500%20Mormon%20volunteers%20were,Thursday%2C%20July%2016%2C%201846.

"Moroni Hides the Plates in the Hill Cumorah." The Church of Jesus Christ of Latter-day Saints Gospel Library. https://www.churchofjesuschrist.org/media/image/moroni -buries-plates-b417feb?lang=eng.

Soukup, Elise. "The Mormon Odyssey." Newsweek, March 13, 201.0 https://www.newsweek .com/mormon-odyssey-121109,

"Style Guide–The Name of the Church." The Church of Jesus Christ of Latter-day Saints Newsroom. http://newsroom.lds.org/ldsnewsroom/eng/style-guide.

"Summer Travel Series: Mormon Battalion Historic Site." The Church of Jesus Christ of Latter-day Saints. https://newsroom.churchofjesuschrist.org/article/summer-travel -series-mormon-battalion-historic-site.

Tanner, Jerald, and Sandra Tanner. "Mormon Inquisition? LDS Leaders Move to Repress Rebellion." Salt Lake City Messenger. https://www.utlm.org/newsletters/no85.htm.

INDEX